Lecture Notes in Computer Science 942

Edited by G. Goos, J. Hartmanis and J. van Leeuwen

Advisory Board: W. Brauer   D. Gries   J. Stoer

Springer

Berlin
Heidelberg
New York
Barcelona
Budapest
Hong Kong
London
Milan
Paris
Tokyo

Günter Böckle

Exploitation of Fine-Grain Parallelism

Springer

Series Editors

Gerhard Goos
Universität Karlsruhe
Vincenz-Priessnitz-Straße 3, D-76128 Karlsruhe, Germany

Juris Hartmanis
Department of Computer Science, Cornell University
4130 Upson Hall, Ithaca, NY 14853, USA

Jan van Leeuwen
Department of Computer Science, Utrecht University
Padualaan 14, 3584 CH Utrecht, The Netherlands

Author

Günter Böckle
Zentralabteilung Forschung und Entwicklung, SiemensAG
Otto-Hahn-Ring 6, D-81739 München, German

E-mail: Guenter.Boeckle@zfe.siemens.de

Library of Congress Cataloging-in-Publication Data

Böckle, Günther, 1949-
    Exploitation of fine-grain parallelism / Günther Böckle.
        p.   cm. -- (Lecture notes in computer science ; 942)
    Includes bibliographical references (p.   ).
    ISBN 3-540-60054-X (Berlin : acid-free paper). -- ISBN
    0-387-60054-X (New York : acid-free paper)
    1. Parallel processing (Electronic computers)   I. Title.
    II. Series.
    QA76.58.B63   1995
    004'.35--dc20   95-30348
                                                                  CIP

CR Subject Classification (1991): D.3.4, D.3.2, B.1.4, B.6.1, B.2.1, C.1.2, D.1.3,
F.1.2

ISBN 3-540-60054-X Springer-Verlag Berlin Heidelberg New York

© Springer-Verlag Berlin Heidelberg 1995
Printed in Germany

Typesetting: Camera-ready by author
SPIN: 10486363   06/3142-543210 - Printed on acid-free paper

Preface

The driving force for many research efforts is to provide higher performance for applications of computer systems. There are many computer systems architectures promising a high performance potential, chiefly among them parallel architectures. A whole zoo of parallel system architectures has been developed so far and many of those, although of intelligent design did not survive in the market. One of the main reasons for such failures is that the performance potential of such an architecture cannot be used efficiently by a sufficient number of applications.

This book presents methods to solve the problem of bringing the performance potential of parallel architectures to the applications so that the applications can use this potential efficiently. The focus is on parallelism on the instruction-set level which provides a high performance potential for a great variety of applications, not just the quite restricted sets of applications we see for many coarse-grain parallel architectures.

These methods have been developed in course of a project at Siemens Corporate Research and Development Department. A cooperation with the Institute for Computer Science at Munich Technical University was installed to join the forces for the development of corresponding methods and tools. This cooperation was then entered into a national research program at the Technical University, the Sonderforschungsbereich 342 "Methods and Tools for the Usage of Parallel Architectures".

Acknowledgements

Many people helped to do all the work presented in this book, however the actual project team was always quite small. We had help from our partners at the Institute for Computer Science at Munich Technical University, several Dimplomarbeiten (master thesis) were made in this project.

I would like to deeply thank all those who contributed to the joined effort, above all the team members who did all an excellent job: Klaus Hahne, Jörg Schepers, Christof Störmann, Karl-Josef Thürlings, Siegfried Trosch, and Isolde Wildgruber.

Special thanks to Wolfgang Karl, our partner at Munich Technical University and to all the others, mainly: Uli Baumann, Ralf Karl, Michael Hardieck, and Martin Liebl.

Table of Contents

1 Introduction **1**

2 Kinds of Parallelism **3**

   2.1 Classification by Structural Items 4

   2.2 Classification by Items Processed 5

   2.3 Classification by Instruction and Data Stream Parallelism 6

   2.4 Classification by Memory Organization 7

3 Architectures for Fine-Grain Parallelism **8**

   3.1 Vertical Parallelism 8

   3.2 Horizontal Parallelism 9

      3.2.1 VLIW Architecture 9

      3.2.2 Superscalar Processor Architectures 11

   3.3 Classification of Pipelined Processor Architectures 12

   3.4 Other Architectures for Fine-Grain Parallelism 15

      3.4.1 Conditional Execution 16

      3.4.2 History 17

4 VLIW Machines **18**

   4.1 Multiflow TRACE 18

   4.2 IBM's VLIW Processor 19

   4.3 Cydra 22

   4.4 LIFE (Philips/Signetics) 24

   4.5 The XIMD Architecture 26

5 Constraints on VLIW Architectures **28**

6 Architectural Support for Exploitation of Fine-Grain Parallelism 32

   6.1 Dynamic Instruction-Scheduling 32

7 Constraints for Instruction Scheduling **38**

   7.1 Data Dependences 38

   7.2 Off-live Dependence 38

8 Instruction-Scheduling Methods **40**

   8.1 Local Instruction-Scheduling 42

8.2   Global Instruction-Scheduling 42

8.3   Global Scheduling Methods Based on Local Scheduling 43

    8.3.1   Trace Scheduling 43

    8.3.2   Other Global Scheduling Methods 46

8.4   Global Scheduling on the Program Graph 47

    8.4.1   Percolation Scheduling 49

        8.4.1.1   Move_op 50

        8.4.1.2   Move_cj 51

        8.4.1.3   Unify 52

        8.4.1.4   Delete 53

    8.4.2   Extensions to Percolation Scheduling 54

8.5   Loop Parallelization 55

    8.5.1   Loop Unrolling 56

    8.5.2   Software Pipelining 58

    8.5.3   Perfect Pipelining 59

    8.5.4   Integrating Loop Parallelization and Instruction Scheduling 61

9   Developing Instruction-Scheduling Methods   **62**

10   Tools for Instruction Scheduling   **63**

10.1 The C Compiler 64

11   The Machine Model   **65**

12   The Horizontal Instruction-Scheduler   **67**

12.1 The Interface Compiler - Scheduler 67

12.2 The Scheduler's Front-end 68

    12.2.1   Mapping rtls to Machine Instructions 70

    12.2.2   Flow Graph, Pointer Targets and Call Graph 74

    12.2.3   Registers and Register Renaming 75

    12.2.4   Memory-Access Analysis 81

    12.2.5   Data-Dependence Analysis 90

    12.2.6   Inserting Representatives for Multicycle Operations 92

    12.2.7   Data-Flow Analysis 96

    12.2.8   Standard Optimizations 101

12.3 The Scheduler's Central Part 103

    12.3.1   Loop Parallelization 104

    12.3.2   Partitioning the Program Graph into Regions 104

    12.3.3   Extended Percolation Scheduling - Core Transformations 106

12.3.3.1   Standard Core Transformations....................................   106
12.3.3.2   Core Transformations for Multicycle Operations   110

12.3.4   Extended Percolation Scheduling - Structure   115

12.3.5   Extended Percolation Scheduling - Control Tactics   117
12.3.5.1   Node-Oriented Tactics   117
12.3.5.2   Operation-Oriented Tactics..   120
12.3.5.3   Which Tactics for what Application?.........................   121
12.3.5.4   Control Tactics for Specific Code Patterns................   121
12.3.5.5   Control Tactics Considering Resources   123

12.3.6   Extended Percolation Scheduling - Control Strategies   124

12.3.7   Moving Operations out of Regions and Functions   125

12.3.8   Resource Management   128

12.4 The Scheduler's Back-End   129

12.4.1   Register Allocation   129

12.4.2   Interactions Between Register Allocation and Instruction
Scheduling   134

12.4.3   Rescheduling   135

12.4.4   Assignment of Operations to PEs   137

12.4.5   Instruction-Word Generation   138

12.4.6   Debug Information   140

13   Resource Management   142

13.1 Machine Description   144

13.2 Operators and Functions for Resource Management   146

13.3 Resource Allocation   147

13.4 Resource Assignment   148

13.4.1   Assignment of Processing Elements   148

13.4.2   Assignment of General Resources   152

14   Exceptions   156

15   Vertical Instruction-Scheduling   158

15.1 Vertical Core Transformations   159

16   Conclusion   164

17   References   165

1 Introduction

Research and development of new computer architectures are driven by many objectives, such as increasing system performance for often not-yet known new applications, adapting a processor system to new functionalities, and realization of new computing models. The most challenging new architectures are parallel systems. There is already quite a zoo of parallel architectures and there is a variety of ways to classify them. Quite a few of these architectures exist only conceptually because it is rather expensive to develop actually running systems. Many of the parallel architectures are especially suited for particular classes of applications (mainly numerical ones); and it is possible to achieve impressive performance for such applications. However, there are only few parallel architectures equally well suited for standard programs - often standard sequential programs will not run at all or only with poor performance.

Much effort is invested into research in compiler techniques to make programming parallel machines easier - but we are still not able to achieve sufficient performance for standard, sequential programs on parallel machines. An architecture especially suited for a particular application will only survive if there are sufficient users of this application, willing to pay for such a machine. Therefore, we have to provide attractive performance and ease of programming for a sufficient number of customers for a price (which is determined also by architectural complexity) they are willing to pay.

This book presents methods for automatic parallelization, so that programs need not to be tailored for specific computer architectures by the programmer. These methods are dedicated to a particular class of parallel architectures. Here, we focus on fine-grain parallelism where the items processed in parallel are machine instructions, not processes as in coarse-grain parallel architectures. Such a kind of parallelism is offered by most new microprocessor architectures and by several special architectures, e.g. super-scalar and VLIW (Very Long Instruction Word) architectures. The best prospect for high performance, however, will be offered by a combination of both, coarse and fine-grain parallelism.

The book is intended for compiler writers, for computer architects, and for students to demonstrate the manifold complex relationships between architecture and compiler technology. The various problem areas which have to be considered for scheduling shall be demonstrated.

The main topics presented are:

- Architectures for fine-grain parallelism.
- The specific architectural provisions to support fine-grain parallelism.
- Software methods for parallelization by instruction scheduling.
- New parallelization methods based on Percolation Scheduling.
- A new systematic approach to resource management.

After a classification of parallel computer architectures in *section 2*, architectures for fine-grain parallelism are described in *sections 3 - 6*. These sections present hardware methods to extract parallelism from programs to increase performance. Still more efficient methods can be provided by software. *Sections 7 - 8* present such software methods for transforming application programs so that the parallelism offered by the architecture can be exploited by the combined efforts of hardware and software parallelization. *Sections 9 - 12* describe methods and algorithms in more detail which have been implemented in tools for fine-grain parallelization, so that applications can benefit from the parallelism without changes to their source programs. *Section 13* presents methods for resource scheduling, an important topic which has mostly been neglected in research and development of parallelization methods. In *section 14* we take a look at the problems which arise for exception handling when instructions are reordered and, finally, *section 15* offers methods for instruction scheduling for deeply pipelined architectures.

2 Kinds of Parallelism

Parallel processing is offered by machines using from just a few up to many thousands of processors. These machines are organized in various kinds of architectures - there is a huge variety in the zoo of parallel computer architectures, different parallel computing models, etc. Thus, for understanding the world of parallel architectures we need a systematic approach, by classifying the different kinds of parallelism.

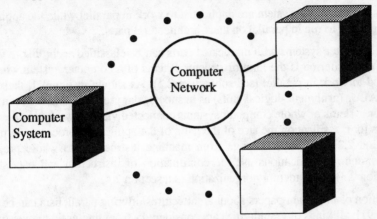

1. Duplicating whole computer systems

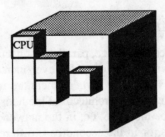

2. Duplicating parts of computer systems, at least CPUs

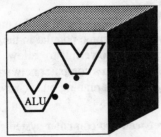

3. Duplicating parts of the CPU, e.g. ALUs

Figure 1: Parallelism by Replication

There are two major ways computer architecture can achieve parallelization:

i. Separating the functionality:

The processing of a single instruction is separated into different parts f1, f2, ..., fn so that at any time (theoretically) one instruction performs part f1, another one part f2, etc. This kind of parallelism, pipelining, is described in subsection 3.1.

ii. Duplicating parts and separating the application:

Parts of a computer system are duplicated to work in parallel while the application is separated to run in parallel on these architectural parts.

Parallel computer systems with duplicated parts can be classified according to various criteria. One criterion is the kind of structural items of a computer system which are replicated to work in parallel (see subsection 2.1). As shown in figure 1, these parts may be ALUs (arithmetic-logical units) as in superscalar processors, CPUs as in multiprocessor systems or whole computer systems connected via a network. Another criterion uses for classification the size of the parts of the application processed in parallel (subsection 2.2). These parts range from machine instructions to whole programs. Other common classifications use the coordination of instruction and data streams (subsection 2.3) or the memory organization (subsection 2.4).

A collection of important papers about architectures offering parallelism can be found in [Lilja 91]; all kinds of granularities are considered - from fine-grain to massive parallelism.

2.1 Classification by Structural Items

From the very beginning of the computer age, parallel architectures were considered as a means to meet the requirements and wishes for ever increasing performance and functionality. Whole computer systems or parts of them are replicated for these purposes. Figure 1 shows a classification of architectural methods to achieve parallelism. The replicated items need not be the same, i.e. in the network of computers we may use different kinds of machines, or in the second case different kinds of CPUs may work in parallel, as well as different kinds of ALUs (Arithmetic Logical Units) in the third case.

The kind of items replicated is used to specify the kind of parallel architecture. Applications on *networks of computers* have become popular in the nineties when the interconnect systems became sufficiently powerful to allow for such applications. Complete computer systems, connected via a computer network, run parts of one common application. The kinds of applications running on such systems have to fulfil particular requirements:

• The amount of data shared between two computer systems must be low so that no huge amounts of data have to be transported between the computer systems which is quite performance consuming.

- The application must be separable into (mostly) independent subproblems which can be processed in parallel; the number of synchronizations between the subproblems must be very low to prevent a significant performance decrease.

The number of applications fulfilling these requirements is quite limited and thus, networks of computers cannot be used for many applications. On the other hand, there are many workstations and PCs available - standard workstations and PCs can be used for this kind of parallel processing. Only a fast network and the software for separating and controlling the parallel processing of the application program are necessary. This may well be the most inexpensive way of coarse-grain parallel processing, and tools for supporting the corresponding parallelization and controlling the processing of the programs, including the control of parallel memory accesses (like e.g. PVM) may turn out very successful.

The "classical" parallelism is realized by *duplicating major parts* of a computer, at least the CPU and often memory. Duplicating only the CPUs results in shared-memory systems and the duplication of memory by giving each CPU its own private memory yields distributed-memory systems.

The goal of processing as much as possible in parallel leads to the reduction of the size of the items replicated. *Replicating parts of the CPU* and often memory was applied already in the sixties in IBM machines (see [Tomasulo 67]) and the CDC 6600 (see [Thornton 70]). Specific control mechanisms are applied to keep these parts (typically ALUs ore memory modules) busy; these may be implemented in hardware (described in section 6) or in software (described in section 8).

2.2 Classification by Items Processed

The classification according to the items processed in parallel, i.e. the granularity, matches to a wide extent the classification according to the replicated structural items. The activity units specifying the granularity, i.e. the chunks of programs processed in parallel, are mostly processes; this kind of granularity characterizes *coarse-grain parallelism*. Such processes may be UNIX processes or threads. Usually, programs running on such machines have to be designed accordingly by specifying explicitly the processes which can be executed in parallel. This is accomplished either by applying languages which offer support for parallelism or with sequential languages, using library routines for specifying the processes. For systems with distributed memory, there is the additional task to map the data to the different processors with their private memories. Performing all this automatically is still a research topic and can only be applied to special program constructs yet. Thus, the task of exploiting coarse-grain parallelism is currently mostly left to the user.

A special kind of parallelism is offered by highly parallel systems with many thousands (or up to millions) of processors. Such systems are useful for specific applications where algorithms can be developed which make use of such a multitude of processors. The tasks of developing algorithms which map problems to such machines and programming them are both left to the user, no general methods exist so far.

Architectures with coarse-grain parallelism offer significantly higher performance than sequential systems for applications which can be expressed by parallel algorithms with corresponding mapping to parallel processes. Such applications are mainly numerical and database programs. For most other applications significant performance increase due to coarse-grain parallelism can only be found in some special cases.

Fine-grain parallelism is specified by a granularity of items on the instruction level; these may either be high-level or machine instructions. Fine-grain parallelism has been used traditionally in vector processors. These are mainly useful and efficient for numerical applications with e.g. matrix manipulations. There are compilers for vector processors which perform the parallelization, mostly for loops, automatically.

Fine-grain parallel processing on the machine-instruction level has proven to be efficient for numerical applications, but it can also be used efficiently for general-purpose programs. Its main feature is that parallelization is performed automatically without requiring the programmer to change any sequential program. The traditional architecture for fine-grain parallelism uses "vertical" parallelism by overlapping the various steps of the execution of machine instructions in processor pipelines. Several machine instructions are processed concurrently, each in another pipeline stage.

In the mid-eighties the first standard microprocessor architectures with "horizontal" parallelism occurred, the first one being the Apollo PRISM. Such a "superscalar" processor contains several processing elements which work concurrently to execute machine instructions simultaneously. This kind of parallelism has been used before on the microinstruction level in horizontally microprogrammed architectures. The experiences in this area led to the development of Very Long Instruction Word (VLIW) machines (see [Ellis 85] and section 4).

Automatic parallelization for coarse-grain machines means splitting application programs into parallel processes and distributing data. For fine-grain systems it means reordering the machine instructions so that the processing elements can be kept busy, i.e. instruction scheduling. Reordering of instructions is also applied by compilers for optimizations.

2.3 Classification by Instruction and Data Stream Parallelism

Michael Flynn proposed a simple model for classifying computers by specifying the parallelism in instruction and data streams. He chose four classes of computer systems:

- Single instruction stream, single data stream (SISD)
- Single instruction stream, multiple data stream (SIMD)
- Multiple instruction stream, single data stream (MISD)
- Multiple instruction stream, multiple data stream (MIMD)

In practice, however, these classes overlap. The first class specifies standard, serial uniprocessors. The second class, SIMD, is composed of parallel processing units which are all synchronized and are controlled by a single instruction and a single program counter (PC). The Connection Machine II is a popular example of a SIMD machine while e.g. vector processors do not classify (according to [Hennessy/Patterson 90]).

There are no real full MISD machines, however, decoupled or systolic architectures may somehow qualify for this classification (see subsection 3.4).

Most parallel architectures belong to the MIMD class, ranging from multiprocessor systems to parallel systems with millions of processors. They all are characterized by independent, unsynchronized processors which have their own, separate program counter each and process different instructions simultaneously. Synchronization is mostly performed explicitly by the programs, not the processors.

For architectures studied in the following there is no unique class in this scheme. E.g. VLIW processors may be characterized as SISD, SIMD or MIMD, whatever characteristic is used for classification.

2.4 Classification by Memory Organization

An important characteristic of processor architectures is the way memory is accessed. If several processors (or processing units) access the same memory modules (and addresses) then they may work on the same data which means that they also have to synchronize their accesses to these data. Such architectures are called shared-memory architectures.

If processors have their own, private memories (and memory addresses) then either data have to be passed around or the part of the program processing these data. In the latter case, only one processor may access particular data while in the former case several processors may access the same data which will have to be duplicated and copied to their private memories. All these machines have a distributed-memory architecture.

The shared-memory architecture is easier to program than the distributed-memory architecture - no shuffling around of data has to be inserted into programs and for particular multiprocessor systems, most of the synchronization task is performed by coherent caches. A combination of shared and distributed memory is offered by distributed architectures with virtually-shared memory. The advantages of both architectures can be used - the simple computing model of shared-memory systems and the performance advantages of distributed-memory architectures. Mostly, virtually-shared memory is implemented so that one processor is the owner of a particular set of data. This processor is the only one to write the data but it can pass the right to read the data (and the data themselves) to other processors. If another processor wants to write the data, it has to become its owner. Big data sets usually are partitioned so that only small sections have to be copied to the memories of other processors. All activities concerning distribution of data and access rights are transparent to the user, they are managed by virtually-shared memory management. This virtually-shared memory is most convenient for users of distributed-memory machines, however its performance is crucial for its application.

3 Architectures for Fine-Grain Parallelism

There are two kinds of fine-grain parallelism, distinguished by the way the activity units overlap parallel processing. The items considered for parallelism are machine operations. On most computer architectures, the execution of a machine operation is separated into several phases, implemented as the different stages of a processor pipeline. We call this "vertical parallelism". The basic hardware unit for processing a machine instruction is called a processing element (PE). When several of these PEs can start and execute machine instructions in parallel, we call this "horizontal parallelism".

Def. 1: Vertical Parallelism

A pipelined processor offers *vertical parallelism* if the execution of a machine instruction is separated into several stages and several instructions may be active at the same time in different phases of their execution.

Def. 2: Horizontal Parallelism

A processor with n (n > 1) processing units which can start and execute several machine instructions at the same time offers *horizontal parallelism*.

Some constraints on the architecture imposed by parallelization methods are described in section 7.

3.1 Vertical Parallelism

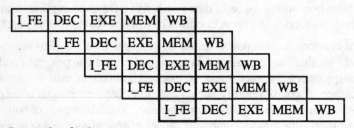

I_FE: Instruction fetch
DEC: Read source registers and decode operation code
EXE: Instruction execution
MEM: Memory access
WB: Write result back to register file

Figure 2: Base Architecture Pipeline

Vertical parallelism is the kind of instruction execution applied by the classical pipelined machines. Figure 2 shows how the pipeline of the MIPS R2000/3000 processor works, as an example of a basic processor pipeline. Each (internal) clock cycle a new instruction is fetched and each clock cycle one instruction can be completed; thus, five instructions may be processed concurrently, each in another pipeline stage. Often the pipeline of a base architecture is simplified by omitting the memory (MEM) phase.

This kind of architecture is also relevant for our further considerations. There is a trend towards deeper pipelines; the MIPS R3000 had five pipeline stages while the MIPS R4000 has already eight. The higher the number of pipeline stages, the higher the degree of parallelism and thus, the higher the peak performance. However, with increasing pipeline depth we have an increasing probability for encountering two dependent instructions in the pipeline concurrently. If an instruction detects in its RF pipeline stage (see figure 2) that one of its source operands is not available because another instruction producing this operand is not yet completed, the pipeline has to be stopped and no new instruction is started until this operand is available. There may be many reasons for such pipeline stalls, due to exceptions or busy resources, most of the latter in the floating-point pipeline.

Thus, increasing the processor pipeline depth does not bring the benefit implied by the pipeline structure itself, i.e. the number of pipeline stages, due to pipeline stalls. Section 15 shows how the performance of machines with deep pipelines can be increased by instruction scheduling.

3.2 Horizontal Parallelism

The processing elements of a machine with horizontal parallelism may themselves offer vertical parallelism using pipelining. Then, the time between issue and completion of an instruction may last several clock cycles (in contrast to just one like in the Multiflow TRACE machines, see [Colwell et al 88] and subsection 4.1). The instruction fetch phase for a pipelined horizontally parallel processor is common for all instructions executed concurrently.

A typical example for horizontal fine-grain parallelism are VLIW (Very Long Instruction Word) machines which were first developed in the context of horizontally microprogrammed machines.

3.2.1 VLIW Architecture

In Very Long Instruction Word (VLIW) architectures we have n processing elements (PEs) working in lock-step (tightly synchronized). In this context, the word "operation" describes a single machine operation processed by one PE. An "instruction" is used to describe the set of operations issued concurrently.

Each clock cycle a new instruction word is fetched from the instruction cache; such an instruction consists of n fields, each containing one operation. The first operation of an instruction word is executed by the first PE, the second operation by the second PE, etc. Obviously, such a machine is most efficient if we can keep the PEs busy.

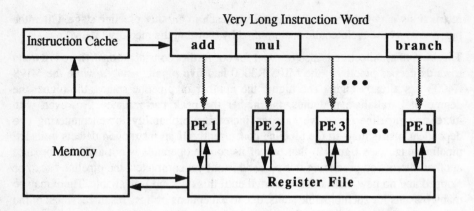

Figure 3: VLIW Architecture

This architecture is an example how hardware and software can cooperate to achieve high performance. Software methods described in section 8 are applied to reorder the intermediate code of a program and compact it into the very long instruction words so that high performance can be achieved by executing many operations in parallel. The main feature of VLIW systems is not just the architecture - it is the combination of hardware and software methods which allow to use the resources efficiently.

A look at the architecture in figure 3 shows some properties which yield constraints on architectural variety. All PEs have to access one common register file concurrently, which means that we need 2*n read ports and n write ports to the register file. This is quite costly with respect to chip space; however, if we can't integrate PEs and register file on the same chip then we have to pay the penalty with increased register access time or reduced clock frequency. There is a trade-off between chip space and performance. Considering the space for integration, it may be most efficient to use a clustered architecture with e.g. 4 PEs together with one register file on each chip. However, if one PE needs an operand from another cluster's register file, it has to be copied to its own register file first; this will cost at least one additional clock cycle. For determining an architecture with sufficiently high performance for particular applications, a thorough analysis has to be performed using samples of this application as workload. Several architectural enhancements have been proposed to overcome this problem, e.g. "shadow" registers as duplicated register files (see [Rau 88]) or funnel files (see [Labrousse/Slavenburg 88]).

Further architectural constraints of VLIW architectures are discussed in section 7.

VLIW methods for supporting high PE utilization and thus exploiting the performance offered by such an architecture are based on instruction scheduling. The programs running on a VLIW machine are first compiled like any program on a conventional machine. The intermediate-code representation of the compiled program is then reordered and grouped ("compacted") into tuples of operations which can be executed in parallel. Each group contains up to n operations; it is then mapped to one instruction word, filling the blank fields with noops. More on instruction scheduling is presented in section 8.

3.2.2 Superscalar Processor Architectures

Superscalar processors have multiple processing units like VLIW architectures. However, they use dynamical instruction-scheduling to exploit instruction-level parallelism. This means that the machine operations are reordered by hardware during a program's run time.

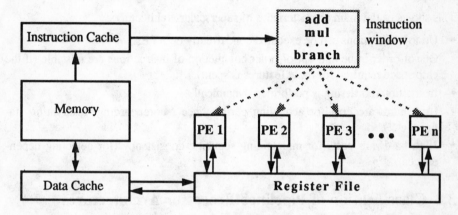

Figure 4: Superscalar Processor Architecture

Figure 4 shows a basic superscalar processor architecture. Like in VLIW architectures, there are n processing elements; in superscalar processors these are usually heterogeneous. The instructions are the standard machine operations, no long instruction words as in VLIW architectures; thus, superscalar processors are mostly binary compatible to the sequential members of the processor family they belong to. Each clock cycle, a set of machine instructions is fetched, decoded, and inserted into an "instruction window", a set from where the instructions to be executed are selected. The instructions are reordered dynamically in the instruction window by mapping them to particular PEs, e.g. an *add* operation to an integer ALU, a *mul* operation to a multiplier, a *branch* operation to a branch PE. The instruction window may be implemented as set of local buffers for the operations waiting for execution on a particular PE, called reservation stations (see [Johnson 91] and subsection 6.1).

The logic controlling the mapping of instructions to PEs has several tasks. For each instruction in the window we have to check prior to execution if its source operands are available. If they are currently being computed by a preceding instruction, we have to wait until these operands are available in some registers (e.g. in bypass registers). Thus, we have to keep track about registers which are targets of operations started but not completed yet and of operations which have to wait for operands. Scoreboarding is a common technique for this purpose (see [Johnson 91] or [Hennessy/Patterson 90]).

With this method we can cope with true dependences between instructions (read-after-write dependences, see definition in subsection 7.1). However, for avoiding errors due to other dependences, anti- (write-after-read, see def. 4 on page 38) and output- (write-after-write) dependences, we need some other technique. Dynamic register renaming is used for this purpose. If an instruction wants to write to a register which is currently in use (read or written) by a preceding instruction, then its destination operand is renamed and another register is used as destination for this instruction. However, this means that all future uses of this register as source operand have to be renamed the same way, until another write to this register is performed. Reorder buffers are needed for each PE to accomplish renaming (see [Johnson 91] and subsection 6.1).

This shows us the main characteristics of superscalar architectures:

- Up to n operations can be executed concurrently on n PEs.
- Out-of-order issue and out-of-order completion of instructions are possible (if the chip space required for these features is spent).
- Instruction reordering is performed dynamically.
- High hardware cost for achieving performance (scoreboarding, reservation stations, etc.).
- High hardware costs for maintaining semantic consistency (for detecting dependences).

3.3 Classification of Pipelined Processor Architectures

The architectures described above can be classified with respect to their pipeline functionality like in [KarlW 93]. Figures 5 - 7 demonstrate the differences of such architectures expressively.

Figure 2 above shows the pipeline of a base architecture like e.g. the MIPS R3000 while figure 5 presents a "*superpipelined*" architecture, the MIPS R4000. A superpipelined architecture is constructed from a base architecture by splitting the pipeline stages as far as possible. The goal is to increase the clock frequency accordingly (i.e. dependent on the number of gates in the now smaller pipeline stages). A comparison of figure 2 with figure 5 shows how the pipeline stages were split. The first stage was split into two stages for instruction cache access and TLB access, register fetch and decode remains one single stage as well as the execution stage and the write-back stage, while the memory access stage is split into three stages. The distribution of the logic in the different pipeline stages is sufficiently uniform to allow for high clock frequencies.

A *superscalar* processor architecture executes several instructions in parallel using several pipelines (in corresponding PEs) working concurrently. However, mostly the pipelines are specialized to perform particular operations only, there is an ALU, a memory access unit, a multiplication unit, etc. Figure 6 shows the schematic representation of a superscalar processor architecture pipeline structure with four PEs. Each clock cycle, four instructions are fetched, each one is decoded separately, the source registers are fetched separately, and the instruction execution is performed in parallel on all four PEs. Of course this is only possible if the instructions can be processed on the particular PE, i.e. if we have one single memory access unit then we can keep the four PEs only busy if one (and only one) of the four instructions fetched is a memory access instruction.

IF	IS	RF	EX	DF	DS	TC	WB							
	IF	IS	RF	EX	DF	DS	TC	WB						
		IF	IS	RF	EX	DF	DS	TC	WB					
			IF	IS	RF	EX	DF	DS	TC	WB				
				IF	IS	RF	EX	DF	DS	TC	WB			
					IF	IS	RF	EX	DF	DS	TC	WB		
						IF	IS	RF	EX	DF	DS	TC	WB	
							IF	IS	RF	EX	DF	DS	TC	WB

IF: *Instruction fetch, first part* - instruction cache access and instruction TLB access
IS: *Instruction fetch, second part* - instruction cache access and instruction TLB access
RF: *Register fetch* - instruction decode, source register fetch, instruction tag check
EX: *Instruction execution* - ALU, data virtual address calculation, instruction virtual address calculation for branch operations
DF: *Data cache access, first part* - for load/store operations
DS: *Data cache access, second part* - for load/store operations
TC: *Data tag check*
WB: *write* the result *back* to the register file

Figure 5: Pipeline of an Architecture with Vertical Parallelism (MIPS R4000)

In contrast to superscalar processors we have just one instruction word to fetch per clock cycle in VLIW processors, all operations belonging to one very long instruction word are fetched in parallel. The PEs decode and fetch the source operands separately, as well as instruction execution and writing back the destination operand. Figure 7 shows the structure of a VLIW pipeline. However, VLIW machines need not be pipelined as e.g. the TRACE machines (see subsection 4.1) show. In [KarlW 93] these architectures are classified according to the more detailed Bode classification, and bounds for their processing power are determined.

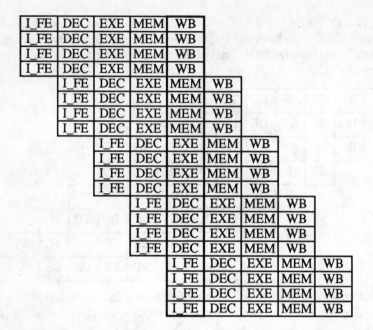

Figure 6: Superscalar Processor Pipeline Structure (with four PEs)

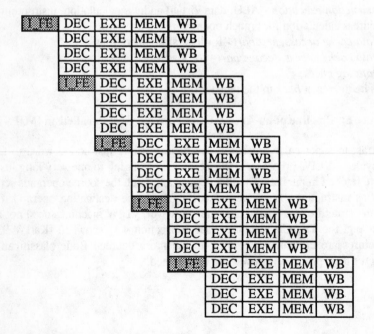

Figure 7: VLIW Processor Pipeline Structure

3.4 Other Architectures for Fine-Grain Parallelism

Several architectures exploiting fine-grain parallelism have been developed. *Decoupled access / execute architectures* are intended for floating-point applications (see [Windheiser/Jalby 91]). They separate the memory access from computations. They consist typically of two processors, one for address generation and one for floating-point computations. The processors communicate through a network of queues. Examples of decoupled access / execute architecture are the Astronautics ZS-1 and the Structured Memory Access (SMA) machine. The Astronautics ZS-1 consists of four main modules: splitter, access processor, execute processor, and memory.

The splitter fetches instructions from the instruction cache and dispatches them to the appropriate processor, using one issue queue for each processor. Thus, the splitter can work ahead of the processors. The splitter is also responsible for processing branch instructions. The access processor generates memory addresses and performs integer arithmetic. The access processor fetches instructions from its issue queue if there are no unresolved dependences on preceding instructions. Four queues are used to communicate with the memory: a load-address queue containing addresses for load operations, a store-address queue containing addresses for store operations, a load queue, and a store queue for the data loaded to or stored from memory by the access processor. The execute processor performs floating-point arithmetic; it fetches instructions from its own issue queue (where they were inserted by the splitter) and has an own load queue and store queue for loading data from memory and storing them. For copies between the two processors, there are two queues for copies in both directions. The queues allows the two processors, the splitter, and the memory unit to work independently (restricted by queue size). For exploiting the fine-grain parallelism, the compiler performs loop unrolling and instruction scheduling (see section 6).

The *iWarp* is a system architecture intended for signal, image, and scientific computing. The processor was developed as a joint effort between Carnegie Mellon University and Intel Corporation (see [Borkar et al 88]). An iWarp system is composed of a collection of iWarp cells. They may be arranged as a ring, a torus, an array for systolic processing or other topologies. An iWarp cell consists of an iWarp component and its local memory. Figure 8 shows the major functional units of an iWarp cell.

The pathway unit builds together with four input and output ports the communication agent to connect iWarp cells. Logical busses are multiplexed on each physical bus so that 20 incoming pathways can operate simultaneously in any single iWarp component. The pathway unit performs the routing for one and two-dimensional configurations of iWarp processors. The output channels of the pathway unit can be accessed by reading and writing from specific registers which are assigned to the corresponding ports (see figure 8). The computational unit contains a floating-point adder, a floating-point multiplier, and an integer/logical unit. Each iWarp cell contains a register file with 128 registers of 32 bits length. The memory unit consists of an off-chip local memory for data and instructions and an on-chip program store.

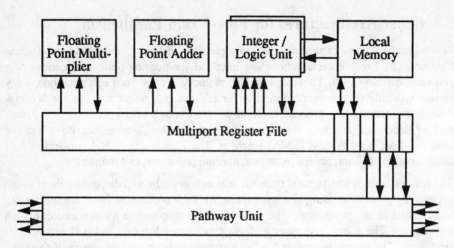

Figure 8: iWarp Component Architecture ([Borkar et al 88])

Two operation code formats are offered: one 96-bit, very long instruction word which controls all processing units and a small, 32-bit instruction word for operations on a single processing unit. A very long instruction word takes two clock cycles for its execution and can initiate 9 operations: one floating-point addition, one floating-point multiplication, two integer operations or three address calculations with memory accesses, two read operations from the input channels, two write operations to the output channels, and one branch operation to a loop header. Register bypassing (a path directly from the output of a processing element to the inputs of all processing elements) provides the results of operations as inputs to succeeding operations.

The parallelism in programs is exploited by the W2 compiler which was developed at Carnegie Mellon University. It supports programming for explicit coarse-grain parallelism and provides software-pipelining techniques for fine-grain parallelism.

3.4.1 Conditional Execution

An important architectural feature is the support for the computing models of conditional execution or speculative execution. In the classical (absolute) computing model we have one (or more) program counter(s) determining which instruction(s) to process next. The flow of instructions, they may be processed in parallel or not, is only changed by a well-defined set of instructions: {branch, jump, call, return, syscall} and by exceptions. When the instruction determining the change of instruction flow is a conditional branch, the corresponding condition has to be evaluated before the branch can be executed. For parallel architectures this may be a significant performance obstacle - often many instructions might be processed in parallel, but they have to wait for a single thread of execution which has to be processed for the evaluation of such a condition.

These problems lead to the following idea: Suppose, we have an architecture with sufficient resources (PEs, busses, registers etc.). Why can't we process both successor paths of a conditional branch (the TRUE and the FALSE successor paths) and, after having evaluated the branch's condition, throw away the results of the path which will not be taken?

This idea is the base of the conditional-execution model. However, there are still some problems to solve. The instructions of both successor paths of such an architecture will write to the same registers, and whoever writes last will determine the registers' contents. Thus, these register contents will generally be unpredictable. To avoid this, we need duplicated registers: each processing elements writes to its own sets of registers and after the branch's condition is evaluated, the register file of the path which will be continued is marked as valid and the other one, containing the results of the wrong path is marked as invalid. An interesting solution to this register-file problem is implemented in the Cydra architecture; see subsection 4.3.

Now we can extend these ideas (as in [Hsu 86]). We mark each single instruction with the result of one or more previous conditional branches. This instruction will only be processed (i.e. its results will only be marked as valid) if this mark is set as TRUE. These "guarded" instructions are used in the LIFE architecture described in subsection 4.4.

We might even assign each single instruction the contents of condition-code registers which were set by evaluations of branch conditions and use masks and expressions combining the masks with the condition-code register's contents to decide if the instruction's result will be valid. This is used in IBM's VLIW architecture described in subsection 4.2.

3.4.2 History

In the architecture newsgroup in usenet, an interesting architecture was mentioned. In the mid-sixties, the IBM ACS (Advanced Computer System) was designed. Each clock cycle, seven instructions could be issued out-of-order, including three fixed-point and three floating-point instructions. The architecture had a 96-entry target-instruction cache where instructions at target addresses of branches were stored to reduce the penalty for taken branches.

The architecture offered some more interesting features: a register-renaming scheme, 24 condition-code registers, conditional writeback bits allowing to conditionally skip register-file writebacks, a scheme for a variable number of branch-delay slots, dynamic branch-prediction used for prefetch, and a scheme for multithreading two instruction streams. Regrettably, the project was cancelled in 1968 and many of these good ideas had to be reinvented.

4 VLIW Machines

Only a few actual VLIW machines have been built. The most famous one is the family of Multiflow's TRACE machines, see [Colwell et al 88] and [Clancy et al 87]. These architectures are described below. Their method for compacting code to create the very long Instruction Words, increases the number of ports and Scheduling, is described in subsection 8.3.1. Multiflow and Cydrome, who built the Cydra machines, were small companies which didn't survive. However, VLIW is discussed intensively in the architecture community and Hewlett Packard and Intel have announced that they are building a processor on VLIW basis together.

4.1 Multiflow TRACE

The Multiflow TRACE machines are the best-known VLIW computers. They were built by the team of Josh Fisher who developed the Bulldog compiler (see subsection 8.3.1) and the Trace Scheduling method for global instruction-scheduling. The TRACE computers were built as two families, the /200 and the /300 families. Each family comprises three members, the 7/200, 14/200, 28/200, and similarly for the /300. They perform 7, 14 or 28 operations per clock cycle. Figure 9 shows the principles of the TRACE 7/200 architecture.

Very Long Instruction Word:

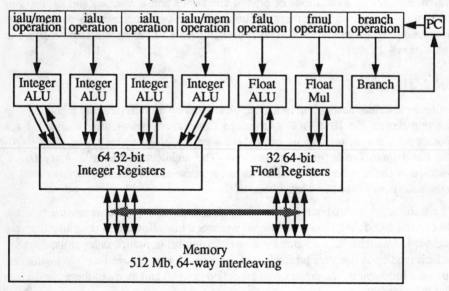

Figure 9: TRACE 7/200 Architecture ([Colwell et al 88])

The TRACE 7/200 applies a 256-bit very long instruction word comprising seven operations, four of them integer, two floating point and one branch operation. These seven operations are executed in parallel. The clock cycle is split into two minor cycles. Each minor cycle, a new instruction is issued; an integer operation takes one full cycle to complete while floating-point operations take longer.

The 7/200 module can be doubled to create a 14/200 machine which has a 512-bit instruction word comprising 14 operations. Similarly, doubling the 14/200 yields a TRACE 28/200 with 28 operations in a 1024-bit instruction.The 7/200 CPU consists physically of three boards, one integer board, one floating-point board, and one board containing program counter, interrupt logic, and interrupt hardware. A pair of integer / floating-point boards is connected with a special 32-bit bus for data exchange without using the (slower) backplane. Each board is equipped with a register file of 64 32-bit general-purpose registers; on the floating-point board these are organized as 32 64-bit floating-point registers. Twelve busses are connected to a board allowing four read and four write accesses to the registers per minor cycle, as well as four bus-to-bus transmissions. Additionally, there are bypasses from write ports to all read ports.

At the beginning of an integer operation, the destination register and its register bank are determined. This may be the local register bank on the integer board, the register bank on the associated floating-point board, or the register bank on another integer board (for the 14/200 or 28/200). The integer boards contain additionally a TLB (a "translation lookaside buffer" for mapping virtual to physical memory addresses) with 4K entries and process tags for 8K-byte pages.

The floating point processors comply with the IEEE 64-bit standard. The floating-point board contains a store buffer of 32 32-bit registers. For store operations the addresses come from the integer board and the data from the store buffer on the connected floating-point board. This helps to avoid conflicts between stores and other operations.

A TRACE machine may contain up to eight memory controllers, each of which controls up to eight memory banks. A fully equipped system contains 512 Megabytes of physical memory. The memory banks are interleaved (the data are spread among the banks), allowing parallel access to all memory banks. Up to four memory accesses per minor cycle can be performed (on a 28/200), one per integer board. The memory banks are managed by software at compile time with no additional hardware as e.g. in vector processors. This allows very simple and fast busses. For accesses where the compiler knows the memory module at compile time, these fast mechanisms are used, so that the busses need no arbitration hardware, queues for data, hardware for synchronization, and interrupts. For accesses to statically unknown addresses, another (slower) mechanism is applied.

A special Unix operation system was developed allowing the use of all Unix tools. Additionally, many application programs for the main application area of these machines, numeric computing, were developed.

4.2 IBM's VLIW Processor

At IBM's T. J. Watson Research Center a VLIW computer was developed not only for scientific applications like the TRACE machines but also for general-purpose applications. This architecture supports multiway branching and conditional execution. The computing model applied is based on tree-shaped instructions; see [Ebcioglu 88] and [KarlW 93]. In [Ebcioglu 88] an architecture with 16 processing elements is described, however later this was reduced to eight processing elements in the prototype.

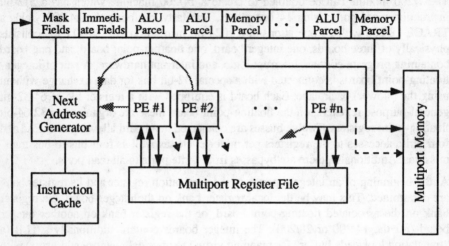

Figure 10: IBM's VLIW Architecture ([Ebcioglu 88])

These processing elements are identical ALUs for integer and floating-point operations. There is a central register file with 64 33-bit registers. The register file is implemented in bit-slice technique and contains 24 ports (for 8 PEs) so that each processing element can read two operands and write one operand in the register file in each cycle.

The ALUs contain integer pipelines, however their floating-point part is not pipelined. The results of ALU operations are written back to their destination registers in the cycle following their computation, however a bypass network provides the results for usage by all ALUs in the cycle after computation.

The architecture is a 33-bit architecture with the 33rd bit characterizing an operation as interruptible or uninterruptible. This mechanism provides the ability of conditional execution. When e.g. a division operation is moved by the instruction scheduler ahead of the conditional branch testing the denominator for 0, an interrupt would occur whenever the denominator is 0 because the division is now processed in any case. However, this architecture can cope with this case: The moved division operation is then marked as uninterruptible which causes the result register to be marked in its 33rd bit as containing the result of an operation which caused an exception. This result may be used in further uninterruptible operations and will be propagated accordingly. When an interruptible operation (one which was not moved above the conditional branch) uses that value, this indicates that the path with the division is actually taken, the interrupt will finally occur. Each operation exists in both versions, interruptible and uninterruptible, and it is the compiler's task to use interruptible and uninterruptible operations accordingly.

The memory is composed of eight banks and allows four concurrent accesses, i.e. an instruction word may contain four memory-access operations.

Each processing element is assigned a two-bit condition-code register where one bit is used to characterize an undefined value. A conditional-branch operation decides upon the contents of all condition-code registers about the next instruction address. Each instruction word may contain up to three conditional branches, allowing each instruction to have up to four successors.

The computing model is based on instructions having the form of a tree of operations as shown in figure 21 on page 48. The nodes of the tree represent compare operations (resp. conditional branches) and the edges represent the other operations occurring between the compare operations. The tree's leaves are labels of the successor instructions, i.e. L1, ..., L4 in figure 21. The processing of such an instruction tree starts by choosing an execution path through the tree. This is performed by evaluating the compare operations top-down. These comparisons are performed in parallel. Next, the operations at the edges of the chosen path are executed, i.e. their results are marked as valid while operations on other paths are invalid. Afterwards, processing continues at the successor determined by the chosen path through the instruction tree.

The instruction word has a length of 537 bits and contains mask fields in addition to the operations. Each processing element is assigned a 4-bit "transfer enable mask" to characterize the place on the instruction-tree path of the corresponding operation. The compiler sets bit i of this mask ($i \leq 4$) if the operation is on the path to the i-th successor label (leaf of the tree). Now, if at the beginning of an instruction execution, the contents of the condition-code registers determine the path to the i-th successor of the instruction word as the one to be taken, only operations with the i-th bit of the mask set may write their results to their destination registers. This mechanism supports the conditional execution model.

The branch conditions are represented as expressions of the contents of the 8 condition-code registers. For each conditional-branch operation in the instruction tree there are two 8-bit masks to code these expressions, for the TRUE-path and the FALSE-path, respectively. These masks specify two subsets of the set of condition-code registers; condition-code register i belongs to the first subset if the i-th bit of the first mask is set. The branch condition evaluates to TRUE if all condition-code registers specified by the first of these sets are TRUE, and all condition-code registers of the second set contain the value FALSE (compare figure 21 and the expressions thereafter on page 48). The mask can also specify that the content of a condition-code register is not relevant for the comparison. The branch-target addresses are specified in three of the six 32-bit immediate fields of the instruction word. The output of the first processing element may also be specified as branch-target address to execute computed branches.

A variant of Percolation Scheduling (see subsection 8.4.1) is used to extract parallelism from application programs during compilation. The nodes of the program graph contain trees of operations which are independent, according to the computation model (see subsection 8.4.2). Loop parallelization is combined with instruction scheduling to allow operations from different loop iterations to reside in the same instruction word (see subsection 8.5.4).

4.3 Cydra

The Cydra 5 was built by Cydrome, Inc. (see [Rau 88], [Rau 92] and [Rau/Yen/Towle 89]). Called a „Departmental Supercomputer", it is a heterogeneous multiprocessor system for engineering and scientific applications. The Cydra system, as shown in figure 11, consists of three kinds of processors: interactive processors for general-purpose applications, I/O processors, and a numeric processor with a VLIW architecture. The processors are all connected to a central bus, together with the memory system and a service processor for the console. The numeric processor offers some good design ideas which found their way into later designs of other systems; its architecture is shown in figure 12.

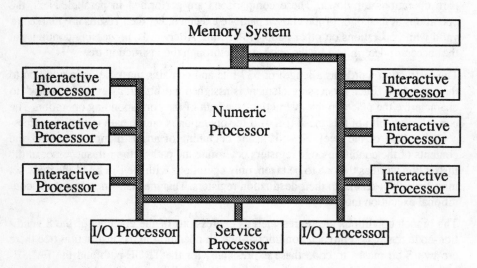

Figure 11: Cydra 5 System Architecture ([Rau/Yen/Towle 89])

The general-purpose subsystem is tightly integrated and shares memory with the numeric processor. A Unix operating system was developed for the interactive processors.

The numeric processor is based on the "Directed Dataflow Architecture". In a pure dataflow architecture, all operations can be executed as soon as their input operands are available. The Cydra system schedules the operations at compile time so that an operation is executed when their input operands are (presumably) ready. Access to the register file is a bottleneck whenever there are several processing elements. Theoretically, two read ports and one write port are necessary for performing parallel processing (like in the IBM VLIW). Cydra uses a Context Register Matrix with a register file of 64 registers of 32 bits length at each crosspoint (see figure 12). Each row can be written be a specific processing unit and all register files have identical contents. Each register file can be read by a single processing unit, the one at its column in the matrix. The register files of a row can be read in parallel, thus each row is equivalent to a single multiported register file with one write and multiple reads per cycle. Each single register file can process one read and one write access per cycle. This architecture allows conflict-free access for each processing unit.

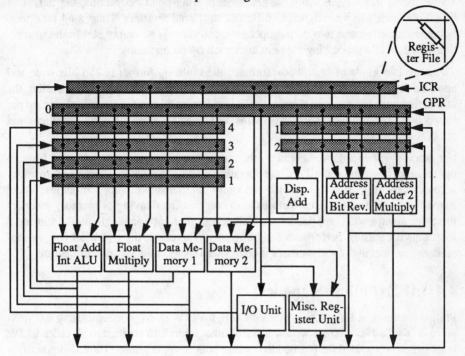

Figure 12: Cydra 5 Numeric Processor Architecture ([Rau/Yen/Towle 89])

Additionally, there is a general-purpose register file (GPR) which can be read by all processing elements in a cycle and written by all, but only one at a time. The processing units are separated into two clusters, a data cluster (left in figure 12, registers no. 1 - 4) and an address cluster (on the right hand side in figure 12, registers no. 1 - 2) for address calculations. The Context Register Matrix is split accordingly. This split reduces the number of register files necessary for concurrent accesses.

A frequent element of numeric applications are loops; often they influence a program's run time significantly. Cydra has specific architectural support for loop processing. Just like a compiler creates a stack frame for each procedure, in Cydra an iteration frame is allocated for each loop iteration dynamically at run time. This allows several iterations to be processed concurrently. The context registers are accessed with an instruction-specified displacement from an Iteration Frame Pointer which is incremented each time a new iteration is initiated. The displacement is computed at compile time.

Instruction scheduling is supported additionally by hardware offering conditional-scheduling control. Each operation uses a third input, a predicate which determines whether the instruction will be executed. The predicate specifies a register in the boolean Iteration Control Register file (ICR) (see figure 12). They contain e.g. the boolean results of conditional branches in loop bodies.

The instruction set is similar to standard RISC architectures; only read and write operations access memory. For double-precision floating-point operations, the halves of 64-bit operands can be assigned to different, unrelated registers. Thus, a 64-bit operation has four input and two output operands, and there is an empty slot in the instruction schedule of a processing element after each 64-bit operation.

There are two kinds of instruction formats: the multi-op format is 256 bits wide and contains seven operations, six for the processing elements and one for controlling the instruction unit; for sequential code, the uni-op format allows for a single operation per instruction. The multi-op format contains 18 Context Register Matrix specifiers and six ICR specifiers.

For processing dependences correctly the compiler marks a register as "busy" from an operation overwriting it until the last operation reading this value. Concurrent memory accesses are supported by pseudo-randomly interleaved memory modules where requests are queued. For architectures with constant interleaving of memory modules there are always some applications which access preferably a single module inside a loop thus decreasing performance significantly. Therefore, the overhead for pseudo-random interleaving of the memory modules was spent in the Cydra architecture.

4.4 LIFE (Philips/Signetics)

Philips Research at Palo Alto produced LIFE, a VLIW microprocessor using a CMOS process (with e-beam direct-write-on-wafer lithography). In contrast to all other VLIW machines it is intended for (embedded) scalar integer applications. The LIFE processor contains six functional units, however in a general sense of „functional unit". These are two ALUs, one memory interface, one branch unit, one register file, and a constant generator (see figure 13). The specific, most interesting characteristic of this processor is its „multiport memory". This memory contains the result from operations on the functional units and provides the input operands for the functional units. It is a kind of a general bypass network, allowing for fast access to operands. Each functional unit is connected to a register file with separate read and write ports. The ports' addresses are directly controlled from the instruction word. The register file's write port is connected to a multiplexer which selects each cycle the output of (at most) one functional unit to be written into its register file. This combination of register file and multiplexer is called a „funnel file". The compiler determines during compilation for each output operand of an operation on which functional unit this operand will be used in future; this operand is written into the funnel file of that specific functional unit as soon as it is produced. The funnel-file system is insofar no full multiport memory as only one value can be written into a given funnel file per cycle. However, collisions are determined by the compiler and solved by scheduling the operations accordingly.

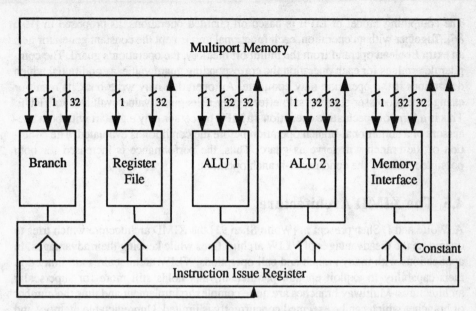

Figure 13: LIFE Processor Architecture ([Slavenburg/Labrousse 90])

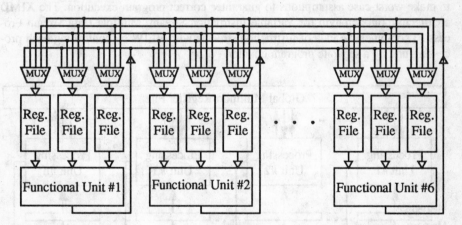

Figure 14: LIFE Multiport Memory ([Slavenburg/Labrousse 90])

The instruction set is rather small, comprising about 40 operations. Memory is accessed via read and write operations and the register file (used as a functional unit) is accessed via "readreg" and "writereg" operations. The instruction word has a length of 200 bits for the six functional units and each clock cycle a new instruction may be issued. The LIFE architecture is customizable for specific applications. It may contain a smaller or larger number of functional units; other units, e.g. a multiplier may be added.

The computing model of LIFE is based on guarded operations, as proposed in [Hsu 86]. Together with an operation, each functional unit except the constant generator gets an extra Boolean operand from the multiport memory, the operation's guard. The compiler determines for each operation the corresponding guard value, a conditional which determines if the operation may complete. An operation may write back its result or change the processor state by side effects only if its guard value evaluates to TRUE. This is a form of speculative execution - a LIFE processor may e.g. start with both successors of a conditional-branch operation before the condition is evaluated. The condition of the branch will serve as guard. Thus, the performance is increased for both possible results of the conditional-branch operation.

4.5 The XIMD Architecture

A. Wolfe and J. Shen present in [Wolfe/Shen 91] the XIMD architecture which tries to overcome the disadvantages of VLIW architectures while keeping their advantages. In applications with many branch and call operations, VLIW architectures are limited in their capability to exploit enough parallelism; this holds still more for superscalar architectures. Multiway branches are quite complex to implement and thus the number of branches which can be executed concurrently is limited. Unpredictable memory and peripherals behaviour may decrease performance because a parallelizing compiler has to make worst-case assumptions to guarantee correct program execution. The XIMD architecture (an acronym for Variable Instruction Stream, Multiple Data Stream Processor) combines the idea of instruction streams with VLIW by controlling each processing unit by a separate program counter.

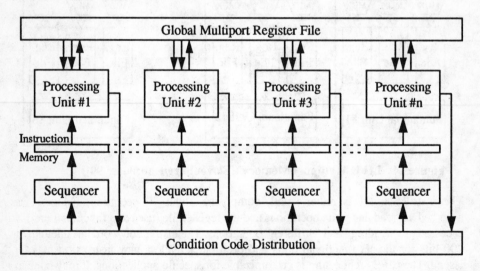

Figure 15: XIMD Architecture ([Wolfe/Shen 91])

XIMD can split its processing units among one or more instruction streams; the number of these instruction streams can be varied dynamically at run time, however based on a scenario generated by the compiler.

Figure 15 shows the basic XIMD architecture. It is similar to a VLIW architecture, but the instruction sequencer is duplicated for each processing unit. Condition-code information is distributed to each of the sequencers. The sequencers may operate identically for a VLIW operation mode or separately for a MIMD operation mode. The compiler tries to resolve dependences as far as possible during compilation time and additionally, it can generate code for explicit synchronization between instruction streams.

The very long instruction words are separated into instruction parcels, each of which controls one specific processing element. Each instruction parcel comprises a control operation (conditional or unconditional branch) and a data operation. For non-branching operations, the control operation denotes just a branch to the subsequent operation. The instruction parcels of one instruction word need not reside at the same address, each processing element may branch to a different address. The computing model allows the compiler to implement a variety of synchronization mechanisms, barrier synchronization as well as more complex synchronization mechanisms.

5 Constraints on VLIW Architectures

VLIW architectures are based on several principles:

- Keeping the hardware simple so that it can be made fast.
- Offering sufficient hardware resources for parallelism.
- Extracting parallelism from the application programs statically by software.
- Hardware support for synchronization or sequencing is only applied when software cannot predict application-program behaviour statically and when (the necessary) worst-case assumptions would cost too much performance.

1. Keeping Hardware Simple

Depending on the kind of application, 4 - 16 processing elements can be kept busy, supposing that the scheduler can extract sufficient parallelism. Hardware has to provide fast busses to memory modules and register banks. The busses may be simple, in the TRACE machines they did not need arbitration logic because the scheduler determined bus usage statically at compile time. Thus, the busses could be made fast.

2. Memory Accesses

For many machines and applications, memory access is a bottleneck, in VLIW and superscalar processors even more than in scalar processors because we have to feed several processing elements at a time with data from memory. Hardware has to provide sufficient memory bandwidth, e.g. using multiport memory like in the IBM VLIW or with memory modules accessible in parallel like in the TRACE machines. However, accesses to multiple memory modules have to be distributed among these modules so that not all memory accesses are addressed to one single memory module for particular applications. This can be implemented e.g. by using (pseudo-) randomly interleaved memory modules like in the Cydra or by assigning random addresses.

Since memory access is a major bottleneck, as much information as possible should reside in registers. This holds for scalar processors, too, but on the one hand, the problem is harder for fine-grain parallel processors since we have more processing elements to feed while, on the other hand, for VLIW processors it is easier to address more registers because we can increase the number of bits to address registers in an instruction word. That cannot be done in standard architectures where instruction formats have to be compatible to earlier processors of the same family.

3. Register Files

In VLIW architectures we can spend more bits per operation to specify source and destination registers which allows for bigger register files. While standard microprocessors usually don't have more than 32 registers, the TRACE machines provide 64 integer and 32 floating-point registers, i.e. 6 bits to specify an operand for an integer operation. In the IBM VLIW and Cydra, 64 integer registers are provided, too (per register file in Cydra).

However, all processing elements must have access to all registers - and these accesses should be possible concurrently. Real concurrent access requires e.g. three ports for each processing element on the register file (two for source operands and one for the destination operand) like in the IBM VLIW. This is a huge hardware investment, and other VLIW architecture developers tried to get along with less.

A specifically elaborate solution to the register problem is presented in the Cydra architecture: Each processing elements has a set of register files and the result of an operation is written into the corresponding register in all register files in parallel. Thus, all processing elements have always access to all operands produced by all processing elements. This is again a significant hardware investment.

However, using many ports or duplicated register files means that register files cannot be kept on chip - and crossing chip or even board boundaries increases access time and by that decreases performance significantly. And many ports and duplicate register files mean not only more hardware, but more cost and more heat.

A solution to these problems is clustering the PEs and providing separate register files for each cluster like e.g. Multiflow did with their TRACE machines. The scheduler has then to assign operations to processing elements so that an operation using the contents of a register should run on a processing element assigned to the corresponding register file. Whenever a processing element uses an operand from a register file not assigned to its cluster, the register contents have to be transferred to its own register file. The scheduler has to create these transfer operations explicitly during or after the assignment of operations to processing elements. Whenever possible, the transfer operations are assigned to PEs which are idle during the cycles the transfer has to be made. However, it will not always be possible to find idle processing elements just during these cycles. Then, an instruction word will have to be inserted which contains one single operation for transferring the contents of one register to another register - and all other processing elements will be idle when this instruction is processed. Of course, scheduling may be restarted to avoid this, but after scheduling we have to assign operations to processing elements again - and the whole process will start over again. Considering all this, clustering processing elements and assigning register files to specific clusters may decrease performance in some cases and increase scheduling time significantly.

Assigning operations to processing elements before scheduling like in the TRACE machines (see subsection 8.3.1) reduces these problems somewhat. However, it reduces also the available parallelism: two operations assigned to the same processing element cannot be scheduled in the same cycle, even if they are otherwise independent.

In the following, a suggestion for solving this problem is described:

- All register files are connected via a common bus, the XMIT bus.
- Each operation is assigned a transfer bit.
- When the result of an operation O is later needed in another register file, this transfer bit is set by the scheduler for the operation O. The scheduler knows at compile time in which register files the operation's result will be needed.

- On one processing element connected to the destination-register file, a Receive operation is performed. This might be done without using any PE; however, even if a PE has to be used, the Receive operation can be scheduled accordingly, as we assume here.
- When executing a Receive operation, the destination register file uses the Xmit bus as input; the register number receiving the data is e.g. specified in the Receive operation.
- There is one cycle delay when there is no bypassing between different PEs from different clusters.
- Having only one XMIT bus means that only one transfer per cycle is possible.

4. Bypassing

Simulations showed that a significant portion of all operand accesses is made via bypasses. Dispensing bypasses would decrease performance significantly. Many of the architectures described above have considered that, like e.g. the IBM VLIW which has an elaborate bypassing network. Many new ideas about methods for bypassing went into the design of the LIFE processor; the result of an operation flows into the "funnel files" of the processing units where this result will be needed later and such results wait in queues and will be accessed when they are needed.

Again, such a solution will be expensive concerning hardware investment, space, and heat, when many processing elements are involved. The solution to this problem is again: clustering. The architecture provides bypasses, linking the output of one processing element to the inputs of all other processing elements (and itself) in the cluster. Accesses crossing clusters will be performed via the register file and thus need an additional cycle. The scheduler can consider this by separating corresponding operations far enough, however only after processing-element assignment.

5. Multiway Branches

A significant characteristic of VLIW architectures is the ability to process more than one conditional-branch operation per cycle. In the TRACE machines, each module can perform one conditional branch, thus four of them can be performed by the TRACE 28/200 in parallel. A shrewd computation model which processes a series of conditional branches during each instruction is used by the IBM VLIW. In general, however, such multiway branches are pretty costly; see e.g. [Fisher 80]. For the instruction-scheduling methods described in sections 12ff, multiway branches similar to those in the IBM VLIW are used.

In our base architecture, each processing element uses two condition-code bits which are set by Compare operations. A Branch_pattern operation is used by the compiler whenever more than one conditional-branch operation has been moved into one node of the program graph, i.e. the successor of a very long instruction word depends on several conditional-branch operations. Each possible successor is specified by the corresponding condition code (cc) values of the comparisons. One of the successors is e.g. taken if:

the first cc states TRUE, the second one FALSE, and the third one TRUE.

Thus, we get a specific pattern, the sequence of all condition-code registers must assume for each specific successor. A Branch_pattern operation contains as immediate value a pattern; when the operation is processed, this pattern is compared with all condition codes and the branch is taken if the sequence of condition codes corresponds to this pattern. For those condition codes the branch does not depend on, don't-care patterns may be used.

6 Architectural Support for Exploitation of Fine-Grain Parallelism

The architectures described in section 3 offer the capability to execute several machine instructions concurrently. However, how efficiently can the potential of such architectures be used by software? The performance which can be achieved depends on the utilization of the processing elements, the higher and the more uniformly the utilization of the PEs, the higher also the performance achievable.

In VLIW systems the machine operations are reordered statically at compile time to find a sufficient number of independent operations which can be packed into the long instruction words to keep the PEs busy. Superscalar processors reorder the instructions inside a window dynamically at run time to find instructions to utilize the PEs. The following subsection describes methods for hardware-based dynamic scheduling. However, the number of instructions considered for reordering is quite limited and therefore, we have not many candidates for reordering. Applying static scheduling at compile time so that a superscalar processor always gets instructions in its window which can be processed in parallel at execution time can increase its performance significantly. Also processors with deep pipelines can benefit from instruction scheduling: reordering the instructions so that two dependent (or exception-causing) instructions are separated far enough so that they will not occur in the pipeline together, will reduce the number of pipeline stalls and thus increase performance. Sections 8ff describe methods for static instruction-scheduling.

6.1 Dynamic Instruction-Scheduling

Scheduling instructions dynamically during execution requires a series of hardware features. The abstract representation of a superscalar processor in figure 4 has to be refined to show the modules necessary for scheduling instructions dynamically (compare [Johnson 91]). Figure 16 shows more details of the integer part of a superscalar processor architecture. A similar structure may be added for floating point.

The requirements for a processor with hardware instruction-scheduling for parallel execution are different from sequential processors. These differences mainly refer to instruction fetch, instruction issue, exception handling and the task of detecting and tracking dependences.

1. Instruction window and reservation stations:

While figure 4 shows a central instruction window holding the instructions for all processing elements, in figure 16 this window is split into reservation stations, one for each processing element. In an architecture with a central window, the operations for all N processing elements, together with their (up to 2N) operands, have to be sent to their processing units in one cycle. The reservation stations need only to be filled at the average execution rate, rather than the peak execution rate for a central window. A reservation station holds decoded instructions until they are free of dependences and its processing element is ready to execute an instruction. However, a central window can choose among more instructions to issue to a processing element and thus yield higher performance. In [Johnson 91] several methods for implementing a central window are suggested, emphasizing the usage of a reorder buffer. Such a reorder buffer is content-addressable and needs no reordering of its contents.

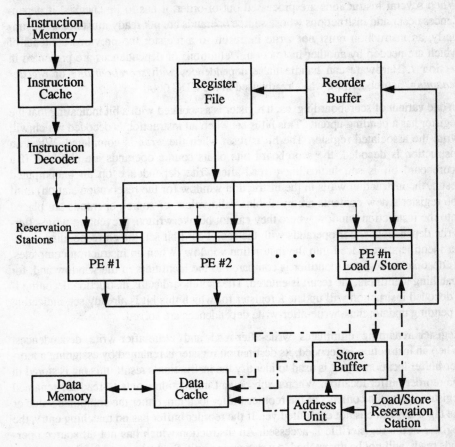

Figure 16: Superscalar Processor Architecture, Detailed

2. Exception handling:

A superscalar processor may issue instructions out of order. After returning from an exception, the previous order of instructions has to be restored to reset the register file to the contents at exception time and to reprocess those instructions which were not completed when the exception occurred. After mispredicted branches (see below), the register contents have to be restored or instructions from the non-taken path of the branch prevented from overwriting registers. In [Johnson 91] several methods are proposed for recovering from mispredicted branches and exceptions: checkpoint repair, history buffer, reorder buffer, and future file. Figure 16 shows a reorder buffer which receives the results of the instructions from the processing elements. The register contents with the results of instructions which completed in order, up to (but excluding) the first uncompleted instruction are copied from the buffer to the register file.

3. Dependence mechanisms:

When several instructions are processed out-of-order, it has to be checked if dependences occur and instructions whose source operands are not ready must not start; similarly, an instruction must not write its result to a register the previous contents of which are needed by another instruction. Definitions of dependences are presented in section 7. Hardware can handle these dependences with *scoreboarding* or *register renaming*. Scoreboarding was already used in the CDC 6600.

In one variant of scoreboarding, each register is associated with a bit indicating that the register has a pending update. This bit is set when an instruction is decoded which will write the associated register. The bit is reset when the write is completed. When an instruction is decoded, the scoreboard bits of its source operands are checked. If a scoreboard bit is set, indicating a read-after-write dependence on an uncomputed result, the instruction waits in the instruction window (or the reservation station) until the register's new contents are available. Valid values of source operands are placed into the instruction window where they cannot be overwritten, preventing write-after-write dependences. For operands with the scoreboard bit set, the corresponding register identifiers are placed into the instruction window. When an instruction completes, its destination-register identifier is compared to the identifiers in the window and, for matching identifiers, the result is entered. The scoreboard stalls instruction decoding if a decoded instruction will update a register for which this bit is already set, indicating a pending update; thus, write-after-write dependences are solved.

Register renaming eliminates write-after-read and write-after-write dependences. When an instruction is decoded, its destination register is renamed by assigning a reorder-buffer location. A tag is used to identify the instruction's result; this tag is stored in the reorder-buffer location. When a subsequent instruction wants to read the renamed register, it gets the contents of the reorder-buffer location, either the computed value or the tag if the value is not computed yet. If the reorder buffer has no matching entry, the register in the register file is accessed. An instruction which has not all source operands ready will not be dispatched to a processing unit. Several entries for the same register may occur in the reorder buffer at the same time because several instructions may write the same register. An instruction reading this register will get the most recent value. The other values are retained for exception handling.

4. Instruction fetch:

The flow of instructions through a processor is impeded by conditional branches. In general-purpose applications, branches occur pretty often, about every third to fourth instruction; on a typical RISC processor about 20% of a dynamic instruction sequence are taken branches. When several instructions are processed in parallel, the branch delay (the time between decoding a branch instruction and decoding the target instruction) increases because the branch instruction itself is decoded earlier (there are several instructions fetched per cycle) and the branch outcome depends on preceding instructions which have to be completed for determining the branch successor.

For decreasing branch latency, branch prediction is used; this may be accomplished by hardware or software. A traditional method for hardware branch prediction is the usage of a branch-target buffer. This buffer contains for each branch instruction its predicted outcome and the target address. After each access the branch-target buffer is updated. An alternative to a branch-target buffer with similar accuracy but less space consumption is to include branch-prediction information in the instruction cache. Each block in the instruction cache contains information about the next block to be fetched and the next instruction in this block to be executed.

There are various branch prediction algorithms; a trade-off has to be made in order to decide between prediction accuracy on the one hand and overhead w.r.t. implementation space and impact on cycle time on the other hand. Current two-bit counter algorithms used on UltraSPARC, Alpha, etc. reach about 86% prediction accuracy on SPECint92 benchmarks. With new branch-prediction algorithms (two levels, branch correlation) 96% may be reached.

5. Instruction decode:

The instruction-decode stage comprises many activities in a superscalar processor; therefore, in some cases it is separated into several stages. These activities are:

1. Fetch the source operand values or tags from the reorder buffer, using the most recent entries. If there are no corresponding entries, fetch the values from the register file.

2. Assign a new tag for the destination register of the instruction.

3. Allocate a processing unit and a slot in the corresponding reservation station or in the instruction window. Enter the corresponding data: operation code, source operand values or tags, and tag of the destination operand.

4. Allocate a slot in the reorder buffer and enter register identifier, tag, and program counter (for exception restart).

6. Instruction issue:

When a processing unit completes an instruction, its reservation station or the instruction window is checked if there is an instruction for this processing unit with all source operands available. In this case, the corresponding instruction is issued to this processing unit. Similarly, when an instruction is decoded and all its source operands are available, it is checked if a suitable processing unit is ready and it is issued to that unit. Finally, when an instruction completes, it is checked if there is an instruction in the instruction window or any reservation station waiting for the value computed by that instruction. In this case, it is also checked if a corresponding processing unit is idle to issue that instruction.

7. Instruction completion:

1. Write the result into the reorder buffer; the entry is identified by the corresponding tag.

2. Check if there is an instruction waiting in the instruction window (resp. in any reservation station) for this result tag. In this case start the instruction issue process.

3. Check if there is an instruction decoded in the current cycle needing the result; in this case, bypass the result to this instruction.

4. If an exception occurred, send tag, result and exception type to the reorder buffer.

8. Instruction retirement:

The retirement actions may be performed multiple times per cycle, triggered by instruction completion.

1. Check the oldest entry in the reorder buffer. If it is valid (i.e. the instruction is completed) and no exceptions are indicated, write the value into the specified register; in case of a store instruction write the data to the store buffer and the address to the load/store reservation station.

2. If an exception is indicated by the corresponding reorder buffer entry, save the PC, flush the buffer (logically) above that instruction (i.e. the instructions issued later) and invoke an exception handler by restarting the decoder with the exception-handler address.

3. In case of a mispredicted branch, flush the reorder buffer above that instruction (i.e. the instructions issued later) and restart the decoder with the correct address. (This activity will usually occur as early as possible).

9. Loads and Stores:

Memory accesses represent the main bottleneck in current computers. In architectures with multiple load/store units the memory dependences have to be checked; out-of-order execution may reverse the ordering of loads and stores even if there is only one processing unit for loads and stores. Loads are performance critical - if data do not arrive in order, the processor will have to wait. Thus, a load/store reservation station can be used combined with a store buffer, allowing load instructions to be served before store instructions if there are no dependences; this is called "load bypassing". If a store instruction is followed by a load instruction to the same address, the value may be derived from the store buffer (if the store is still waiting there) without accessing the data cache or memory. This optimization is called "load forwarding".

In [Johnson 91] various architectures for load and store handling are presented. The architecture of figure 16 is suggested there, with a combined load/store reservation station holding the memory addresses and a store buffer for the data to be stored. The following activities can be added to the activities of the pipeline stages described above:

When a load or store instruction is decoded, its address register value or tag (if the value is not ready yet), together with the address offset are entered into the load/store reservation station (for other addressing modes the additional data for address determination are entered, too). For a store instruction, the data to be stored is placed into the store buffer. The loads and stores are issued in order from the load/store reservation station to the address unit when their address-register values are valid. The address unit places store addresses into the store buffer and sends load addresses directly to the data cache, thus allowing loads to bypass stores. Before sending loads to the data cache, they are checked for dependences on the stores in the store buffer. In case of a dependence, store data are returned directly from the store buffer, thus realizing a load forwarding.

The architecture described above is only one example of a superscalar architecture. There are many variants, e.g. branches may be processed in the instruction decoder like in the RS 6000 or instruction combining (pairing) is used like in the Pentium processor.

7 Constraints for Instruction Scheduling

The main constraints for instruction scheduling are dependences; they are introduced in this section.

7.1 Data Dependences

We consider two machine operations, O1 and O2 where O1 precedes O2 in the program text. Two dependent operations must not be interchanged or executed concurrently because the program semantics would be altered, otherwise.

Def. 3: True dependence

> There is a *true dependence* between two operations O1 and O2 (in short form written as: O2 δ^t O1) if O2 has a source operand which is destination operand of O1 and which is not written between O1 and O2 in the operation sequence. This is also called *read-after-write dependence* or *flow dependence*.

The instruction sequence "a = z + 5; x = x + a;" shows such a true dependence; the value of a has to be determined before calculating the new value of x in the second instruction.

Def. 4: Anti-dependence

> There is an *anti-dependence* between two operations O1 and O2 (in short form written as: O2 δ^a O1) if O2 has a destination operand which is a source operand of O1 and which is not used between O1 and O2 in the operation sequence. This is also called *write-after-read dependence*.

The instruction sequence "x = x + a; a = z + 5;" shows such an anti-dependence; for calculating the new value of x the original value of a has to be used, not the one determined in the second instruction.

Def. 5: Output-dependence

> There is an *output-dependence* between two operations O1 and O2 (in short form written as: O2 δ^o O1) if both operations have the same destination operand. This is also called *write-after-write* dependence.

Data dependences are barriers for instruction reordering - the sequence of dependent instructions has to be maintained to preserve program semantics. There is also another kind of dependence, *input dependence* or *read-after-read dependence* between two operations reading the same source operand; this kind of dependence is not relevant for our further considerations because it does not prevent reordering.

7.2 Off-live Dependence

There is yet another kind of dependence relevant for instruction scheduling which does not belong to the standard types of dependences defined above. We consider a conditional branch operation cj and its successors on its TRUE- and FALSE-paths.

Def. 6: Off-live-dependence

There is an *off-live-dependence* between a conditional jump operation cj and an operation O which is a successor of cj in one of its two successor paths, if O writes to a variable which is read by an operation in the other successor path of cj (before being written on that path).

The following example shows an off-live dependence in C representation and incorrect reordering when that is not considered:

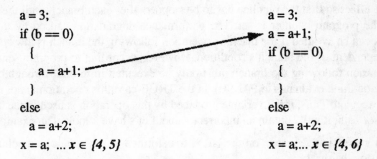

```
        a = 3;                                  a = 3;
        if (b == 0)                             a = a+1;
        {                                       if (b == 0)
            a = a+1;                            {
        }                                       }
        else                                    else
            a = a+2;                                a = a+2;
        x = a;  ... x ∈ {4, 5}                   x = a;... x ∈ {4, 6}
```

Figure 17: Off-live Dependence and Incorrect Reordering

The variable x gets in the TRUE-successor path the value 4 and in the other (the FALSE) path the value 5, as shown on the left-hand side in figure 17. Now let's reorder the statements: consider the instruction "a = a+1". It must not be moved ahead of "a = 3" because there is a true dependence. However, if we move it before the conditional jump "if (b == 0)" (and after the assignment "a = 3") then the variable x will get the value 6 if the FALSE-path is taken (as shown on the right-hand side in figure 17), violating program semantics.

For our further considerations we need the definition of basic blocks:

Def. 7: Basic Block

A *basic block* is a sequence of instructions with at most one entrance to the sequence (at its beginning) and at most one branch operation (at the end of the sequence).

Thus, only the first instruction of a basic block may have preceding instructions outside the block; it is the only instruction in the block which may have more than one predecessor and the only one which may have a label (which is actually used). A conditional or unconditional branch must not occur in the middle, it can only be the last instruction of a basic block. Call instructions may be considered as a special kind of branches which return to their origin. For our purposes call instructions may occur inside basic blocks, not only at the end of a basic block; this is made possible by interprocedural program analyses, see subsection 12.2.7.

8 Instruction-Scheduling Methods

The methods for fine-grain parallelization are based on reordering intermediate or machine code so that groups of instructions are formed which can be executed in parallel.

Instruction scheduling is a well-known method to exploit processor power; it was already applied in the CDC 6600. It became popular again with the emergence of RISC architectures. In these pipelined processors, branches need mostly two cycles to take effect so that the pipeline has to be stopped after each branch until the new value of the program counter is set. The performance degradation caused by this pipeline stall can be avoided if the machine operation following the branch is always executed, independent of the branch's condition. However, according to program semantics, the operation following the branch must only be executed in the fall-through case (i.e. if the condition evaluates to FALSE); in the TRUE-case this operation is not intended to be executed. Thus, if the variable produced by this operation is used in the TRUE successor path, it will contain an incorrect value. Let's have a look at an example:

The instruction sequence on the left is transformed to the symbolic machine instructions on the right:

a = 5;	a = 5;
if (x ≤ 0) then	jump_if_greater_0 x, L1;
{ a = a - 1;	a = a - 1;
b = 4; }	b = 4;
else	jump L2;
{a = a + 1;	L1: a = a + 1;
b = 12; }	b = 12;
$\Rightarrow a \in \{4,6\}$	L2: ... $\Rightarrow a \in \{4,5\}$

Figure 18: Branch Delay Slot

The second instruction, "a = a - 1" in this example is executed independent of the value of the variable "x" because the program counter is set to its new value two cycles after the issue of the jump instruction - and thus, this instruction (a = a - 1) which is placed in the "delay slot" is executed before the target instruction of the branch. Thus, in the TRUE-case (x > 0) the value of "a" is calculated incorrectly, as 5 instead of 6.

One method to maintain program semantics is to implement a check-and-stall algorithm in hardware; however, this is costly and may increase processor cycle time. According to RISC philosophy, architecture has to be developed towards decreasing cycle time; thus, maintaining semantic consistency is performed by software where it is less costly.

Correct program semantics is guaranteed by scheduling a machine operation immediately after the branch which will be executed in any case, e.g. one originally preceding the branch operation. This may also be an operation which is executed in one path after the branch and does not change semantics in the other path, i.e. by writing a variable (as its destination operand) which is not used in that path afterwards, and which causes no exception.

Similar to branch delay slots, as these cycles after branches are called, are load delay slots. After a load operation the variable fetched from memory cannot be accessed, at least for the succeeding cycle. For this case, instruction scheduling tries to move instructions using loaded data away from the load operations to ensure that the correct data are used.

In the early RISC processors scheduling was necessary to maintain semantical correctness. However, in later versions of the processors the number of delay slots varied and hardware methods had to be applied to ensure binary compatibility (compare e.g. MIPS R4000 vs. R3000). For these architectures, scheduling is no longer necessary for maintaining semantical correctness, however it can improve performance.

Several instruction-scheduling methods for filling delay slots have been developed, see e.g. the basic paper on instruction scheduling for RISC processors, [Hennessy/Gross 83]. There are also scheduling methods which were developed for specific processors, e.g. for the IBM RS 6000 in [Warren 90].

Similar scheduling methods are used in the field of hardware synthesis. Algorithms used in this area are described in [Paulin/Knight 89]. In [Breternitz 91] an extension of Ebcioglu's version of Percolation Scheduling (see below in subsection 8.4.2) is used for the synthesis of application-specific processors.

The main requirement for parallel execution is data and control independence, for two dependent instructions have to be executed successively. All instruction-scheduling methods perform program analysis first to determine dependences between instructions. Then the scheduling process is performed in particular regions; the size of these regions determines the number of candidates available for reordering. This size is an important factor for the performance achievable by scheduling.

Basic blocks are very convenient units for scheduling because inside a basic block only data dependences have to be considered, no off-live dependences. Otherwise, moving an instruction from one successor path of a branch instruction before the branch (which means also to another basic block) may change a variable read in the other path of the branch instruction and thus alter program semantics, i.e. we have to consider off-live dependences. These off-live dependences can be identified by data-flow analysis. Thus, for reordering instructions globally, i.e. beyond basic-block boundaries, data-flow analysis is necessary which can be quite time consuming. Therefore, many reordering methods use local scheduling inside basic blocks only, although global scheduling has a higher parallelization potential by considering more instructions for reordering.

8.1 Local Instruction-Scheduling

Methods for local instruction-scheduling have already been developed for early IBM mainframes. Optimal scheduling is NP-hard (see [Hennessy/Gross 83]); optimal algorithms can therefore not be used in practice, except for quite small basic blocks. A series of near-optimal algorithms have been developed; these can be divided into two classes, one using List Scheduling and the other using selection heuristics.

The basic conditions to be considered for scheduling are data dependences. For local scheduling these are represented in a data-dependence graph, a directed acyclic graph (DAG) (see [AhoSethiUllman 88]). For each basic block one DAG of data dependences is constructed where the nodes represent instructions, and with an edge from node N1 to N2 if the instruction represented by N2 is dependent on N1. The nodes and edges of the DAG may be attributed with execution times of instructions and other information.

List Scheduling computes in a first pass priorities for each instruction in the DAG, thus linearizing it and sorting it according to these priorities. In a second pass, instructions are selected considering dependences and execution times. The selection algorithms use one pass only to select the next instruction to be scheduled; several selection criteria with different priorities may be used.

A series of local scheduling algorithms was developed by D. Bernstein, e.g. in [Bernstein 88]; they all are based on List Scheduling and use different methods to determine the priorities of the instructions in a DAG. The basic algorithm using such selection criteria was defined by Gibbons and Muchnick in [Gibbons/Muchnick 86]. A variant of this algorithm was developed for the IBM RS6000 architecture [Warren 90]. An overview of these methods can be found in [Krishnamurthy 90].

Local scheduling methods are compared and assessed in [Schepers 92]. More performance than with standard instruction-scheduling methods will be gained if also pipeline stalls, e.g. due to resource usage, are considered for scheduling. In [Schepers 92a] a nearly optimal method is presented which considers a variety of processor characteristics.

In current developments the focus is on algorithms which consider caches and TLBs (Translation Lookaside Buffers) in order to decrease the number of (primary and secondary) cache misses, TLB misses, and disk accesses. The reason for this emphasis on cache behaviour is that in current processors memory access is mostly the main bottleneck for system performance. Additionally, the differences of the access times to primary caches, secondary caches, and memory are very high, so that these algorithms try to get primary cache hits for as many accesses as possible.

8.2 Global Instruction-Scheduling

Scheduling globally, i.e. beyond basic block boundaries, offers far more instructions as candidates for scheduling; these are e.g. all instructions in a loop body or even more if loop unrolling or scheduling between functions is performed.

Since 1981 several global scheduling methods have been published, mostly for horizontal microcode compaction. The following papers present such methods:

[Aiken 88], [Aiken/Nicolau 88a], [Banger et al 89], [Bernstein/Rodeh 91], [Böckle 92], [Chang/Lavery/Hwu 91], [Danelutto/Vanneschi 90], [Ebcioglu 90], [Ebcioglu/ Nicolau 89], [Fernandes et al 92], [Fisher 81], [Fisher et al 84], [Franklin/Sohi], [Grishman/Bogong 83], [Hahne et al 89], [Hendren/Nicolau 89], [KarlW 93], [Keckler/Dally 92], [Lah/Atkins 83], [Lam 90], [Linn 83], [Melvin/Patt 91], [Nakatani/ Ebcioglu 90], [Nakatani/Ebcioglu 90a], [Nicolau 84], [Nicolau 85], [Nicolau/Fisher 81], [Nicolau/Fisher 84], [Nicolau/Potasman 90], [Nicolau/Pingali/Aiken 88], [Paulin/ Knight 89], [Schubert 90], [Su/Ding/Jin 84], [Su/Ding 85], [Wall 86], [Werner 91].

Two classes of global scheduling methods can be distinguished. Algorithms of the first class partition a program's flow graph into regions of traces or trees and apply a local scheduling method like List Scheduling to these regions. At the boundaries between the regions the program semantics may be altered by these methods, thus it must be reconstructed by (usually quite costly) bookkeeping methods (see 8.3.1). The second class comprises methods which apply scheduling to the "program graph" where the nodes contain independent operations which can be executed in parallel and are attributed with dependence information. Semantics-preserving transformations for reordering are provided and reordering is separated from strategies controlling reordering so that no bookkeeping is necessary.

A scheduling method which can be used for speculative-execution architectures (see subsection 3.4.1) is presented in [Hsu/Davidson 86]. Instructions which must not be moved across some branches, e.g. particular stores, are transformed to *guarded instructions*, characterized by a boolean value specifying the condition for such a move. This *decision tree scheduling* reorders a complex of basic blocks, making efficient use of these guarded instructions.

8.3 Global Scheduling Methods Based on Local Scheduling

8.3.1 Trace Scheduling

The most important method of this class is *Trace Scheduling*. It was developed by J. Fisher (see [Ellis85], [Fisher 81], [Fisher et al 84]). Originally, it was employed for horizontal microcode compaction. Later, this method was also used on the instruction-set level for exploitation of fine-grain parallelism. Fisher described such architectures in [Fisher 83], [Fisher 84], [Fisher 87] and [Fisher/O'Donnell 84]. At Yale university, the ELI project provided the base for the TRACE-family of VLIW machines which offered quite high performance for numeric applications (see subsection 4.1). The results of the ELI project are described in [Ellis85].

During this project the BULLDOG compiler was developed which was the base for the TRACE compilers (see [Ellis 85] and figure 19). This compiler performs many standard optimizations as well as memory-reference disambiguation and Trace Scheduling. Memory-reference disambiguation helps to parallelize memory accesses. At

compile time the address in memory which will be accessed by a load or store statement is often not known. In these cases, a store operation must not be exchanged or
being processed in parallel with another memory access because it may refer to the
same address. Memory-reference disambiguation finds out whether two memory
accesses may refer to the same address. Memory-bank disambiguation is used to determine if two memory accesses refer to two distinct memory banks and can thus be executed in parallel (if hardware offers two distinct paths to these two memory banks).

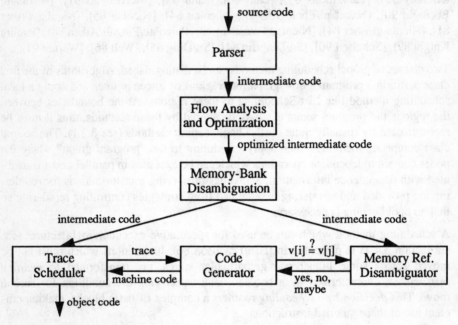

Figure 19: Bulldog Compiler Structure

After disambiguation, the compiler selects the regions to be considered for parallelization. In local scheduling methods these regions are basic blocks. Fisher's basic idea for
global scheduling was:

- Consider large portions of code for parallelization, more than just basic blocks.
- Make those parts of a program faster which are executed frequently (this is also the
  basic idea of RISC).
- Assign weights to the operations according to their execution frequencies.
- Construct traces in the program by starting with a frequent operation and add its
  predecessors and successors, taking at each conditional branch the most probable
  successor.
- Consider each trace as a sequential block and reorder operations w.r.t. dependences
  inside the trace so that as many operations as possible can be processed in parallel.
- Compact operations which can be executed in parallel to very long instruction
  words.

The Bulldog compiler implements these ideas. The intermediate code of the program to be compiled is conveyed to the Trace-Scheduling part of the compiler as a flow graph for each function (see [Aho/Sethi/Ullman 88]). First, each operation and each edge in this flow graph is assigned a weight, according to the estimated number of times it will be executed at run time. The weights are computed according to the following algorithm:

$$g(S) = 1 \qquad \text{for the first node S of the flow graph}$$

$$g(O) = \sum_{e \in in(O)} g(e) \qquad \text{for an operation O and the set } in(O) \text{ of incoming edges e joining in O}$$

$$g(H) = \text{Iterations}(H) * \sum_{e \in in(H)} g(e) \qquad \text{for a loop header H with } Iterations(H) = number\ of\ (estimated)\ loop\ iterations$$

$$g(e) = g(O) * prob(e) \qquad \text{for an exit edge e of operation O, taken with probability prob(e).}$$

Algorithm 1: Trace Scheduling: Execution Weights

If no directives are given by the programmer or no other heuristics for determining weights are available, the probability for each successor of a conditional branch operation is assumed as a default value of 50%. For loops, the number of iterations is used to determine the weight; where no loop boundary is known, a fixed number, e.g. 100 loop repetitions are assumed.

After weight determination, trace selection is performed. The node with the highest weight in the flow graph is selected first. List Scheduling is used to build the trace (see e.g. [Ellis 85]). The trace is enlarged by adding nodes forward and backward. It is enlarged forward by taking the trace's last node and adding the successor with the highest weight. The forward enlargement ends if no such successor can be found or if the successor belongs to another trace or if the edge to the successor is the back-edge of a loop. Similarly, the trace is enlarged backward. The trace will not contain a loop back-edge so that all operations inside a trace belong to at most one loop iteration; allowing several iterations inside a trace would complicate the scheduler significantly.

In contrast to local scheduling methods, scheduling traces can change program semantics as shown in figure 20.

Let the instruction sequence on the left in figure 20 be transformed to the sequence on the right side; the trace was chosen e.g. on the TRUE-path of the conditional jump "if (e) then" and the statement "i:= n+1" was moved behind the jump. This move is possible in Trace Scheduling, however, it changes program semantics: In the FALSE-path of the conditional jump the value of i is *not* n+1 as it should be, because the statement "i := n+1" is now only executed in the TRUE-path. Thus, we have to restore correct program semantics; this can e.g. be performed by adding a statement "i:=n+1" in the FALSE-path of the conditional jump, just before the statement "k:= i+5". Adding this statement to restore program semantics is called *bookkeeping*. The compiler's book-keeping phase can be quite costly - all possible changes of program semantics due to scheduling have to be detected and repaired - and it is thus the major drawback of Trace Scheduling. The insertion of this correction code may increase code size substantially and even cause code explosion. Several methods to limit code increase are discussed in [Ellis 85].

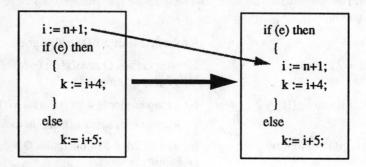

Figure 20: Bookkeeping

The traces are in turn conveyed to the code generator where the statements are compacted to very long instruction words.

The Bulldog team from Yale university founded Multiflow Corp. and created TRACE, a family with two series of VLIW machines comprising three machines each, with 7, 14, and 28 operations per instruction. These machines had a very good price/performance ratio and remarkable performance for scientific code. These machines are described in [Colwell et al 88] and in [Clancy et al 87]. The architectures and methods are described in [Fisher 81], [Fisher 83] [Fisher 84], [Fisher 87], [Fisher/O'Donnell 84], and [Fisher et al 84]. Methods for Trace Scheduling and correctness proofs can be found in [Nicolau 84]. The research in [Nicolau/Fisher 84] showed that there is sufficient inherent parallelism in programs to justify the development of VLIW machines.

8.3.2 Other Global Scheduling Methods

The code size increase and danger of code explosion in Trace Scheduling was a major motive for developing other global scheduling methods.

The ITSC (Improved Trace Scheduling) method ([Su/Ding/Jin 84]) reduces the amount of code-size increase due to bookkeeping by separating a trace's operations into two sets with different scheduling priorities, starting with operations on the critical path and the operations dependent on those.

The tree-method ([Lah/Atkins 83]) reduces the amount of code increase in Trace Scheduling by separating a program's flow graph into "top trees" which contain mainly nodes which are not join or leaf nodes, and in "bottom trees" which contain mainly nodes which are not start nodes or fork nodes. First top trees are scheduled, then bottom trees.

The SRDAG method ([Linn 83]) allows for more parallelization potential. Single-rooted directed acyclic graphs (SRDAGs) are considered for scheduling, not just sequential traces. However, bookkeeping is more complex than in Trace Scheduling.

8.4 Global Scheduling on the Program Graph

Other kinds of global scheduling methods were developed to overcome the major drawback of Trace Scheduling: the costly bookkeeping. During the Bulldog project at Yale University A. Nicolau developed *Percolation Scheduling* [Nicolau 85], a method performing instruction scheduling on the *program graph*, a generalized flow graph. This graph is defined as:

Def. 8: Program Graph and Conditional Tree

The *program graph* is a directed graph $PG = (\overline{N}, \overline{E}, \overline{CT})$ with a set $\overline{N}$ of nodes, a set $\overline{E}$ of edges, and a set of conditional trees $\overline{CT}$. A node $N \in \overline{N}$ contains a set of symbolic operations which can be executed in parallel (i.e. which are independent). There is an edge from a node N to a node N' if the operations in N are executed before those in N', i.e. the edges represent the control flow of the program.

The *conditional tree* in a node N of PG is a tree $CT = (Nc, Ec, \{T,F\})$ with a set Nc of nodes which represent the conditional jumps in N. The edges are labeled with T or F, representing the TRUE or FALSE successor of a conditional jump. There is a T-edge from a node cj1 $\in$ Nc to a node cj2 $\in$ Nc if cj2 is executed after cj1 and if the condition in cj1 evaluates to TRUE and there is a F-edge from a node cj1 $\in$ Nc to a node cj2 $\in$ Nc if cj2 is executed after cj1 and if the condition in cj1 evaluates to FALSE.

The expression *independent* in def. 8 refers to particular dependences, relative to the architecture of the machine used. In an architecture with pipelined processing elements we have operations writing their destination operands in the same clock cycle as others read their source operands. If inside this clock cycle writing is always performed before reading and if exception processing guarantees a proper restart, operations reading a register r and operations writing the same register r may be placed in the same program-graph node. The conditional tree represents the flow dependences inside a program-graph node. In conditional-execution architectures (see subsection 3.4.1) the edges are attributed with the non-branch operations performed on the paths emanating from a conditional jump.

Each operation inside a program-graph node is executed by a specific processing element. Thus, on a machine with n processing elements, only program-graph nodes with up to n operations are executable. The number of operations in a node specifies the degree of parallelism represented by the node. Thus, the higher the number of operations in a node, the higher the performance of the program represented by the program graph.

```
if (a > 3) then        c1
  {x1 = y1 + 5;
   if (b > 4) then     c2
     {   x2 = y2 + 1;
      L1:  ..... }
   else
     {   x3 = y2 - 1;
      L2:  ..... }
  }
else
  {x4 = y3 + 5;
   if (c > 4) then      c3
     {   x5 = y4 + 1;
      L3:..... }
   else
     {   x6 = y4 - 1;
      L4: .....}
  }
```

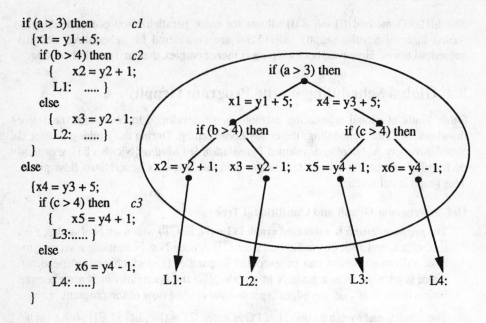

Figure 21: Program-Graph Node and Conditional Tree

Figure 21 shows a a program section which can be represented inside one program-graph node. We assume that the statements at labels L1, L2, L3, and L4 reside in successor nodes. For standard architectures, the operations in the program-graph node are not structured, they all are processed in the same clock cycle. However, the successor node depends on the evaluation of the comparison c1 ("a > 3"), c2 ("b > 4"), and c3 ("c > 4") inside the node.

We continue processing at label

- L1 if (c1 = TRUE) and (c2 = TRUE)
- L2 if (c1 = TRUE) and (c2 = FALSE)
- L3 if (c1 = FALSE) and (c3 = TRUE)
- L4 if (c1 = FALSE) and (c3 = FALSE).

Branching to L1 and L2 is independent of c3 and branching to L3 and L4 is independent of c2.

In conditional-execution architectures such operations can be placed inside one node even if they are dependent. Let's assume that the operation before label L2 is "x2 = y2 - 1" instead of "x3 = y2 - 1". This operation is processed concurrently to the operation "x2 = y2 + 1", writing to the same destination. In the original program, both statements will not be executed in parallel because they are on different paths in the program flow. In conditional-execution architectures, both operations are processed in parallel, however, only the one on the actually taken path may write its results to the destination registers, i.e. the operation determined by the value of condition c2 (for c1 = TRUE). Such an architecture allows for far more parallelism than standard "absolute"-execution architectures. For these architectures the edges of the conditional trees are labeled by the non-branch operations while for standard architectures the conditional trees are determined by the branch operations only and are just used to determine the successor node.

Some more technical expressions used in this context are (according to [Aho/Sethi/ Ullman 88]:

Def. 9: Start Node, Top Node, Leaves, Heads and Tails of Edges:

Each program graph has exactly one *start node* (or *top node*) which has no incoming edges, i.e. the operations in this node will be processed first.

Nodes without outgoing edges are called *leaves*.

If a → b is an edge, b is the *head* and a is the *tail* of this edge.

In FORTRAN programs, "ENTRY" statements may cause the creation of several top nodes per program graph. We can derive a single-rooted program graph by inserting a dummy node as common predecessor of all ENTRY nodes.

The program-graph nodes may be annotated by several attributes like the set of variables read and written by operations in the node or information about liveness of variables.

8.4.1 Percolation Scheduling

The basic idea of Percolation Scheduling is to increase parallelism and performance by moving operations "up in the program graph", i.e. from a node to preceding nodes; thus, nodes towards the bottom of the graph are emptied and can be deleted. Operations are moved upwards in the graph so that they are processed as early as possible.

The method is structured in several layers; the bottom layer offers basic *core transformations* which move an operation to the preceding node(s), unify operations, and delete nodes. The upper layers are described quite abstractly in [Nicolau 85] - they perform instruction reordering to parallelize loops and select the nodes the core transformations are applied to. More specific and detailed new definitions of the actions being performed in two levels above the core-transformation layer and extensions of the core transformations are presented in subsection 12.3.3 - 12.3.6.

The upper layers as described in [Nicolau 85] are:

Layer 1, the *Support Layer*, contains analysis methods like e.g. memory disambiguation and standard optimizations like e.g. dead-code removal.

Layer 2, the *Guidance Layer*, contains rules directing the applications of the core transformations. In [Nicolau 85] this is characterized as the major difference to Trace Scheduling where we have just a single rule (for trace picking) and which is inseparable from the actual transformation mechanism (whereas in Percolation Scheduling the latter is comprised in the lowest level).

Layer 3, the *Enabling Layer*, consists of transformations that allow the core transformations to process arbitrary graphs and enables them to exploit coarser-grained parallelism, e.g. within nested loops.

Layer 4, the *Meta Layer*, consists of transformations that use the core transformations to exploit coarser parallelism, e.g. partial loop/module overlapping.

Layer 5, the *Mapping Layer*, takes the partial schedule created by the other levels and fits it to the given architecture (e.g. register and memory bank allocation, resource management, etc.).

The following subsections describe the core transformations. Enhancements to these transformations are described in subsection 12.3.3.

8.4.1.1 Move_op

The *move_op* core-transformation is used to move an operation, which is no conditional jump, from a node in the program graph to a preceding node. Figure 22 and algorithm 2 show how an operation op'_i is moved from a node N to a preceding node M.

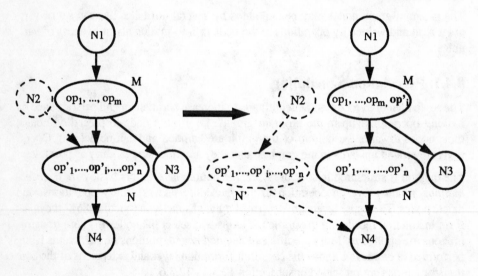

Figure 22: *Move_op* **Core Transformation**

Move_op Core Transformation:

- Is there any true or anti-dependence between op'_i and any operation op_k in M?

  yes: • no move possible; exit.

  no: • Does op'_i write to a variable which is live in N3 (or in the subgraph headed by N3)?

      yes: • No move possible (off-live dependence); exit.

no: • Insert op'i in M and adjust all corresponding attributes in M.

   • Has N any other predecessor besides M (like N2)?

      yes: • Make a copy N' of node N, including all attributes and edges.

         • Relink all edges from node(s) N2 to N' instead of N.

   • Delete operation op'$_i$ from node N.

   • Recompute data-dependence and liveness information for all nodes where changes occurred.

Algorithm 2: *Move_op* Core Transformation

8.4.1.2 Move_cj

Conditional jumps have to be treated separately from other operations because they change control flow and have more than one successor. There is a special core transformation for conditional jumps, "move_cj", shown in figure 23.

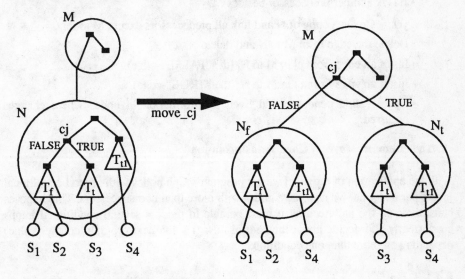

Figure 23: *Move_cj* Core Transformation

We want to move a conditional jump cj from a node N to a preceding node M. In figure 23 we see the conditional tree in node N with the square nodes representing conditional-jump operations. For standard (i.e. absolute-execution) architectures the other operations in node N are all completely executed. In conditional-execution architectures (see subsection 3.4.1) these operations are attributed to the edges in the conditional tree; they all start execution but only those on an edge for which the conditions evaluate to TRUE may write their results back.

For each conditional jump we have a left ("FALSE") subtree T_f, containing all successors on the FALSE-edge. Similarly, there is a right ("TRUE") subtree T_t. If we want to move cj to M then we only have to check read_after_write dependences because a conditional jump does not write any variable (which may be read as operand by another operation and had to be considered here). The operations in successors of cj which are now inside N, i.e. its subtrees in N, will reside after the move in different nodes.

A simplified version of the algorithm for move-cj is shown below in algorithm 3.

Move-cj Core Transformation:

- Does cj read a variable which is written by any operation in M?

    yes: • no move possible; exit.

    no: • Build a copy N_f of N and delete cj and its "TRUE" subtree T_t in N_f.

    • Build a copy N_t of N and delete cj and its "FALSE" subtree T_f in N_t.

    • Insert cj in M at the bottom of M's conditional tree, where the successor link to N was before.

    • Has N another predecessor besides M?

        yes: • Create a copy of N and link all predecessors except M to that.

    • Delete the edge from M to N and delete N.

    • Insert an edge from cj in M to N_f (the "FALSE"-edge).

    • Insert an edge from cj in M to N_t (the "TRUE"-edge).

    • Update all dependence and liveness information in nodes where changes occurred.

Algorithm 3: *Move_cj* **Core Transformation**

With the application of move_cj we get program-graph nodes with several conditional jumps per node, i.e. we now have nodes with more than two successors. This imposes constraints on the architecture: it must be able to process several conditional jumps concurrently and decide about the control flow (i.e. the next program-counter value) depending on more than one condition.

8.4.1.3 Unify

This core transformation unifies copies of operations in neighbour nodes and moves the unified operation to a common predecessor. Application of move_op and move_cj may create many copies of operations for particular application programs. These copies do not increase program run time, however they increase code size and thus the instruction cache miss rate which in turn may decrease program run time.

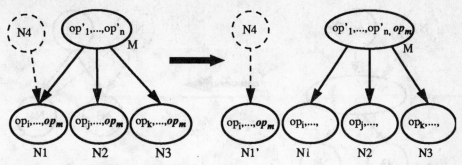

Figure 24: *Unify* **Core Transformation**

Unify **Core Transformation:**

We have a node N1 containing an operation op_m and a predecessor M of N1.

- Are there any true or anti-dependences between op_m and any operation in M?

  yes: • No unify possible; exit.

- Does op_m write a variable live in another successor of M, and is this liveness not caused by a copy of op_m?

  yes: • No unify possible; exit.

- Are there any copies of op_m in other successors Ni of M?

  yes: • For each of these Ni with another predecessor besides M:
  - • Make a copy Ni' of Ni.
  - • Relink the edges from these predecessors to Ni so that they point to Ni' now.

- Insert op_m in M.

- Delete op_m in all Ni

- Update liveness information in all nodes changed.

Algorithm 4: *Unify* **Core Transformation**

8.4.1.4 Delete

The main purpose of all core transformations is to gain performance by filling the upper nodes in the program graph and deleting lower and intermediate nodes. Deleting a node means saving at least one clock cycle in program run time (and accordingly more if the node is in a loop).

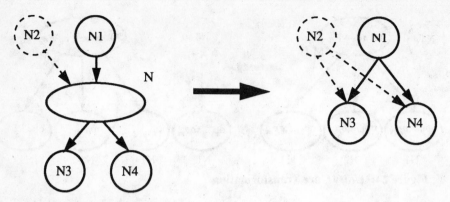

Figure 25: *Delete* **Core-Transformation**

Delete Core Transformation:

We want to delete a node N in the program graph.

• Does N contain any operation?

   yes: • No delete transformation possible; exit.

   no: • Relink all predecessors of N to the successors of N.

        • Delete N and the edges to N.

    Algorithm 5: *Delete* **Core Transformation**

8.4.2 Extensions to Percolation Scheduling

Several high-level transformations for Percolation Scheduling are presented in [Aiken 88]. There, A. Aiken shows that *Trace Scheduling* can be expressed using only the Percolation Scheduling core transformations. Thus, he gets a simpler and more comprehensive algorithm than the original (described e.g. in [Fisher 81] and [Ellis 85]). He used this description to derive Compact_global, a generalization of Trace Scheduling. Several scheduling algorithms based on the core transformations are described in [Aiken/Nicolau 88a].

Aiken defines the *migrate* core transformation and shows that it is the best strategy for moving a single statement (under certain conditions). Migrate moves an operation as far in the program graph as dependences allow and tries to unify as many copies of this operation as possible. Restrictions by busy resources are not considered on the path by migrate except in the destination node; thus, blocking an operation unnecessarily due to exhausted resources in an intermediate state can be avoided.

The migrate transformation was used to define *Compact_global*, a generalization of Trace Scheduling. Compact_global selects traces and moves operations in the program graph together with their copies as highly up as possible, including moves between different traces. Aiken shows in [Aiken 88] that a program graph transformed by Trace

Scheduling along a particular trace has no higher degree of parallelism than the same program graph using Compact_Global on the same trace. However, for general cases, i.e. not restricted to a particular trace, this is not valid because the program graphs constructed this way are not comparable in general.

In [Ebcioglu/Nicolau 89] an interesting version of Percolation Scheduling is presented. It is based on the IBM VLIW architecture (see subsection 4.2) using a speculative-execution model. This scheduling method can be used for other execution models as well. It is the only version of Percolation Scheduling where *resource management* is integrated in the scheduling algorithms. Resource management controls the usage of machine resources so that each operation finds sufficient resources available like processing elements, busses, registers, etc. Methods and algorithms for resource management are presented in section 13.

In Ebcioglu's version of Percolation Scheduling, for each node N in the program graph the set of all operations in successor nodes which can be transferred into N without violating dependences is determined as the set *unifiable_ops(N)*. The program graph is then traversed top-down (breadth-first), choosing for each node N the operations which will be moved there, out of the set unifiable_ops(N). Criteria for choosing the operations are priorities determined by the execution probabilities or the number of dependent operations. N is filled until the first resource is exhausted. This method is very thorough, and the compacted programs will presumably be near optimum. However, determining the sets unifiable_ops for each node N and updating them after each move is very costly and thus, even in the IBM VLIW scheduler it has not been implemented. The methods actually implemented in IBM's VLIW scheduler are described in [Nakatani/Ebcioglu 90] where a window (defining a specific number of operations) is used inside which the application of the Percolation Scheduling core transformations is performed.

8.5 Loop Parallelization

In many programs, mainly scientific applications, a significant portion of the execution time is spent in loops. Therefore, optimizing these loops means optimizing a significant part of the program's execution time. Vector processors use this fact to achieve their performance advantage over sequential machines for programs spending significant time in (parallelizable) loops. The main idea of loop parallelization is: we can process loops fast if we execute several iterations in parallel. This works fine for loops where we can predict the number of iterations but has some drawbacks for statically unpredictable loops where the number of iterations is unknown and where the program may jump out of the loop, perhaps at several places.

Loops can be parallelized on the source-code level or on the machine (resp. intermediate) code level. The former is often characterized as medium-grain parallelism.

For optimizing loops there are also a series of standard compiler techniques, e.g. loop fusion, strip mining, loop interchanging, loop unrolling (see [Aho/Sethi/Ullman 88]). The latter is also an important technique for loop parallelization.

8.5.1 Loop Unrolling

The central idea of loop unrolling is to execute several iterations of a loop concurrently; figure 26 shows a loop unrolled N times, so that each iteration can be executed on a separate processor.

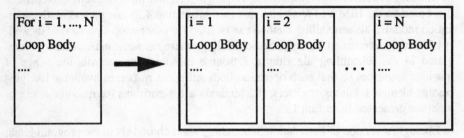

Figure 26: Loop Unrolling

However, this is only possible if there are no data dependences; in the example shown in figure 26 we can execute the first iteration on the first processor, the second iteration on the second processor, and so on - all in parallel (if they are independent). However, for loops there is yet another dependence which has not been mentioned yet. This is shown in the following example:

a[0] = c;

For i = 1, ..., N

   a[i] = a[i-1] + 2;

In the first iteration the value of a[1] is determined, in the second iteration the value of a[2], and so on. For the determination of a[1] we use the value of a[0], for the determination of a[2] we use the value of a[1], and so on. This means that we cannot start with the determination of a[2] before a[1] has been computed, and generally, we cannot start with the i-th iteration before the (i-1)st iteration is finished. And this actually means that we cannot parallelize the loop at all.

Dependences like this one, where the value causing the dependence is "carried" from one iteration of the loop to the next iteration are called *loop-carried dependences*. For a more formal definition see [Zima/Chapman 91].

We get an unrolling factor of k if k copies of the loop body exist after unrolling (k ≤ N, N being the number of iterations). However, we still cannot use the full potential of parallelism offered by unrolling: each of the unrolled loop bodies uses the same registers and variables, thus we have dependences between the registers used (not only the loop-carried dependences). Here, register renaming will help to exploit the inherent parallelism (for a more detailed description and the corresponding algorithms see subsection 12.2.3). Loop unrolling with register renaming is shown in the following example:

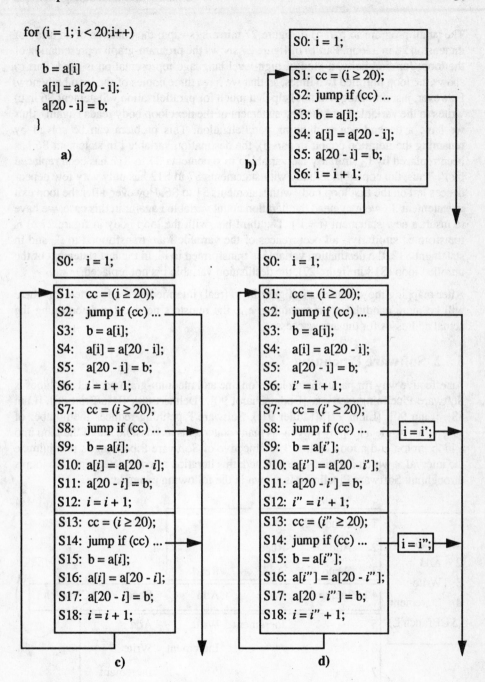

```
for (i = 1; i < 20;i++)
    {
    b = a[i]
    a[i] = a[20 - i];
    a[20 - i] = b;
    }
```

a)

b)

S0:	i = 1;
S1:	cc = (i ≥ 20);
S2:	jump if (cc) ...
S3:	b = a[i];
S4:	a[i] = a[20 - i];
S5:	a[20 - i] = b;
S6:	i = i + 1;

c)

d)

Figure 27: Loop Unrolling with Register Renaming

The small program in part a) of figure 27 mirrors (swaps) the contents of an array of dimension 20 in a loop. Part b) of figure 27 shows the program-graph representation of the loop; for simplicity, a kind of high-level language representation is used. Part c) shows the loop unrolled two times, so that we have three copies of the loop body now. However, just unrolling will not help that much for parallelization - Statement S6 in c) writes to the variable i and the first statement of the next loop body reads i again - thus we have a dependence prohibiting parallelization. This problem can be solved by renaming the iteration count; in part d), the destination variable i in statement S6 has been replaced by i', similarly the variable i in statements S7 to S12 has been replaced by i'. Thus, the copied loop body with statements S7 to S12 has only very few dependences left on the first loop body with statements S1 to S6. However, after the loop exit in statement S8 we may need the iteration count variable i again; in this case, we have to insert a new statement (i = i'). The third box with the loop body in figure 27 c) is transformed similarly - all occurrences of the variable i are transformed to i", and in statement S12, the destination variable is transformed to i". In the last statement of the unrolled loop (S18 in figure 27), the destination variable i is not replaced.

After mapping the statements in figure 27 to (real) intermediate-code statements there will be more candidates for renaming, e.g. the registers needed for determining the actual addresses for the array accesses.

8.5.2 Software Pipelining

An effective way for parallelizing loops on fine and medium-grain parallel machines is Software Pipelining (see e.g. [Bodin/Charot 90], [Dehnert 88], [Hsu/Bratt 88], [Lam 88], [Lam 90], [Liebl 92], [Müller 91]). Software Pipelining reduces the number of statements inside a loop by moving as many statements as possible out of the loop into a loop prolog and a loop epilog. The objective of Software Pipelining is to minimize the interval at which iterations are initiated; this iteration interval determines the loop's throughput. Software Pipelining is shown in the following example:

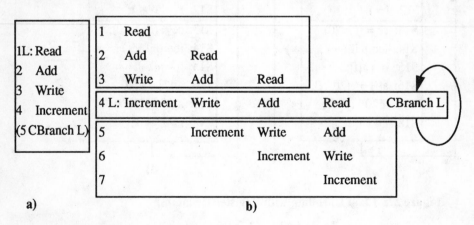

Figure 28: Software Pipelining

Part a) of figure 28 shows the body of a loop; the value of an array element is read from memory, a constant is added, the result is written back to memory, and the iteration variable is incremented; in the loop, all array elements are increased by this constant. Part b) of figure 28 shows the loop after application of Software Pipelining. The loop is unrolled and written in the column near the previous loop body in a pipelined fashion, considering dependences so, that no data dependent (loop-independent or loop-carried) operations occur in the same horizontal line. The original loop body in a) comprises 5 statements; all 5 occur in line 4 of part b), albeit of different iterations. In an architecture with 5 processing elements we can process the loop with one cycle per loop, as shown in line 4 of figure 28, part b). The increment of the i-th iteration, the write of the (i+1)st, the Add of the (i+2)nd, and the Read operation of the (i+3)rd iteration are processed in parallel; each clock cycle a new iteration can be started, processing the conditional branch to the loop header in parallel. The statements in lines 1 - 3 form the loop prolog and the statements in lines 5 - 7 the epilog of the loop, while line 4 represents the loop body.

8.5.3 Perfect Pipelining

Aiken and Nicolau developed Perfect Pipelining, a technique to minimize loop execution time; this and similar techniques are described in [Aiken 88], [Aiken/Nicolau 88], [Aiken/Nicolau 88b], [Aiken/Nicolau], [Nicolau 87], [Nicolau 88], [Nicolau/Pingali/ Aiken 88], [Schwiegelshohn 89], [Schwiegelshohn et al 90] and [Schwiegelshohn et al 91]. Perfect Pipelining tries to optimize software pipelining in combination with scheduling techniques. This is performed by unrolling the loop, compacting (parallelizing) it as far as possible, and searching for common patterns in the resulting code to find the optimal new loop body.

Figure 29 shows an example for Perfect Pipelining with three instructions A, B, and C where A_i denotes the i-th iteration of A. The loop in part a) is unrolled 5 times and the statements compacted (i.e. parallelized) as far as dependences (here loop-carried dependences) permit; the resulting graph is shown in part b). In this graph we see a loop prolog comprising the top three boxes and a loop epilog, comprising the three boxes at the bottom. In the figure's centre there are two boxes with statements D_j, C_{j+1}, B_{j+2}, A_{j+3}. If we unroll the loop body further and compact it as before, we will get the same structure: a loop prolog of three boxes, a loop epilog of three boxes, and boxes of the same structure in the centre. We can then combine the centre boxes into a loop again and get in part c) of figure 29 an optimized loop where the size of the loop body is minimized. The algorithm for Perfect Pipelining is thus, in a general description:

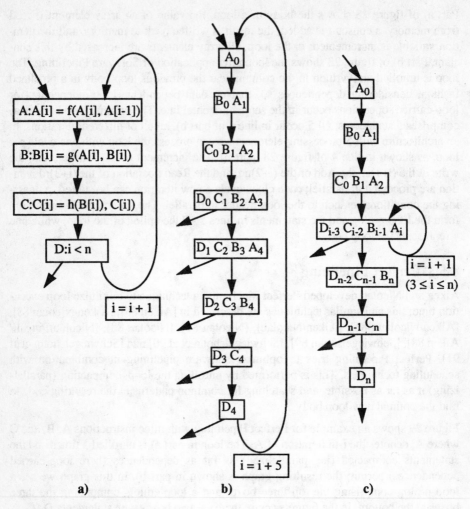

Figure 29: Perfect Pipelining

- Repeat while no common patterns are found between the nodes in the loop's centre:
    - unroll the loop;
    - compact the loop;
    - compare the nodes in the loop's centre;
    - find common patterns.
- Roll back the loop around the common nodes in the loop's centre.
- Form the loop epilog.

   Algorithm 6: Perfect Pipelining

However, it is quite hard to find such common patterns and for specific kinds of loops (mostly irregular ones), Perfect Pipelining cannot be applied.

8.5.4 Integrating Loop Parallelization and Instruction Scheduling

In [Aiken/Nicolau 88] the Percolation Scheduling core-transformations are used to compact the nodes; a combined processing of Perfect Pipelining and instruction scheduling is described in [Ebcioglu 87], [Ebcioglu/Nakatani 89], and [Ebcioglu/Nicolau 89]. Their method is called "Enhanced Pipeline-Percolation Scheduling"; it was developed for an architecture using speculative execution.

9 Developing Instruction-Scheduling Methods

The following sections describe instruction-scheduling methods and the variety of things which have to be considered for their development and application. Additionally, a set of tools is recommended as an environment to apply, tune, and assess these methods. The motivation for developing such methods is based on the question how competitiveness can be achieved in the three main areas of computing:

1. PCs:

   Based on a given HW platform try to get most performance for particular application areas and support high-level user interfaces for the end-user by hiding all activities providing performance.

2. Workstations:

   Performance is the key for competitiveness - try to provide as much performance as possible.

3. Mainframes:

   Usage and exploitation of new HW for supporting the features of mainframe applications without sacrificing compatibility.

For all three areas we have the problem that new hardware is being developed which cannot be fully used by application programs yet. These new processors offer fine-grain parallelism and, as shown above, instruction-scheduling methods promise most success for exploiting the potential of the new hardware. So far, scheduling has proven its suitability for delivering high performance for applications in the numerical and technical domain. One of the main tasks of this book is the description of scheduling methods for the far bigger area of general-purpose applications.

The methods described in the following provide support for the following objectives:

- Creation of an environment for the development, testing, assessment, and tuning of instruction-scheduling methods.
- Development, test, assessment, and tuning of instruction-scheduling methods for various applications, mainly in the general-purpose area.
- Specification of hardware features which support scheduling and which promise most performance in combination with such software methods.

The following sections describe, based on the experience from this project, what has to be considered and what has to be undertaken for instruction scheduling.

10 Tools for Instruction Scheduling

Figure 30 shows a set of tools for building an environment supporting the objectives above:

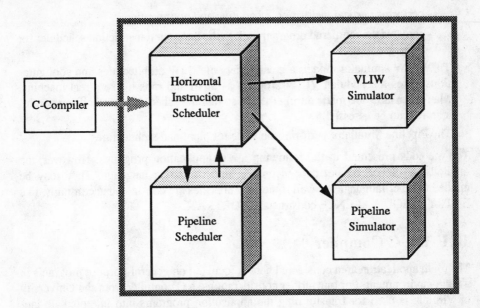

Figure 30: Tools for Fine-Grain Parallelism Exploitation

For developing, implementing, testing, and evaluating instruction-scheduling methods tools like those shown in figure 30 are needed. The application area chosen for the developments is based on general-purpose programs on workstations; such programs are typically written in C. The system architectures considered are a variety of VLIW and superscalar architectures as representatives of horizontal parallelism, and also pipelined architectures offering vertical parallelism.

These tools take an application program as object to be tested; this may be one which is specific for particular applications or is used for benchmarking, e.g. one of the SPEC benchmarks.

- The C compiler transforms the program into an intermediate-code representation. This representation is the input to the horizontal instruction scheduler.
- The Horizontal Instruction Scheduler
    - analyses the program to provide all information necessary to optimize and schedule the application program
    - represents the application program in the program graph and in the form used by the pipeline scheduler
    - performs horizontal instruction scheduling and optimization

- generates code and other output which is used as input for the simulators.

- The Pipeline Scheduler

  - gets the representation of the application program from the horizontal instruction scheduler

  - performs vertical instruction scheduling and optimization

  - conveys the reordered program back to the horizontal instruction scheduler for code generation.

- The VLIW simulator models a great variety of VLIW architectures and configurations, takes a scheduled VLIW program as input and runs it like a real machine. Many measures are made during the run so that the scheduling methods and architectures can be assessed.

- The Pipeline Simulator performs the same for pipelined architectures.

The methods presented in the following use C application programs. However, the methods developed do not depend on the kind of source language. They may be applied to other languages as well if their peculiarities are considered accordingly, like ENTRY or EQUIVALENCE constructs in FORTRAN.

10.1 The C Compiler

The main application area considered here is focussed on general-purpose programs in a Unix environment. For our further considerations, a C compiler from the University of Virginia is used for transforming the application programs into intermediate language which will be the input for the horizontal instruction scheduler. This compiler comprises the "*vpo*", the "*very portable optimizer*".

It is not hard to parallelize unoptimized code because there is mostly a lot unnecessary or dead code in such a program; however, this is not a realistic base for assessment. Optimized code was chosen to start with, so that we can evaluate how much performance we can get on top of these optimizations. Most well-known compiler optimizations are offered in a consistent way by this compiler.

The C compiler performs lexical and syntactical analysis of the application program and creates a flow graph for each function. This flow graph is output into a file which is then used as input to the horizontal instruction scheduler. For creating efficient code, the compiler's back-end uses a machine description based on a yacc grammar. This machine description is used with some additions for the scheduler as well. However, the routines for the semantic analysis were changed.

11 The Machine Model

The simulator and the horizontal instruction scheduler have a general machine model which allows to support a great variety of architectures. Basically, the machine model used for the following sections is described by sets of parameters, comprising:

- The number of PEs.

- All PEs are assumed as full ALUs (integer and floating point); resource management specifies PEs as using only subsets of the instruction set and the scheduler's back end maps operations to suitable PEs.

- There are 3 general register files, one for integer, one for single-precision floating point values, and one for double-precision floats. The corresponding entries in the machine description specify symbolic registers; they are mapped to physical registers in the scheduler's back-end; (see subsection 12.4.1). All registers referred to before this mapping in the back-end are symbolic registers. The register files' default size is 512 registers. The single- and double-floating-point registers may be synonyms for the same physical registers as in the MIPS R3000, i.e. d[0] (double) is physically the same register as f[0] combined with f[1] (single).

- For each PE there is a 2-bit condition-code register; all condition-code registers can be accessed by all PEs.

- All PEs are directly connected to all register files.

- The number of memory banks.

- All PEs are connected to all memory banks via separate busses.

- The organization of data on the memory banks may either be contiguous or interleaved.

- The PEs' instruction set is an extension of the MIPS instruction set.

- The compare operations write to the condition-code register of the PE they are executed on.

- The main features of VLIW machines can only become evident if several conditional branch operations can be processed in parallel. The branch operations in the model used are "branch_pattern"- operations; they read all condition-code registers in parallel and consider them all for determining the new program-counter (PC) value. The branch_pattern operation has two operands, a pattern for masking the condition codes, and the new PC value. The mask for each condition-code register may assume the values *TRUE*, *FALSE*, and *Don't Care*.

Example: Consider the program section from figure 21 on page 48. The three comparisons are processed on three different PEs, e.g. on PE1 the comparison "a > 3", on PE3 the comparison "b > 4", and on PE5 the comparison "c > 4". The comparison operation on PE1 sets the condition code register cc1 according to the evaluation result to TRUE or FALSE, similarly in the other PEs. The branch_pattern operation sets the PC (shown using the labels of figure 21) according to the contents of the condition codes registers to:

PC = L1 if [(cc1 = TRUE) ∧ (cc2 = DC) ∧ (cc3 = TRUE) ∧ (cc4 = DC) ∧ (cc5 = DC)]

PC = L2 if [(cc1 = TRUE) ∧ (cc2 = DC) ∧ (cc3 = FALSE) ∧ (cc4 = DC) ∧ (cc5 = DC)]

PC = L3 if [(cc1 = FALSE) ∧ (cc2 = DC) ∧ (cc3 = DC) ∧ (cc4 = DC) ∧ (cc5 = TRUE)]

PC = L4 if [(cc1 = FALSE) ∧ (cc2 = DC) ∧ (cc3 = DC) ∧ (cc4 = DC) ∧ (cc5 = FALSE)]

Here, DC means "don't care", i.e. the corresponding value is not used and the PC is determined independently of the corresponding value. For the other condition-code registers (cc2 and cc4), DC is used for the mask, too.

Restrictions and extensions to this machine model can be described in the input to the resource management (see section 13).

12 The Horizontal Instruction-Scheduler

Figure 31 below shows the basic structure of the horizontal instruction scheduler:

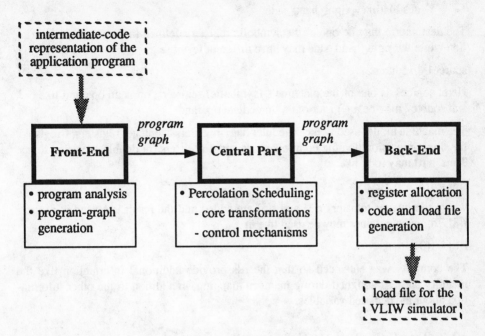

Figure 31: Horizontal Instruction-Scheduler Structure

The horizontal instruction scheduler consists of three parts:

- The front-end which gets the intermediate-code representation of an application program as input, performs program analysis and generates the program graph as central data structure of the scheduler.
- The central part (or middle-end), where transformations are performed on the program graph; these transformations are based on Percolation Scheduling.
- The back-end, where the code for the target machine and the load file to drive the simulators are generated.

12.1 The Interface Compiler - Scheduler

The interface between compiler and scheduler comprises all information about the application program. The statements are represented in a "*rtl*" notation which means "register transfer line". This notation is specified in the yacc description of the target machine.

A rtl may represent a declaration or a symbolic instruction, several classes of which are defined; these are e.g. binary instructions (like c = a + b), loads or jump_and_link instructions. Each instruction class has its own syntax; for binary instructions it is e.g.

>   destination = right_hand_side;

The destination may be one of the symbolic registers defined in the machine description while the right_hand_side may have different forms, e.g.

source1 *op* source2

Here, source1 is one of the machine's (symbolic) registers, op is an operand like "+" and source2 may be a register or an immediate operand.

The machine model used in the scheduler has r-registers as integer registers, f-registers for single-precision floating point operands and d-registers for double-precision floats. Thus, a rtl may look like:

$r[8] = r[3] + r[5]$;

where the integer registers $r[3]$ and $r[5]$ are added and the result is placed in register $r[8]$. Immediate values may be used like in

$r[8] = r[3] - 4$.

The compiler was enhanced so that the rtls provide additional information like the memory address assigned during memory mapping, in addition to the other information about the declared variables.

12.2 The Scheduler's Front-end

The main tasks of the scheduler's front-end is shown in figure 32. It has to provide all information needed for instruction scheduling in the central part. The methods presented in this subsection will be useful for most compilers and architectures, not only VLIW and superscalar.

First, the symbol table information is determined. We want to be able to schedule memory-access statements (loads and stores) like other statements; therefore, we need sufficient information about placement of variables in memory. This information is stored in the symbol table. For each variable in the program we need for scheduling purposes its:

- name
- type
- memory address
- length

Additionally, we need the layout and contents of branch tables (e.g. as created from a switch statement in the compiled program) and similar information.

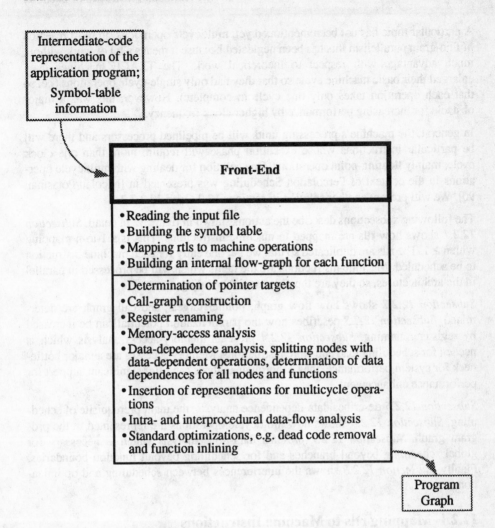

Figure 32: The Scheduler's Front-end

Next, all rtls are read in; the rtls representing declarations are used to extend the symbol table information about the memory addresses assigned. While reading rtls representing symbolic instructions, syntax and semantics of the rtls are checked and corresponding information is created, mainly the sequence of machine instructions corresponding to the rtls.

The task of the front-end is to create the program graph for each function of the application program. This means, we have to ensure that all nodes of the graph contain operations which can be executed in parallel. All rtls, nodes, and functions must get attributes which characterize their data dependence and liveness information. Various kinds of program analyses are to be performed to provide all information necessary for our main purpose - global instruction-scheduling.

A particular topic has not been mentioned yet: multicycle operations. In most research of fine-grain parallelism this has been neglected because it means a lot of work without much advantage with respect to theoretical work. The TRACE machines even enlarged their basic machine cycle so that they had only single-cycle operations (i.e. so that each operation takes only one cycle to complete). However, this was a major obstacle for increasing performance by higher clock frequency.

In general, the machine's processing units will be pipelined processors and there will be particular instructions whose execution phase will require more than one clock cycle, mainly floating-point operations. One solution for dealing with multicycle operations in the context of Percolation Scheduling was presented in [Nicolau/Potasman 90]. We will present another solution in sections 12.2.6 and 12.3.3.2.

The following subsections describe the actions shown in figure 32 in detail. *Subsection 12.2.1* shows how rtls are mapped to machine instructions. This is a 1-to-n mapping with $n \geq 1$. The rtls are duplicated so that we get one entry for each machine instruction to be scheduled. Machine instructions are the items which will be processed in parallel in the architectures, so they are the objects of scheduling.

Subsection 12.2.2 shows how flow graph, pointer targets, and call graph are determined. *Subsection 12.2.3* describes how the parallelization potential can be increased by register renaming. *Subsection 12.2.4* presents memory-access analysis which is needed for scheduling load and store instructions. Memory accesses are a major bottleneck for system performance, thus a thorough analysis can offer significant support for performance enhancement.

Subsection 12.2.5 describes data-dependence analysis, the main prerequisite of scheduling. *Subsection 12.2.6* shows how multicycle operations are represented in the program graph. *Subsection 12.2.7* presents data-flow analysis which is necessary for global scheduling beyond branches and for scheduling beyond function boundaries. Finally, *subsection 12.2.8* shows the interferences between scheduling and optimization.

12.2.1 Mapping rtls to Machine Instructions

This subsection is rather detailed (on the algorithmic level) and may be skipped by those who are not interested in these technical details.

The rtls are the compiler's representations for the program statements on an intermediate level. For execution on a machine, each rtl has to be mapped to one or more machine operations. Other intermediate-code representations will use a similar abstraction level above machine code so that they have to be mapped like the rtls. This mapping is described in the example below.

Example:

The high-level statement "$x = (y \geq 100000)$" is translated by the compiler to a rtl statement of the class "compare_and_set". Its syntax is:

> destination = source1 *rel* source2;

Here, source1 may be an integer register and source2 an integer register or an immediate value, while "rel" is a relation. The rtl will then e.g. look like:

$$r[3] = r[5] \geq 100000;$$

There are two problems to be solved for implementing such a rtl on a machine; firstly, the number has to be loaded, and secondly, the relation ("≥") has to be mapped to a corresponding machine instruction.

In our machine model, the instruction "set_on_less" is used; for immediates requiring not more than 16 bits, the machine instruction "set_on_less_immediate" can be used.

Thus, in our example, first the immediate value 100000 has to be loaded into a register and then the "≥" has to be transformed to a "<".

Loading the immediate:

In the underlying machine model, first the upper 16 bits ("a") of the immediate have to be loaded, and then the lower 16 bits ("b"); i.e. we determine a = 100000 & 0xffff0000 and b = 100000 & 0x0000ffff. The result will be written to a scratch register, e.g. r[2].

Creating the relation:

The comparison with "≥" can be implemented as *set_on_less* followed by an *exclusive_or*.

Thus, we get the sequence (specifying the destination as rightmost operand):

load_upper_immediate a, r[2];

or_immediate b, r[2], r[2];

set_on_less r[5], r[2], r[2];

xor 1, r[2], r[3];

Generally, for each rtl it has to be analyzed if an immediate operand is allowed at this place (i.e. as first or second operand), if it can be used for this kind of operation or if it has to be loaded using other machine instructions. Accordingly, the sequence of machine operations is determined.

This part of the front-end, the mapping of rtls, encompasses instruction selection which is in traditional compilers mostly a task of the back-end. In our case, we have to perform it in the front-end to determine the candidates for scheduling - the instructions which we want to be processed in parallel, as far as possible.

There are several classes of instructions to be considered which are treated separately while the instructions inside a class are treated equally.

• *binary*:

This class encompasses most of the instructions, e.g. most of the arithmetic instructions.

- *compare_and_branch*:

  The instructions in this class compare register contents (or immediates) and branch depending on the comparison's result. The immediates (if there are any) have to be loaded into registers; relations have to be converted, branches which jump always (or never) have to be detected and mapped to jump instructions (or none), the fastest comparison instruction determined, etc. (In some machines, the comparison with 0 is faster than other comparisons.) In the machine model, compare_and_branch operations are implemented as pairs of instructions, namely compare instructions for various relations which set a condition code (according to the PE they are processed on) and branch_pattern operations which read all condition codes and decide depending on their contents upon the new value of the program counter (PC).

- *branch_on_coprocessor*:

  This symbolic instruction branches depending on a floating point comparison.

- *compare_and_set*:

  These instructions compare the operands and place the result (TRUE or FALSE) in the destination register. Only one relation (compare_if_less) is implemented as machine instruction; thus, all other relations have to be mapped to a sequence of instructions comprising this one.

- *convert*:

  Conversions between different floating-point formats (single, double precision).

- *float_compare*

- *jump_and_link*:

  These are essentially the call instructions; saves and reloads of registers at function calls are entered separately by the compiler; the machine model offers no complex call-instructions (because they might decrease parallelism).

- *load*:

  The addressing mode is determined by the compiler; in the scheduler's front-end it has to be determined if immediates have to be loaded into registers before actually executing the load (as above) and if floating point values or integers have to be determined or if unsigned variants of operations are used. Additionally, we try to find out which memory address is accessed; the expression for calculating the memory address and the address' value are determined (if possible) and entered as attributes of the rtl in its program-graph node (see subsection 12.2.4).

- *load_immediate*:

  Loading immediates is implemented by operations like add_immediate or load_upper_immediate followed by or_immediate.

- *move_from_coprocessor*, *move_to_coprocessor*:

  These instructions move data between PEs.

- *jump*:

  Such an instruction sets the value of the next PC to an immediate conveyed as operand; actually, this information is represented by the edges in the flow graph. It would be rather cumbersome to schedule jump operations individually because their dependences are flow dependences, not data dependences. Hence, jumps would have to be changed frequently during scheduling. There is an easy way to deal with jumps: remove all jumps - the information is retained in the flow graph (and thus in the program graph) structure, anyway. At the end of the code generation phase (see section 12.4.5) jumps are inserted at the places where they are needed.

- A special class encompasses *case* instructions. These are mapped to *jump tables* internally. Such a table contains jump operations to the instructions to be executed in the different branches of the case operation. The possible results of the condition to be evaluated in the case statement are mapped to a sequence of integers. The case instruction is implemented by loading the integer corresponding to the condition to be evaluated into a register first and then performing an indirect branch using these register contents as distance to the head of the jump table.

- Other classes, like negate, not, return, store, noop, ...

For some instruction classes, lots of different cases have to be considered, but mostly the algorithm for mapping rtls to machine instructions has the following structure:

First, if one operand is an immediate (or both), it has to be checked if there is an operation for the intended purpose allowing immediate operands. If there is none, the immediate values have to be loaded into registers by creating the corresponding operations as described above. Then, the binary instruction is selected - in case of boolean expressions there may be a sequence of such instructions. Finally, a subsequent instruction for moving data may be necessary.

We will take a closer look at the class encompassing most instructions, which are also those occurring most frequently, the binary instructions. This class encompasses not only most integer-arithmetic instructions, but also most floating-point instructions. For those, just the operands' precision has to be considered and the corresponding single- or double-precision instruction has to be created.

For mapping the rtls to machine instructions, first the left and then the right operand is checked. If the left one is an immediate operand (or if it does not fit into the 16-bit immediate field of a machine instruction) it has to be loaded into a register because the machine model does not allow immediates as left operands. Loading an immediate means creating a "load_upper_immediate" instruction to load its upper 16 bits (if they are not all 0). Then an "or_immediate" instruction is created which will combine the previously loaded 16 upper bits with the 16 lower bits of the immediate operand.

Such immediate operands may be expressions containing the names of variables or constants; in such a case, the expression has to be evaluated, replacing names by the corresponding addresses.

After having determined the operands, the machine instruction can be created. It may belong to one of several types:

- standard (signed operation with register operands only)
- unsigned (unsigned operation with register operands only)
- immediate (signed operation with one immediate and one register operand)
- unsigned-immediate (unsigned operation with one immediate and one register operand).

This is just an outline of the algorithm. For particular cases more effort is invested for creating machine instructions, e.g. for subtractions of immediates the instruction *add_imm* adding the negative immediate is created because subtraction instructions with immediates are not offered by the machine model and because the algorithm described above (in this simplified form) would create two instructions instead of the (faster) single add_imm instruction.

The other classes of operations are mapped similarly, corresponding to the outline described above for binary operations.

12.2.2 Flow Graph, Pointer Targets and Call Graph

The compiler conveys the rtls structured in a *flow graph*; this structure is used as initial structure of the program graph.

Pointers are quite convenient for programming, however, they induce a lot of hardship for compilers and for instruction scheduling. A store operation to a variable in memory must not be moved across a load or store operation referencing the same address; similarly, a load operation must not be moved across a store operation which may reference the same address. Otherwise, memory contents cannot be kept consistent with program semantics. This fact is quite obvious, but how can we determine the address of a load or store operation?

Subsection 12.2.4 presents methods to determine such addresses for non-pointer accesses. For simple pointer accesses this is not too hard either: if a pointer p always references the same variable x, then accesses via p and accesses to x must not be interchanged (if at least one of them is a store operation). However, what happens if we have pointers to pointers? Or pointers to pointers to pointers? In linked lists we may chase down a long chain of pointers until performing eventually the actual access to the data needed.

In [Aho/Sethi/Ullman 88] a method is described to identify the set of those variables which may be accessed via pointers. For each pointer we can additionally determine the set of variables which may be accessed via this specific pointer. Using this information, we can get rules for moving load and store operations:

Consider two memory accesses where at least one is a store operation; how can they be reordered?

- If we have no information about pointer targets, an access via pointer must not be moved across another memory access and, similarly, no memory-access operation must be moved across an access via pointer.

- If we have the set *Pointer_targets* of variables which may be accessed via pointer then an access via pointer must not be moved across an access to a variable v ∈ Pointer_targets, and, symmetrically, an access to v must not be moved across an access via pointer.

- If we can identify for a pointer p the set Targets (p) of variables which may be accessed via p then an access to a variable v must not be moved across an access via p if v ∈ Targets (p), and similarly the symmetric move is not allowed.

Generally, the sets Targets(p) cannot be identified for all pointers p. However, some further observations allow additional movements of operations:

- A pointer p which references only global variables may be moved across accesses to local variables.

- A pointer p which references only local variables may be moved across accesses to global variables.

- Special care has to be taken for pointers conveyed as function parameters; using such pointers, a function f may access a variable local to another function g.

The *call graph* is a basic structure for all interprocedural analyses. Its nodes represent functions and there is an edge from a node N1 representing a function f to a node N2 representing a function g if g is called in f. Recursive function-calls yield a cyclic call-graph. The call graph is needed for interprocedural analyses in the front-end and also in the other parts of the scheduler.

12.2.3 Registers and Register Renaming

First experiments showed that a considerable portion of the parallelism inherent to the application programs could not be exploited due to dependences which could not be resolved. In subsection 7.1, the data dependences are introduced as major constraints for instruction scheduling. However, write_after_write and write_after_read dependences do not represent program semantics - they are only for programmer's convenience or lack of resources. Both dependences occur when we assign a new value to a variable v. But let's assume we assign this new value to a different variable v' - we need not use the name v for this variable any more. If we rename v to v' in the program for this assignment and all further uses until the next assignment of another new value to v, we remove all dependences of the renamed variable to v. Thus, instructions using v may be processed in parallel to instructions accessing v'.

On the intermediate-code level of the rtl statements, there are the same kind of dependences - assigning a variable v fixedly to a symbolic register r means that the dependence between variables is mapped to the same kind of dependence between registers. There are additional sources for dependences on the intermediate-code level, e.g. for the evaluation of expressions. In the simple example:

x = 5 * y[8] + 10 * y[7];

we have just one high-level instruction. However, on the rtl level we need more than two registers for x and y. The (optimized) rtl sequence for this statement may look like:

r[2] = y + 32;   /* Assuming 4 bytes wordlength for y, we have to access the
                        address determined by the start address of y plus a distance
                        of 8*4 for y[8]. */

r[3] = MEM (r[2]); /* The contents of the memory cell containing y[8] is loaded
                        into register r[3]. */

r[4] = r[3] * 5;

r[2] = y + 28;
r[3] = MEM (r[2]);
r[3] = r[3] * 10;
r[5] = r[3] + r[4];

The registers r[2] and r[3] are used for evaluating both expressions, "5*y[8]" and "10*y[7]"; this induces dependences between the evaluation of the two expressions which are not necessary. Using other registers for the second expression (the three statements marked by a bar) allows to process them in parallel to the first three statements.

This shows that register renaming can increase performance by removing anti- and output-dependences; in our experiments this turned out to be significant after the first runs.

The following part of this subsection may be skipped by those who do not want to dive into algorithmic details. The algorithm for register renaming is presented and some information necessary for understanding the algorithm.

Internally, the scheduler uses two passes for renaming, one after call-graph construction for renaming the evaluation of expressions, and the other one after live analysis for general renaming outside expressions.

For most processor architectures particular registers are reserved for particular purposes. The instruction scheduler applies the MIPS conventions; the following ones are important for renaming:

- Registers r[4], r[5], r[6], and r[7] are used for function parameters (if a function has not more than 4 parameters; otherwise, a pointer to the memory address where the parameters are stored is used as parameter).

- Register r[2] is used for a function's return value.

- Some registers contain fixed values or are mostly used for particular contents:
  - r[0] always contains 0
  - r[29] usually contains the stack pointer
  - r[31] usually contains the return-instruction pointer
  - f[0] and f[2] are used for floating-point function results
  - f[12] and f[14] are used for the first two parameters with floating-point values.
- The HI- and LO-registers are used for multiplication and division results only.

The general algorithm, applied after live analysis, cannot utilize these special registers, therefore in the first pass these reserved registers are renamed as far as possible.

The common renaming algorithms work on program dependence graphs and are used only inside basic blocks, see [Liebl 92] and [Müller 91]. Therefore, a new, quite straight-forward, general renaming algorithm was developed (see [Liebl 92]). However, this algorithm uses registers quite offensively and already medium-sized programs need a lot of symbolic registers (their number is defined in the machine description). The reason is that symbolic registers are renamed across the whole application program and no register number is used twice, not even in different functions.

Let's consider two functions f1 and f2. If there is a path in the call graph from f1 to f2 then f1 calls f2 or f1 calls another function which calls another ... which calls f2. Consider the following example:

A symbolic register r[i] was renamed to r[9]:

<table>
<tr><td>f1: ...</td><td></td><td>f1: ...</td></tr>
<tr><td>r[i] = 3;</td><td rowspan="3">renamed to ⟶</td><td>r[9] = 3;</td></tr>
<tr><td>call f2;</td><td>call f2;</td></tr>
<tr><td>r[10] = r[i] + 2;</td><td>r[10] = r[9] + 2;</td></tr>
</table>

If register r[9] is written in function f2, too, then the renaming of r[i] to r[9] in f1 changes program semantics - which is not quite desirable. How can we know if register r[9] will ever be used in f2? Well, that's only possible if f2 is renamed before f1 - or if r[9] is not used as possible renaming target in f2; the latter is the way it is implemented in the algorithm. The former case is only possible in non-cyclic parts of the call graph and is thus not generally applicable.

Some practicable solutions are:

- Rename as far as possible, i.e. as long as there are enough symbolic registers available. Renaming is stopped if there are no more registers available, sacrificing the performance increase possible by further renaming.
- An analysis of the call graph determines for each pair (f1, f2) of nodes representing functions f1 and f2 if they interfere, i.e. if there is a path between them. If f1 calls f2 then the rules are:

- for renaming in f1 no register r[i] may be used as renaming target if r[i] is used (read or written) in f2

- for renaming in f2 no register r[i] may be used which is live after the call of f2 in f1

- all places where calls from f1 to f2 are made have to be considered for renaming

- all pairs of functions have to be considered.

For the following algorithm we need the definition of a "dominator":

Def. 10: Dominator

A node N1 in a program graph *dominates* a node N2 if every path from the graph's start node to N2 passes through N1; N1 is a *dominator* of N2.

We consider each node to dominate itself.

Register renaming is performed according to the general description in the following algorithm; function calls are printed below in italics and bold face is used for function names where they are specified. Some functions are called which are not described further or only partly in the algorithm:

- **Determine_dominators (N):**

  For each node N the set of all nodes N' which dominate N is determined and added as attribute to the node N in the program graph. There are many algorithms to determine dominators, e.g. in [Aho/Sethi/Ullman 88].

- **insert_correction_code (N, r[i], r[j]):**

  Such correction code is needed to maintain program semantics at places where we step from one region of the program graph where r[i] has been renamed to another one where r[i] has not been renamed; such a situation is e.g. shown in figure 27 on page 57 where the statement "i=i' " is inserted.

  This routine is called when we have a node N' with 2 predecessors N and M; a symbolic register r[i] is renamed to r[j] in N (and its predecessors) and not renamed in M. Thus, we have to remap r[j] to r[i]; this is performed by inserting an assignment r[i] = r[j] in node N. This node N is the first parameter of the function insert_correction_code (N, r[i], r[j]).

  The assignment " r[i] = r[j] " is inserted into node N as a rtl if there are sufficient resources in N available and if there are no dependences, e.g. if r[j] is not written in N. The dependence and liveness information has to be updated if the insertion can be performed.

- **rename_expression (op, N):**

  This routine renames the output operand r[i] of operation op in node N and its use as source operand in subsequent operations reading r[i], until r[i] is overwritten again. In the actual implementation, renaming of expressions is performed before the nodes of the flow graph are split. Thus, the nodes contain basic blocks and the evaluation of an expression is performed inside one basic block, i.e. always inside the node N. The sequence of the rtls inside a node is the execution sequence before the rtls are moved. No renaming is performed in nodes comprising call operations.

Algorithm for register renaming:

Generally, the following actions have to be performed:

1. Determine for all nodes N their dominators.
2. Loop across all nodes N and all operations op in N: try to rename op's destination register r:
    2.1 Check all successor nodes of N and collect those in a list L where r will be renamed.
    2.2 Mark all places where correction code has to be inserted.
3. Rename r in N and all nodes in the list L.
4. Insert correction code wherever necessary, i.e. where a mark has been set.

Register Renaming (program_graph):

Ad 1.:

 • Loop across all nodes N of a program graph:
   • *Determine_dominators (N).*

Ad 2.:

 • Loop across all nodes N of the program graph and all rtls "op" in N:
•   *Ad 2.1:*
       • For each operation op writing to an expression-evaluation register r[i]:
         • *rename_expression (op, N)*, rename the expression only.
       • For other operations op writing to a register r[i], which are neither copies of any rtl nor part of multicycle operations:
          • Loop across all successor nodes N' of N (from N down to the leaves) as long as r[i] is not overwritten:
            • Is N' not dominated by N and r[i] live in N'?

            no: • return (no renaming possible or necessary).

            yes: • L = L ∪ {N'} if r is read in N'.

- *Ad 2.2:*
    - Has this N' a successor where r[i] is live and which is not dominated by N?

      yes: • Mark N' to insert correction code.

      • L = L ∪ {N'} if r is read in N'.
    - End loop across all successors of N.

Ad 3.:

- r[j] = *rename_destination_operand (op, N)* (r[j] is the new register name).
- Update node and rtl information (e.g. the set of registers written).
- Loop across all nodes N2 ∈ L and all rtls *op1* in N2:
    - *rename_source_operands (r[i], op1, r[j]).*
- End loop across all rtls in N2 and across all N2.
- End loop across all rtls "op" in N and all nodes N (from 2.).

Ad 4.:

- For all nodes N' where the mark for inserting correction code t is set:
    - *insert_correction_code* (N', r[i], r[j]);

Recalculate the accumulated attributes of the current function "foo" e.g. about registers read and written in "foo", live registers at entrance and exit of "foo", etc.

rename_expression (op, N):

- If there is no call or system_call operation in node N:
    - Loop across all rtls in N:
        - Is there a rtl *op1* where op's destination operand r[i] is dead?

          yes: • Determine the next available renaming target, register r[j] (just the next element of a list of unused registers).

          • r[j] = *rename_destination_operand(op, N).*

          • Loop across all rtls in N from op to op1:

          • *rename_source_operands (r[i], op1, r[j]);*

Special care has to be taken for floating-point single and double registers, which may overlap in particular architectures.

rename_destination_operand (op, N):

- Determine the next available symbolic register r[j] for renaming (single- and double-precision floating-point registers have to be considered accordingly).
- Stop if there are no more registers available.
- Replace r[i] by r[j] as destination operand and in the corresponding attributes of the rtl *op*, e.g. the set of registers written.

- Replace r[i] by r[j] in the corresponding attributes in N, e.g. the set of registers written in N.

(Accumulated information for the function "foo" where N belongs to, cannot just be updated because we don't know here if the register r[i] may be read or written at another place in "foo" or N; this information has to be determined anew.)

rename_source_operands (r[i], op, r[j]):

The symbolic register r[i] has to be renamed to r[j] in operation op as source operand.

- Determine which operands have to be renamed in operation op, according to its syntax.
- Replace r[i] by r[j] as source operand(s) and in the corresponding attributes of the rtl *op*, e.g. the registers read and the sets of live registers.
- Replace r[i] by r[j] in the corresponding attributes in N, e.g. the set of registers read in N;

Algorithm 7: Register Renaming

12.2.4 Memory-Access Analysis

In section 7 the constraints for instruction scheduling were introduced - data dependences and off-live dependence. However, these definitions were developed for symbolic registers. In an actual machine there are dependences between memory accesses to be considered, too. Two memory accesses where at least one of them is a store operation may only be executed in parallel or in exchanged order if we can guarantee that they refer to different, non-overlapping memory areas. For accesses to symbolic registers we always know which register is accessed, however, accesses to memory often do not offer the actual addresses as operands statically.

Such a memory-access analysis may be performed at different representation levels; here, we use the intermediate-code level where we have symbolic registers. At the source-code level, an alias analysis is necessary to get the information needed.

In RISC architectures usually only load and store operations access memory while in CISC architectures other operations may refer to memory addresses, too. In the machine models considered here, only load and store operations may access memory. However, the methods presented here can be extended to CISC architectures.

Memory-access operations mostly use two or three operands to determine the memory address; the most common addressing modes are shown below for store operations:

Constant: Direct (immediate) addressing;
                     example: MEM[2048] = r[5];

register: Indirect addressing, (register deferred or indirect);
                     example: MEM[r[4]] = r[5];

immediate + register: displacement or based addressing (e.g. for local variables);
example: MEM[r[29] + $var] = r[5];

immediate + register +
*   scale * index*:   scaled or indexed addressing;
example: MEM[r[29] + $var + d*r[3]] = r[5];

Other addressing modes are memory indirect (memory deferred), auto increment, and auto decrement.

A literal (constant) in rtl notation may either be a number or a symbolic variable (like "$var" above); the latter specifies the memory address of a user- or compiler-defined variable. The symbolic variable name used in the front-end of the compiler and scheduler is later replaced by the actual memory address of the variable "$var". The scale factor "d" may be used to specify the length of an array element.

Direct addressing mode is used for accessing static data, mostly data created by the compiler or operating system. Register indirect addressing is used e.g. for computed addresses or accesses via pointer. Based addressing is e.g. used for accessing local variables where the register contains the stack pointer and the literal value is the variable's distance from the current stack pointer. It may also used be for accessing arrays if there is no scaled access. The scaled access mode is used for array accesses or e.g. for accessing structured variables like records. In the example above, r[29] may contain the stack pointer, $var is the symbolic name of a local variable, i.e. its address, "d" the length of an array element, and in r[3] we have the array index to be accessed.

The direct addressing mode offers the memory address statically, but for all other addressing modes the rtl notation of a load or store operation does not contain the actual memory address. If we want to schedule load and store operations then the addresses have to be determined at compile time so that these operations can be executed in parallel or in exchanged order.

This means that we have to determine the contents of registers statically at compile time. Thus, in the above example for (register) indirect addressing, we have to determine the contents of register r[4]. There are of course cases where we cannot determine these contents, e.g. when the program chases down a linked list via sequences of pointers; often, it even cannot be reconstructed statically how many accesses via pointer are made e.g. inside a while-loop.

In the following we assume that our machine offers direct, indirect, and base addressing. From the kinds of operands used in a load or store operation we can get information about the kind of variables accessed (depending on the compiler and how it creates memory addresses). A load or store operation always has the form:

load r_{dest}, r_{addr}, *literal*;   ... r_{addr} is the register used to determine the address

store r_{addr}, r_{source}, *literal*;   ... r_{addr} is the register used to determine the address

The different cases are analyzed below:

1. r_{addr} is r[0]:

   In our machine architecture the register r[0] always contains the value 0 as in many RISC architectures.

   1.1 *literal* is a symbolic variable:

   This is a direct access to a simple global variable or the first element of a global array or structure.

   1.2 *literal* is a number:

   This is a direct access to a constant; usually this is used for compiler or operating-system defined variables stored at fixed places in memory.

2. r_{addr} is the stack pointer, resp. the frame pointer r[29]:

   2.1 *literal* is a symbolic variable:

   This is a direct access to a simple local variable or the first element of a local array or structure (if the compiler allocates structures and arrays on the stack).

   2.2 *literal* is a number:

   This is an access to a local constant which resides always at the same place on the stack; this access mode is usually used for items which reside always at the same place on the stack, e.g. compiler-created data like the frame size.

3. r_{addr} is neither r[0] nor the stack pointer, resp. the frame pointer (This is the general case):

   3.1 *literal* is a symbolic variable:

   3.1.1 This is mostly a direct access to a structure or array where *literal* is the name of the array or structure and r_{addr} specifies the distance from the beginning of the array or structure. We have such a direct access if the contents of r_{addr} can be determined uniquely.

   3.1.2 If the contents of r_{addr} cannot be determined uniquely, but as function e.g. of an index, then we may have an ambiguous direct access to array or structure elements. Example: an access to a[2*i+1] inside a loop may be compiled with *literal* as $a (i.e. the start address of the array a) and the contents of r_{addr} are the distances of the accesses from this start address, depending on the loop iteration and the array element size.

   3.1.3 If the contents of r_{addr} cannot be determined then we may have a direct access to an array or structure determined by *literal* where the distance (stored in register r_{addr}) may be determined by other functions in the source program.

   3.2 *literal* is a number:

   3.2.1 If the contents of r_{addr} can be traced back (maybe across arithmetic transformations) to the loading of a symbolic variable, i.e. the start address of an array or structure (a symbolic "load_address" operation), then this is a direct access to an array or structure. The element accessed may be unique or ambiguous; the latter one e.g. if we access a[2*i] in a loop with loop index i.

3.2.2 If the contents of r_{addr} can be traced back to a load operation - there may also occur some arithmetic transformations - then we have an indirect access, i.e. via pointer. The pointer may be unique or ambiguous, e.g. as compiled from a statement like: "x = if (expr) then *p else *q".

3.2.3 If the contents of r_{addr} can be traced back to loading a number and perhaps some arithmetic transformations on that, then we have an indirect access via a pointer which resides at a fixed place in memory; this will mostly be accesses to compiler-generated variables.

3.2.4 In cases where we chase down pointers along lists or graphs or when pointers are passed as parameters to functions, we have generally no chance to determine the address of a memory access (except in some particular cases).

From the list above we can see that there are many kinds of accesses where we can determine the actual address. But how can this determination be performed? First, we check all load and store statements. Starting from there we trace the program graph backwards and try to evaluate the actual contents of r_{addr}. In the following, an algorithm is presented which tries to find the addresses of memory accesses, i.e. an algorithm for memory access analysis.

Readers who do not want to dive into algorithmic details may skip the remainder of this subsection.

After the rtls are mapped to machine instructions we try to determine the memory addresses for each load and store operation of a program graph (there is one program graph per function of the user program). When a rtl is mapped to a load or store operation then the literal for determining the memory address may be not only a name of a symbolic variable, but also a more or less complicated expression. This expression is analyzed and inserted as attribute into the rtl structure in the program-graph node.

For each memory-access operation the memory address is determined and analyzed and the results added as attributes to the rtl of this load or store operation and to the node where the rtl resides. Some of these attributes are:

- The *address* accessed, described as expression.
- The *value* of the address accessed (if it can be determined).
- The *type* of variable being accessed, one of:
  - CONSTANT
  - simple GLOBAL variable
  - simple LOCAL variable
  - ARRAY
  - ARRAY_EXPRESSION: here, an expression is used to determine the literal of the operation

- POINTER
- POINTER_EXPRESSION; here, an expression is used to determine the operation's literal
- ALL; here, all memory addresses may be accessed.
- The *uniqueness* of the access, one of:
- UNIQUE
- EMPTY_AMBIGUOUS; the actual values cannot be determined
- VALUE_AMBIGUOUS; here, the address is one element of a set of determined values.
- A mark specifying if the variable accessed is a *pointer target* (see subsection 12.2.2).
- For variables with ambiguous value we may have several sets of these attributes, one for each possible value.

The following example shows an access which is "VALUE_AMBIGUOUS":

x = if (expr) then a[4] else a[5];

Here, the set of possible values for accesses is

{ (start address of variable a) + 4 * (length of array element),
  (start address of variable a) + 5 * (length of array element) }

For an integer array a this is e.g.: { $a + 16, $a + 20 }.

The load or store operation represented by the rtl has two operands to determine the address: the register r_{addr} and an expression "*expr*" for the literal. Both operands are represented as structures with the same attributes as the memory access itself, especially the type (e.g. LOCAL or POINTER, see above), and the ambiguity (e.g. UNIQUE or AMBIGUOUS). The structures for both operands (i.e. r_{addr} and *expr*) are combined in all attributes to describe the memory access, i.e. the expressions describing the operands are combined as "expression1 + expression2", thereby considering additional unary operations like indirection (i.e. something like "*p" in C). The values are combined by evaluating the expressions and replacing symbolic addresses by their actual values. The type and ambiguity attributes are combined according to the following rules (applied in this order):

- If the type of r_{addr} is "ALL" then the type of the memory access is "ALL".
- If one of the two operands is of type "CONSTANT" then the memory access has the type of the other operand.
- If the type of r_{addr} is "POINTER" and the type of *expr* is "GLOBAL" then the type of memory access is "POINTER"; this kind of access occurs if we access via a pointer inside a structure. Such structures are not allocated on the stack, thus they are not local in the sense used here. This may occur also for arrays which are declared as simple variables (not as arrays) in the application program, but are actually accessed as arrays.

- If the type of r_{addr} is "POINTER" and the type of *expr* is "ARRAY" or "ARRAY_EXPRESSION" then the memory access is of type "ARRAY_EXPRESSION" of the ambiguity "EMPTY_AMBIGUOUS", i.e. we cannot identify statically exactly which array elements will be accessed. This occurs e.g. for an access to the i-th element of an array where i is not a constant but a variable loaded from memory before the access. At compile time we do not know the value of i at run time, therefore it is "EMPTY_AMBIGUOUS" and may assume different values, e.g. inside a loop.

- If the ambiguity of r_{addr} is "EMPTY_AMBIGUOUS" and the type of *expr* is "ARRAY" or "ARRAY_EXPRESSION" then the memory access is of type "ARRAY_EXPRESSION" of the ambiguity "EMPTY_AMBIGUOUS", i.e. we cannot identify statically exactly which array elements will be accessed.

- For all other types of combinations we assume that any arbitrary memory address may be accessed, i.e. the type of memory access is specified as "ALL".

One of the main actions of memory-access analysis is evaluating the contents of the register r_{addr}. How can this analysis be performed? The method is developed using an example:

```
        PC = r[1] > 0, L01            branch_if_greater_0 r[1], L01;
        r[3] = 10;                    add_imm r[3], r[0], 10;
        PC = L02;                     jump L02;
L01:    r[3] = 12;                    add_imm r[3], r[0], 12;
L02:    r[4] = 40000;                 load_upper_immediate r[4], up40;

                                      or_immediate r[4], lo40, r[4];
                                      up40 are the upper 16 bits of the number 40000, and
                                      lo40 are the lower 16 bits

        r[5] = r[4] - r[3];           sub r[5], r[4], r[3];
        r[5] = r[5] << 2;             shift_left r[5], r[5], 2;
        r[6] = MEM[$myvar+r[5]];      load r[6], $myvar, r[5];
```

Figure 33: Example Program for Memory-Access Analysis

In figure 33 we have a small part of a program, in the left column in rtl notation and in the right column there are the corresponding machine operations these rtls are mapped to. The machine language used is oriented at the MIPS instruction set where the destination operand is noted first. Immediates requiring more than 16 bits have to be loaded in a register by loading the upper 16 bits with the instruction load_upper_immediate and then adding the lower 16 bits using the instruction or_immediate. We assume that the address of the variable "myvar", here specified as "$myvar", requires not more than 16 bits, e.g. $myvar = 880.

In the bottom line we have the load operation we want to analyze. This operation loads something from memory and moves the result to register r[6]. The memory address to be accessed is specified by $myvar and register r[5]. The name "$myvar" represents the address of the user-defined variable myvar. The register r[5] is unknown at this place; thus, we will try to evaluate its contents. Before, we will evaluate the literal by searching for the name "$myvar" in the symbol table. There we will find for example that $myvar is an array with start address 880. Such a literal may be specified as an expression applying standard arithmetic (including shift operations). We note the information about this literal:

type = ARRAY;
value = 880
ambiguity = UNIQUE;

Then, we start to analyze the contents of register r[5]. We perform this by tracing r[5] backwards (i.e. upwards) in the program graph.

The method for analyzing the contents of register r_{addr} can be outlined as:

- Go upwards in the program graph until you find r_{addr} as destination operand.
- If the operation found there has only immediate source operands then evaluate them and report the result back.
- If the operation found has one register source operand and one immediate source operand then evaluate that source register in the same way as described here and combine the evaluation result with the immediate source operand to get the result for r_{addr}.
- If the operation found has two register source operands then evaluate them both in the same way as described here and combine the evaluation results to get the result for r_{addr}.

Now we apply the outlined method and develop the steps to proceed for determining the contents of r[5]:

Step 1: On our way up in the program graph we first find the instruction "shift_left r[5], r[5], 2". We note that r[5] is destination operand in this instruction, thus we analyze this instruction next. Checking the source operands we find that there is one register, r[5], and one immediate, 2. Thus, our task has been transformed to the new task: "Find the contents of r[5] and shift them left 2 bits; then convey the result to the caller".

Step 2: On the way up in the program graph we find the instruction "sub r[5], r[4], r[3]" next. The destination operand is r[5], so we have to analyze this instruction. The source operands are r[3] and r[4]. Thus, the objects of our subsequent analyses are r[3] and r[4].

Step 3: The next register to evaluate is r[3]. On our way up the program graph we find two instructions where r[3] is not the destination operand - these are not considered here. The following one is "add_imm r[3], r[0], 12". Here, we have r[3] as destination operand and r[0] and 12 as source operands. We know the contents of r[0] - this is always 0 - thus, we can tell the contents of r[3] here: It is $0 + 12 = 12$. So we can note 12 as the value to convey back as contents of r[3].

Step 4: However, the preceding node where we discovered r[3] as new target, has two predecessors - the one we just checked and another one with the instruction "add_imm r[3], r[0], 10". Here, the same kind of analysis shows that r[3] has the value 10. We return this value, too, to the function which initiated the action in step 4; this is the function executed in step 3.

Step 5: This is a return to the function from step 2 where we initiated steps 3 and 4. We get two results for r[3]: 10 and 12. Both are possible, depending on the condition in the conditional branch operation above ($r[1] > 0$). Thus, r[3] gets marked as "VALUE_AMBIGUOUS" with the values {10,12}.

In step 2 we found out that not only r[3] but also the contents of r[4] have to be analyzed.

Step 6: We climb up the program graph again from the line considered in step 5 and step 2 (" sub r[5], r[4], r[3] "). We find the line "or_immediate r[4], lo40, r[4]", where r[4] is the destination register. The next register to analyze is again r[4], the instruction's source register.

Step 7: Here, we find the instruction "load_upper_immediate r[4], up40" and the evaluation shows that r[4] contains the value of the upper 16 bits of 40000. Combined with the result from step 6 we get the value of 40000 for r[4] which is conveyed back to the function initiating the evaluation of r[4] - the one we left in step 2 (and step 5).

Step 8: In step 2 we noted that the contents of r[3] and r[4] have to be combined as r[4] - r[3] to determine the contents of r[5]. With the values conveyed back from steps 3 and 5, together with step 7 we get the values {39990, 39988} as possible contents of r[5] (as difference of r[4] and r[3]). There are two possible instead of one unique result, therefore, we have to attribute r[5] as "VALUE_AMBIGUOUS". Then these values are conveyed back to the function initiating the current one - to step 1.

Step 9: In step 1 it was noted that the contents of r[5] have to be shifted left, thus we get {159960, 159952} as possible contents of r[5] and the attribute "VALUE_AMBIGUOUS".

Step10: Finally, we can describe the load operation: We have to add the address of $myvar and the possible values of r[5] and get the attributes:

    type = ARRAY

    value = {160840, 160832}

    ambiguity = VALUE_AMBIGUOUS

    expression = "$myvar + ((40000 - {10,12}) << 2)"

The rtl is annotated with these attributes specifying the load operation; they will be accumulated with other attributes to compose the node attributes.

For formulating all this in an algorithm, we get - starting on a high, general level - the following actions to be performed:

4. Evaluate the immediate operand and store its description ("immediate_description").

5. Evaluate the register operand r_{addr} and store its description ("register_description").

6. Combine the two descriptions to determine the "variable_description" of the loaded variable.

Ad 1.:

The data needed for this evaluation are addresses of variables etc. which can be found in the symbol table.

Ad 2.:

This means determining recursively the contents of the register. The algorithm scans backwards until it finds an operation op with this register as destination register. This operation, e.g. an addition of two terms, can later be "enacted", if only its operands can be determined, in our example the two terms of the sum. If one of these operands is an immediate, its value can be determined without further effort. Register operands have to be traced back recursively in the same way. Finally, this tracing back will end at a point where:

- Immediates are loaded (either directly as values or as symbolic addresses or using r[0]).
- A value is loaded from memory.
- A function parameter is used.
- A function value is used (this includes external data e.g. input from a terminal).

In cases where *immediates* are loaded, we can determine their actual values like in 1.

For cases where a value is loaded from *memory*, we can trace it back similarly - at some point in the past this value must have been written to memory. However, wherever we find function calls on the backward analysis we can only continue if we can prove that the called function does not overwrite the memory contents at this specific address - or we have to analyze the called function (and any other function which may be called there) in the same way. A specific class of problems will be encountered with indirect memory accesses, e.g. when accesses via pointers or to arrays are performed. Accesses to arrays can be analyzed without much effort - just the start address and the lengths of the array's dimensions have to be retrieved. An access via pointer requires pointer analysis. The simple classes of pointer accesses can be analyzed, however general pointer analysis is still an unsolved problem.

For *function parameters* we have to analyze the function which called the current function in the same way as the analysis for the register is performed.

A *function value* is the return value of a called function. That function's program graph can be analyzed forward, using the corresponding function parameters if we know them. However, there will be cases where the function values cannot be determined, e.g. where we don't know in which nesting depth of recursively called functions we are currently or in cases where external values are used, e.g. from a keyboard.

Ad3.:

Combining the descriptions means determining the *type* and *ambiguity* of the variable according to the rules on pages 85 and 86. The variable's *value* is determined by enacting the rtls involved and the *expression* combines the operations of these rtls as strings, replacing the register names by their contents which were determined before (as in the example above).

Algorithm 8: Memory-Access Analysis

12.2.5 Data-Dependence Analysis

While the scheduler reads the input file and builds the basic program-graph structure, two rtl-specific attributes are determined: the set of symbolic registers read by this rtl, and the set of symbolic registers written by this rtl.

After memory-access analysis and before the splitting of data-dependent nodes starts, the rtls inside a node may be rearranged so that data-dependent rtls are separated from each other and data-independent rtls are grouped together. Thus, the initial number of program-graph nodes is kept small and the time to perform global scheduling can be limited. The algorithm used for this rearrangement is a Gibbons-Muchnick algorithm of at most quadratic complexity, depending on the number of rtls per node (e.g. for the construction of a data-dependence graph); this is mostly faster than the time needed for global scheduling. More information about local scheduling can be found in [Schepers 92a].

Read-Write Analysis

After this local reordering, data-dependence analysis starts with a read-write analysis. For each program-graph node, the set of registers read as source operands by rtls inside the node is determined together with the set of registers written in the node. Similarly, for each function "foo" the sets of registers read and written inside the function are determined. For each call operation we have to determine the registers read and written by the called function, too. This cannot be performed in a simple loop, however. Consider a function "foo" which calls a function "fum" which itself calls a function "fy" (which itself contains no call operation):

foo → fum → fy

These read and write attributes of functions and nodes are determined iteratively. In the first iteration, only the read and write attributes of "fy" will be correct because "fy" has no call operation. When encountering the call operation to "fum" inside "foo", we will try to determine the read and write attributes of this call operation by adding the corresponding attributes of "fum" - but these are not determined yet! The same holds for the call operation to "fy" inside function "fum". In another iteration we will start over again and take a look at the call operations; this time, the call to "fy" inside fum will get the correct value because the attributes of "fy" are correct now - they were determined during the first iteration. Thus, we get the correct sets for the attributes of the call-rtl - and thus, for the node containing the rtl, too; this will be propagated to the read and write attributes of the function "fum", too. In the second iteration, the sets for "fum" were determined after the call operation of "foo" to "fum" was processed; thus, we need another iteration to determine the read and write attributes for the function "foo".

This means, for getting interprocedural data, we have to iterate the determination of the read and write attributes for rtls, nodes, and functions as long as there is any change in any of these attributes. Loops in the program graph will not cause problems because building the union of a set with itself (which is performed for a recursive call, i.e. a loop in the program graph) will not change the set.

Algorithm for read_write analysis:

- Set all non-leaf nodes (representing functions) in the call graph to "changed".
- Loop while any change in the sets of registers read resp. written in a function occurs:
    - Loop: For each function *"func"* in the call graph, i.e. for each program graph:
      (This loop is performed in postorder so that func's successors, i.e. the functions called by func are processed before func).
        - Is any successor function of func marked as changed?

          yes: • *read_write_analysis (func)*.
        - End loop across all functions in the program graph.
- End loop (while any change occurs).

read_write_analysis (foo):

- Loop: For each node *"node"* in the function "foo" and each call-rtl *"rtl"* in *node*:
    - Enlarge the set of registers read by *rtl* by adding the registers read by the function called by *rtl*;
    - Enlarge the sets of registers read resp. written in *node* by adding the sets of registers read resp. written by *rtl* (i.e. also by the function called by *rtl*);
    - Enlarge the sets of registers read resp. written in "foo" by adding the sets of registers read resp. written by *node* (i.e. also by the function called in *node*); if any of these sets changes, "foo" is marked as changed, otherwise as unchanged.
- End loop (for each node).

Algorithm 9: Read_Write Analysis

After the read_write analysis, the nodes are split as first step towards creating the "real" program-graph nodes. Up to this point, the nodes contain basic blocks; in the "real" program graph, all operations inside a node are processed concurrently, thus they must be independent. Therefore, our next task is to split the nodes so that only data-independent operations reside in each node. The scheduler's front-end is also used for local instruction-scheduling; for this purpose, the program-graph nodes will not be split.

Splitting Dependent Nodes

The splitting of nodes is performed by first scanning all rtls "*rtl*" of each node N sequentially to determine if they are dependent on the rtls previously checked in the node. The dependences checked here are read_after_write, write_after_read, and write_after_write dependences of registers and of memory addresses. The checking of memory-access dependences requires a memory-access analysis as described in subsection 12.2.4. If we detect one of those dependences for *rtl*, the node N is split so that all operations scanned before remain in N, and *rtl* together with all unchecked rtls are inserted into a new node N'.

Similarly, it is checked if there is more than one control-flow operation in N. Such control-flow operations may be: (conditional and unconditional) branches, calls, system_calls, and return operations. Whenever it is detected during the scan that a second control-flow operation resides in the node, the node is split so that the control-flow operations are separated. The new node is inserted after the one which is currently checked, copying all attributes but adjusting the sets of register read and written in the node. All successors of N become now successors of N' while N gets N' as its only successor. The sets for registers read and written in functions may have to be adjusted when the corresponding sets of the nodes change.

12.2.6 Inserting Representatives for Multicycle Operations

As mentioned in subsection 12.2, we need to represent multicycle operations so that they can be scheduled the same way as single-cycle operations. The main reasons for introducing these kinds of representations are:

- Most architectures have multicycle operations.
- The multicycle operations need resources, e.g. processing elements, for more than one cycle and have to be scheduled so that no stalls occur.
- Not representing multicycle representations is only viable for architectures and applications with a very low percentage of multicycle operations. Thus, generally we will have to represent them.
- The operations which may be processed in parallel to multicycle operations are constrained by dependences in the same way as with single-cycle operations.
- A unique approach for dealing with all kinds of operations is desirable.
- Resource usage, dependences, etc. should be expressed in the same way as for single-cycle operations because they represent the same kinds of constraints.

For single-cycle operations, a program-graph node represents all operations which are issued and processed at a particular clock cycle. This means that each clock cycle of program execution (outside loops) is represented by particular program-graph nodes. If we extend this characteristic then we need different program-graph nodes for each clock cycle a multicycle operation is being processed. This can be accomplished by representing a n-cycle operation by n representatives, one for each clock cycle it needs in the execution phase. All other phases of a pipeline are common to all operations and need not be considered individually. Thus, we have n rtls for a n-cycle operation, not just one. The (i+1)st representative must reside in a node which is a direct successor of the node containing the i-th representative.

This means, we have to insert multicycle representatives for each cycle after the first one of the execution phase of a multicycle operation (the first one is already represented). Figure 34 shows the insertion of such multicycle-reps (as they are called) for a two-cycle operation.

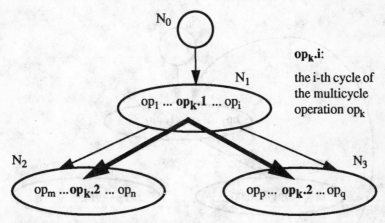

$op_k.i$:

the i-th cycle of the multicycle operation op_k

Let $op_k \in N_1$ be a two-cycle operation:
Change op_k to $op_k.1$ for the first cycle in N_1 and insert representatives for the second cycle in N_1's successors in distance 1 (i.e. in N_2, N_3)
Precondition: op_k is data independent of $op_m...op_n$ and $op_p...op_q$

Figure 34: Insertion of Multicycle-reps

What properties should be given to these multicycle-reps, what values will the attributes assume in the program graph? Let's consider a n-cycle operation op:

• If the representative of the i-th cycle resides in node N then all successor nodes of N will contain representatives of the (i+1)st cycle (compare figure 34).

• If we want to insert a multicycle-rep for operation op into a node N and N contains already a multicycle-rep of op then this may have two reasons:

  i) We are inside a loop comprising less than n nodes.

  ii) There is a join point in the program graph with different numbers of nodes between the corresponding fork point and this join point, i.e. we have an asymmetric "diamond" structure (see figure 36).

Case i) is shown below in figure 35. Nodes N_1 and N_2 form a loop; in this loop we have the operation op_k which needs three cycles in its execution phase. The first cycle is represented in node N_1, the second one in node N_2 and N_3. We could place the third cycle $op_k.3$ in node N_1, too, but this means that we have to process the third clock cycle of operation op_k as part of the first iteration of this loop in the same clock cycle on the same processing element as the first clock cycle of op_k as part of the second iteration in this loop. However, this is usually not possible - only if the execution phases on the processing elements are pipelined themselves (an operation has to be processed completely on a single processing element, it cannot jump to another PE during processing). But even for such sophisticated processing elements, we have to place the third cycle of the execution of op_k in the last iteration somewhere so that it can be processed before the operations in node N_4 if these are dependent on op_k.

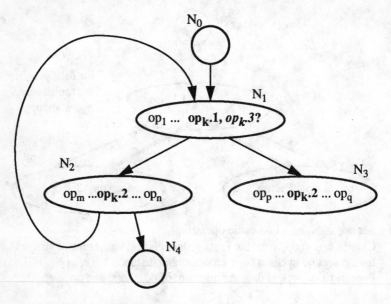

Figure 35: Inserting Multicycle-reps in Loops

Case ii) is shown in figure 36. In this case, we have a diamond structure, i.e. a fork node N_1 and a join node N_5 with two paths from N_1 to N_5. In the example, there are different numbers of nodes in the two paths. We assume a 4-cycle operation op_k. In figure 36 we have to insert $op_k.3$ into N_5 if we take the right path (N_1, N_3, N_5). If we take the left path (N_1, N_2, N_4, N_5) then we have to insert $op_k.4$. As in case i) we have representatives of two different cycles of the same instruction in the same node. However, in this case the two representatives can never coincide - during program execution either the left path is taken or the right path, never both at the same time, even if the diamond structure is part of a loop (in this case, multicycle-reps are placed so that the complete diamond of one iteration will be completed before the diamond of the subsequent iteration is started; see algorithm 10 on page 96). Thus, we allow the two multicycle_reps in the same node concurrently in this case - they will never be processed both at the same time and will thus never occupy the same resources concurrently.

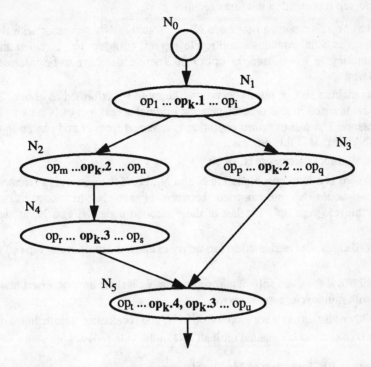

Figure 36: Inserting Multicycle-reps into a diamond structure

- The dependences may be different for different multicycle operations, e.g. the destination register may be live until the last cycle for most multicycle operations. However, for simplicity we assume that all dependence and liveness information is the same for all multicycle_reps of an operation.

- The multicycle_reps of an operation are linked together so that they can be treated all together as a group; there is a link from the i-th multicycle-rep to all successors representing the (i+1)st multicycle-rep (shown as fat arrows in figure 34).

- In many processors we have some operations which need many cycles for execution, e.g. for floating-point multiplication. It would be rather clumsy using separate nodes for each of e.g. 300 cycles of such an operation. Therefore, we introduce aggregate multicycle-reps; they represent k cycles of a multicycle operation and occur only in nodes with no other rtls. They have to be considered accordingly during scheduling, e.g. by expanding them step by step wherever necessary.

insert_multicycle_reps (node, rtl):

The rtl "op" in node N has to be expanded by inserting multicycle_reps in node's successors; for a m-cycle operation we have to insert such multicycle_reps into each node in distance i from N with i = 1, ..., m-1; the rtl in node N is transformed into a multicycle_rep representing the first execution cycle.

- If N has no successors, a new node N' is inserted as N's successor with the same attributes as N. N' contains a multicycle_rep op' of op; for m > 2, either an aggregate multicycle_rep is used for op' or m-2 new nodes have to be inserted in the same way.

- If N contains a call or return operation, the same is performed as above. The last node N' inserted in this process gets the original successors of N now as its own successors. The call or return operation is removed from N and placed in the last node N' inserted in this process.

- Check all direct successors N_s of N:

  - If there is a loop encompassing N and N_s, i.e. if there is a path from N_s to N, new nodes N' are inserted between N and N_s as above, containing multicycle_reps op'. The last of these inserted nodes N' gets N_s as successor now.

  - In all cases not considered so far, we try to insert the multicycle_rep op' into the node N_s:

    - Check if there are sufficient resources in N_s; if there are not, insert new nodes with multicycle_reps as above.

    - Otherwise, insert a copy op' of op in N_s and recalculate the attributes of N_s.

- The whole process is repeated until all m-1 multicycle-reps are inserted.

Algorithm 10: Insertion of Multicycle_reps

12.2.7 Data-Flow Analysis

After having performed all the work described so far in subsection 12.2 we have the application program now represented in program graphs, each rtl mapped to the corresponding machine operations, multicycle rtls represented accordingly, and dependences noted. However, there are still some attributes missing which are needed for scheduling. In def. 6 on page 39 we defined the off-live dependence which has to be checked for moving instructions across conditional branches. This liveness information has still to be determined, and this subsection provides the base for it.

In our dataflow analysis we define sets of symbolic registers and perform operations on these sets. All characteristics defined in this context refer to nodes in a program graph; they are partially derived from [Aho/Sethi/Ullman 88].

Similarly to the data-flow analysis of symbolic registers, the data-flow analysis of symbolic variables is performed. This is necessary to move load and store operations across conditional-branch operations. While we apply *inter*procedural data-flow analysis (beyond functions) for registers, only *intra*procedural data-flow analysis (inside functions) is applied for symbolic variables. Performing this interprocedurally, too, would imply to perform a thorough alias analysis, especially for pointers. Pointers conveyed to functions via parameters can create sets of aliases for symbolic variables and it is quite costly to find out which memory accesses refer to aliases of a particular variable. Moreover, it is not possible to do this generally - chasing down pointer chains cannot be analyzed statically at compile time in many cases. However, there are not that many cases for which it is necessary to perform such an analysis. The cases where instruction scheduling is hampered by the fact that there is no interprocedural data-flow analysis for variables are:

- Moving a specific load or store across a call operation.
- Moving a call operation across such a load or store.
- Moving such a specific load or store above a conditional branch with a call operation in the other branch.
- Moving a call operation above a conditional branch with such a specific load or store in the other path.
- Moving loads or stores for which the address to be accessed is determined outside the current function.

The kind of memory accesses for which these restrictions apply are:

- accesses to a global variable which is a pointer target
- accesses via pointer to global variables
- accesses via pointers which may be conveyed as function parameters.

These restrictions are not that serious to justify the costly alias analysis and interprocedural data-flow analysis for symbolic variables. However, in cases where an implementation of such an alias analysis is available and efficient with respect to run time, it may be usefully applied.

Def. 11: Live registers:

A symbolic register r[i] is called *live* in a program-graph node N when it was defined in a predecessor node of N and is used in N or afterwards in a successor node of N.

A symbolic register is "defined" when it is used as destination register of an operation. It is "used" when it appears as source register of an operation. The predecessor and successor nodes of N mentioned above need not be direct predecessors or successors.

Def. 12: in(N) and out(N):

The set of symbolic registers live at the point immediately before a node N is called *in(N)*. The set of symbolic registers live immediately after N is called *out(N)*.

Def. 13: def(N) and use(N):

The set of symbolic registers defined in N, i.e. those appearing as destination operands in N and not as source operands, is called *def(N)*. The set of variables used in N, i.e. those appearing as source operands in N, is called *use(N)*.

In the previous definitions we assume that a symbolic register, read and written in the same node, is read before it is written; this is the intuitive usage anyway; in the statement

r[i] = r[i] + 5

first, the previous value of r[i] is read, then it is increased by 5, and then the new value is assigned to r[i].

Using all the definitions above and the set "successors(N)" as the set of all direct successor nodes of a node N, we get the standard data-flow equations:

$$in(N) = use(N) \cup (out(N) - def(N)) \qquad \text{(EQ 1)}$$

$$out(N) = \bigcup_{S \in successors(N)} in(S) \qquad \text{(EQ 2)}$$

Data-flow analysis is mostly performed intraprocedurally, i.e. inside functions only. By restricting data-flow analysis to intraprocedural usage, we have borders for applications of this information, i.e. borders across which we cannot move any operation. These borders are all operations which refer to other functions, i.e. the call and return statements. Thus, scheduling is restricted to regions between call and return operations. This might be feasible for scientific code where not many call statements occur compared to other statements, however, in general-purpose code their portion is significant. In [Hennessy/Patterson 90] the number of calls and returns together is reported as 8% on the 8086, using Turbo C, a macro assembler, and Lotus 1-2-3 as benchmark. This means that there are about 10 instructions between two calls or returns, thus we have to restrict scheduling to regions of 10 machine instructions only. For many applications, mainly modern ones, using many small functions, the regions will be even smaller. Therefore, for global scheduling, it is necessary to perform data-flow analysis interprocedurally so that scheduling across call operations is possible.

The first part of data-flow analysis for our purposes is read-write analysis. This has mainly been performed already, compare algorithm 9 on pages 91. We define for each rtl the sets rreads(rtl) and rwrites(rtl), and for each node N similar sets rreads(N) and rwrites(N) as shown there. For each function f we calculate similarly the sets rreads(f) and rwrites(f) of all symbolic registers read and written in f, according to the following data-flow equations:

$$rwrites(f) = \bigcup_{N \in f} (rwrites(N) \cup (rwrites(g)) \quad \text{for all functions g called in N} \qquad \text{(EQ 3)}$$

$$rreads(f) = \bigcup_{N \in f} (rreads(N) \cup (rreads(g))) \quad \textit{for all functions g called in N} \quad \text{(EQ 4)}$$

We can now determine the standard sets for data-flow analysis:

$$use(N) = rreads(N); \tag{EQ 5}$$

$$def(N) = rwrites(N) - rreads(N); \tag{EQ 6}$$

These equations are obvious for nodes without call instructions. But what happens with calls? We don't know in node N which registers will be used or written in a function "foo" called in N. But beyond that - we don't know which path will be taken in "foo", because a register r[i] may be written in one path only and may not be used in another path through "foo". We thus cannot determine the sets use(N) and def(N) exactly - we have to make some estimates. These estimates must be conservative, we may assume more registers being live in a function as actually are, but choosing a non-conservative estimation may assume a register as being dead which is actually live; if we move an operation across a call with such a register we will change program semantics if this operation writes to that register. Thus, it is absolutely necessary to make conservative assumptions because instruction scheduling must not change program semantics.

A conservative approach for the set use(f) of a function f called in node N is *in(N)*, the set of registers live before N. A register in in(N) may be read on a single path through f only, however since we don't know which path through f will be taken, we have to assume that it is live in f. The set def(f) is harder to derive.

The goal of all calculation here is to find the set of registers live in a node N, which is *in(N)*; we make a conservative estimation which gives us a superset of in(N). According to equation EQ1 we have to determine the sets def(N) and out(N) in order to get in(N). A conservative estimation for def(N) has to keep this set small - looking at equation EQ 1 shows that we must only subtract those registers from out(N) which can definitely not be live; these are the registers which are written on *each* path through f. However, there may be some of these registers which are live at the exit of f - these must be excluded. Thus, we get the equation:

$$def(f) = dead(f) \cap must\_mod(f) \tag{EQ 7}$$

In this equation, must_mod(f) is the set of registers written on each path through f. This kind of analysis, the datasensitive mod-analysis, is described in [Callahan 88].

For determining the set must_mod(f) we perform a must_mod analysis; we calculate the sets must_mod(N) for each node N in f. For this purpose we define:

Def. 14: must_mod(N)

A symbolic register r is in the set must_mod(N) of a program-graph node N if it is modified on each path from (the beginning of) node N to the function's end.

We initialize must_mod(N) with rwrites(N); then it is extended by the following equation:

$$must\_mod(N) = must\_mod(N) \cup \bigcap_{s \in successors(N)} must\_mod(s) \cup must\_mod(f), \qquad (EQ\ 8)$$
$$f\ called\ in\ N$$

The set $must\_mod(f)$ is then the set $must\_mod(N_r)$ of the root node N_r of function f.

Next, we have to determine the set $out(f)$. Here, we have information flowing from the caller to the callee (i.e. the called function), whereas above (in equation EQ 8) we have information flowing from the callee back to the calling function. The variables live at the end of a function are just the variables live at the end of all nodes containing calls:

$$out(f) = \bigcup_{g\ calling\ f} \bigcup_{N} out(N) \quad for\ all\ nodes\ N\ containing\ a\ "call(f)" \qquad (EQ\ 9)$$

Now, we have got all equations together and can summarize (the sets $rreads(N)$, $rwrites(N)$, $rreads(f)$, and $rwrites(f)$ have been determined before):

Algorithm for Interprocedural Data-Flow Analysis:

- Initialize for each node N of each function f (in postorder, so that the successors of N are processed before N):

    $use(N) = rreads(N);$

    $def(N) = rwrites(N) - rreads(N);$

    $in(N) = use(N) \cup (out(N) - def(N));$

    $out(N) = \bigcup_{S \in successors(N)} in(S);$

    $must\_mod(N) = rwrites(N);$

- Determine (like in equation EQ 8) in a loop across all functions in postorder (i.e. so that functions called by f are processed before f):

$$must\_mod(N) = must\_mod(N) \cup \bigcap_{s \in successors(N)} must\_mod(s) \cup must\_mod(f),$$
$$f\ called\ in\ N$$

- Determine for each function f the set $dead(f)$ as complement of $live\_regs\_at\_entry(f)$ which is itself the set $in(N_r)$ for the root node N_r of f:

    $dead(f) = \{all\ registers\} - in(N_r);$

- Enlarge the sets iteratively in a (postorder) loop across all functions f:

    $def(N) = def(N) \cup ((dead(f) \cap must\_mod(f)) - use(N));$

    $use(N) = in(N);$

    $in(N) = use(N) \cup (out(N) - def(N));$

Algorithm 11: Algorithm for Interprocedural Data-Flow Analysis

12.2.8 Standard Optimizations

The code used for instruction scheduling should be optimized - it makes no sense optimizing performance using scheduling alone, scheduling redundant operations is not effective either. However, there are some interferences between standard compiler optimizations and instruction scheduling.

A popular compiler optimization like common-subexpression elimination needs an additional register to hold the subexpression. Let's have a look at an example:

x = 2 * (a + b);

y = a + b + c;

Here, the compiler will e.g. assign x to register r[5] and y to r[6]; the intermediate-code program with and without common-subexpression elimination (in the actual code, the multiplication will be represented as a shift operation) will then be:

r[5] = a + b;		r[7] = a + b;
r[5] = r[5] * 2;	with common-	r[5] = r[7] * 2;
r[6] = a + b;	subexpression	r[6] = r[7] + c;
r[6] = r[6] + c;	elimination	

Parallelized with 2 PEs:

without CSE:

```
r[5] = a + b;        r[6] = a + b;
r[5] = r[5] * 2;     r[6] = r[6] + c;
```

with CSE:

```
r[7] = a + b;        - - -
r[5] = r[7] * 2;     r[6] = r[7] + c;
```

Figure 37: Interference of Scheduling with Standard Optimizations

In both cases we need two cycles on two PEs, however with common-subexpression elimination we need an additional register - a scarce resource taking into account that scheduling increases register life-time and, thus, the number of registers live concurrently. A good register allocator may in some cases eliminate the need for an additional register - but e.g. not in the one above (unless we use three cycles instead of two). Generally, in the presence of several PEs we have the opportunity to compute such expressions anew in parallel to other computations. Thus, common-subexpression elimination will not often provide significant optimization if combined with instruction scheduling.

There are some more interferences between standard compiler optimizations and instruction scheduling. Loop-invariant motion may show the same kinds of interferences with instruction scheduling as common-subexpression elimination, and loop unrolling may interfere with a specific loop unrolling combined with instruction scheduling (compare e.g. [Ebcioglu/Nakatani 89]).

There are also optimizations which interfere in positive direction with instruction scheduling, e.g. dead-code elimination, where the number of operations to schedule is reduced. Another of these optimizations is function inlining - having the code of a called function copied into the calling function provides us with all data *intra*procedurally now and we can get more information in our analyses for supporting scheduling. This correlation gives us the place where function inlining has to be performed: before data-dependence and data-flow analysis so that we can determine the dependences and liveness information!

12.3 The Scheduler's Central Part

The scheduler's front-end delivers a program graph for each function of the application program to the central part. All information which can be gathered about the program is added as attributes to the program graph - to its nodes, the rtls inside the nodes, and to graphs (i.e. functions) as a whole. In the central part the program graph is transformed by instruction scheduling so that the program's run time is decreased by increasing the fine-grain parallelism. Figure 38 shows the main tasks performed in the central part:

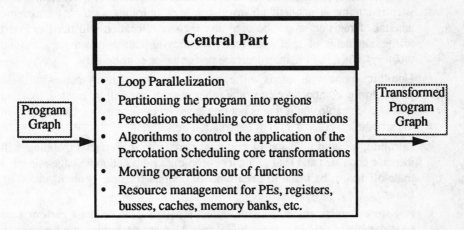

Figure 38: The Scheduler's Central Part

The subsections of 12.3 present all the activities performed in the scheduler's central part as shown in figure 38. These are mostly transformations on the program graph using all the information gathered in the scheduler's front-end.

Subsection 12.3.1 describes the methods for loop parallelization, belonging to the higher levels of Percolation Scheduling. *Subsection 12.3.2* shows how a function's program graph is split into regions inside which scheduling can be performed without affecting application-program semantics.

Subsection 12.3.3 presents extended versions of Percolation Scheduling's core transformations, e.g. for capturing multicycle operations. *Subsection 12.3.4* presents a new structure of the levels of percolation scheduling. *Subsection 12.3.5* describes new scheduling-control tactics which determine *from where, how far,* and *to where* operations are moved by applying the extended core transformations. *Subsection 12.3.6* shows scheduling-control strategies, another one of these new levels of Percolation Scheduling. They determine the sequences of nodes on which the scheduling-control tactics and core transformations are applied.

Subsection 12.3.7 describes how operations can be moved from one region to another one and from one function to another. Finally, *subsection 12.3.8* presents some hints for resource management, a topic which has been neglected so far in most research on fine-grain parallelism. A systematic approach for resource management, including methods and algorithms, is presented in section 13.

12.3.1 Loop Parallelization

The central part starts with parallelizing the coarse- or medium-grain structures, mainly loops. Methods like loop unrolling, Software Pipelining or Perfect Pipelining may be applied here (see subsection 8.5). Several problems have to be considered:

- Loop unrolling (which is also used in the other methods) is only efficient if register renaming is applied; however, for high unrolling factors, an extreme amount of registers might be used and register allocation will need to insert many statements of spill code (code for moving data between registers and memory). This, in turn, may decrease performance considerably.

- Unrolling loops with jumps will cause the creation of many copies of these jumps during compaction; copies of other instructions will be created, too, and lead to code explosion if that is not prevented by corresponding mechanisms in the scheduling-control level of Percolation Scheduling.

- Unrolling without a fusion of common parts like in Perfect Pipelining will increase code size and lead to higher cache-miss rates and more page misses; a trade-off has to be made to determine an optimal (or near optimal) unrolling factor.

- Register renaming combined with Perfect Pipelining can decrease performance considerably in certain cases, while it may increase performance otherwise. In figure 27 on page 57 the copy statements ($i = i'$ and $i = i''$) had to be inserted. If they cannot be moved outside the loop they will decrease performance. Perfect Pipelining tries to create small loop bodies with a high number of iterations, while loop unrolling creates loop bodies with a small number of iterations each; thus, in the former case, the significance of an inserted statement w.r.t. performance is a lot higher than in the latter.

More about these problems can be found in [Liebl 92].

12.3.2 Partitioning the Program Graph into Regions

Instruction Scheduling is performed inside regions of the program graphs. There are particular borders which must not be exceeded for scheduling, e.g. at loops. Using the standard scheduling mechanisms along back edges of loops might move an operation from one loop iteration to another iteration and thus change program semantics (note that the iteration index is different). All loop scheduling is performed in a previous phase, anyway, according to subsection 12.3.1. The program graphs under consideration here have the loops already unrolled and parallelized as far as possible.

Thus, regions must not extend beyond loop boundaries. There is another construct in the program graph which prevents scheduling, namely irreducibility. This is defined below according to [Aho/Sethi/Ullman 88]:

Def. 15: Reducible Graphs, Forward Edges, Back Edges

A program graph is called *reducible* if and only if its edges can be partitioned into two disjoint subsets, called forward edges and back edges, with the properties:

The *forward edges* form an acyclic graph in which every node can be reached from the top node.

The *back edges* {e | e = M → N, with nodes M, N} have the property that the "head" N dominates the "tail" M (see def. 9 on page 49 and def. 10 on page 78).

Loops are characterized by their back edges. The nodes on the path(s) from the head of a back edge to its tail represent the loop body and the back edge itself represents the transition to a new iteration of the loop.

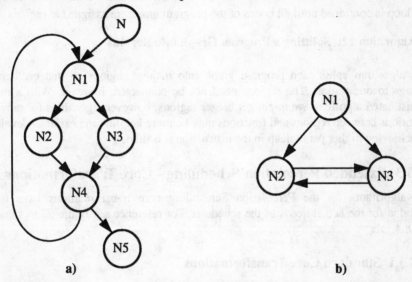

Figure 39: a) Program Graph with Loop, b) Irreducible Program-Graph

In figure 39a) the nodes N1, N2, N3, and N4 form a loop with (N4 → N1) as back edge; all other edges are forward edges. In b) the edges N2 → N3 and N3 → N2 are no back edges and the graph consisting of nodes {N1, N2, N3} is cyclic and not reducible.

Scheduling in a irreducible program-graph may change program semantics. Thus, regions have to be reducible parts of program graphs.

A simple, however a bit strict algorithm was used to determine the regions so that each loop is in a separate region and that regions consist of irreducible graphs.

Splitting a Program Graph into Regions:

We determine a set R of regions, represented by their header nodes: R = {H_1, ...,H_n}. Each header node is linked to the other nodes in its region, building sets R_1, ..., R_n.

- Insert the program graph's root node N_r as first node in the set of region headers and into the first region:

  $R = \{N_r\}$ and $R_1 = \{N_r\}$.

- Loop across all regions R_i:
  - Take the region's last node N and loop across all successor nodes S of N:
    - Are all predecessors of S elements of this region?

    yes: • Add S to the region as its last node: $R_i = R_i \cup \{S\}$;

    no: • Add S to end of the list of region headers: $R = R \cup \{S\}$.

    - $\{S\}$ becomes a new region.

The loop is continued until all nodes of the program graph are assigned to regions.

Algorithm 12: Splitting a Program Graph into Regions

This algorithm splits each program graph into disjoint regions so that each node belongs to one region. The regions need not be connected, however. With a more sophisticated algorithm we might get bigger regions, however algorithms for moving operations between regions and functions may be more helpful (and easier to develop) for achieving higher parallelism in the instruction schedule.

12.3.3 Extended Percolation Scheduling - Core Transformations

The algorithms for the Percolation Scheduling core transformations have been extended for the actual needs of the scheduler. For reference see figure 22 in subsection 8.4.1.1.

12.3.3.1 Standard Core Transformations

The move_op core-transformation has been extended to comprise the unification of the operation op to be moved with copies of op, too. Below there is a general description of the extended move_op core transformation. Other changes have been added, we try e.g. to move an operation to as many predecessors as possible in one transformation. For predecessors requiring the creation of a copy node, only one single copy node is made and all these predecessors are linked to that single copy node. Both measures limit the code increase due to scheduling and the number of nodes to be allocated. Figure 40 shows the effects of the algorithm.

In this move_op core transformation, we try like in algorithm 2 on page 51 to move an operation op'_i from a node N to a preceding node M in the program graph. Copies of op'_i may reside in M or in any "neighbour node" of N, i.e. successors of M like N_3 in figure 40. There will be an off-live dependence between op'_i and M w.r.t. these op_ks in cases where destination and source registers in op'_i are the same. To delete nodes in this algorithm, the *delete* core transformation is used which checks if the node N is empty and deletes it in that case, relinking the predecessors and successors. The additions to algorithm 2 on page 51 are marked by printing them in italics.

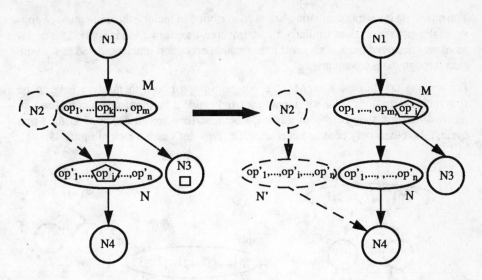

Figure 40: Move_op, Extended Version

Move_op Core-Transformation:

- Is there any (including off-live) dependence between op'$_i$ and M?

  yes: • *Is there a copy op$_k$ of op'$_i$ in M?*

    yes: • *Remove op$_k$ from M; if M is empty, delete it and exit.*

    no: • *Are all these dependences off-live dependences and is there a copy op$_k$ of op'$_i$ in all successors N3 of M (N3 ≠ N)?*

      yes: • *Remove all copies of op'$_i$ in M's direct successors (e.g. N3) except N and delete empty successors of M.*

      no: • no move possible; exit.

- Insert op'$_i$ in M and add all corresponding attributes.

- Has N any other predecessor besides M (like N2 in figure 40)?

  yes: • *Try to move op'$_i$ to all these predecessors in the same way as it is moved to M. If this is not possible,* make a copy N' of node N, including all attributes and edges, *unless such a copy has been made before.*

    • Relink all edges from node(s) N2 *where op'$_i$ cannot be inserted* to N' instead of N.

- Delete operation op'$_i$ from node N.

- Recompute data-dependence and liveness information for all nodes where changes occurred.

  Algorithm 13: Move_op Core-Transformation, Extended Version

The move_op core-transformation has been extended to include the unification of copies of the same operation; similarly, the *delete* core-transformation is applied for nodes an rtl was removed from. This saves considerable execution time compared to separate runs through the program graph.

For moving conditional branches, the program-graph nodes themselves have to be structured internally. So far, all operations (rtls) inside a program-graph node form an unstructured set; they belong to this node because they are all executed in the same cycle, this is their only common characteristic. Now let's take a look at figure 41:

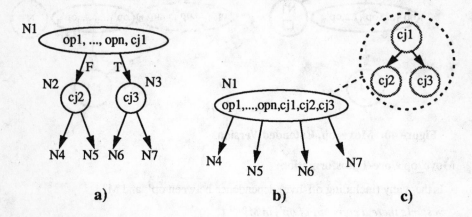

Figure 41: Conditional Trees

Nodes N2 and N3 are successors of node N1; node N2 is only executed if the conditional jump cj1 in N1 evaluates to FALSE (i.e. the left successor), while node N3 is executed if cj evaluates to TRUE (right successor). We assume that the left successor of a conditional branch is always the FALSE-successor and the right successor is taken if the condition evaluates to TRUE. Now let's assume that the conditional branches cj2 and cj3 in nodes N2 and N3 in part a) can be moved to node N1 which has then 4 successors; in our example nodes N2 and N3 can be deleted (see part b) of figure 41). Successor node Ni, i = 4, ..., 7, is then only executed if particular condition codes evaluate to particular values:

N4 is only executed if: cj1 = FALSE and cj2 = FALSE

N5 is only executed if: cj1 = FALSE and cj2 = TRUE

N6 is only executed if: cj1 = TRUE and cj3 = FALSE

N7 is only executed if: cj1 = TRUE and cj3 = TRUE.

Thus, we get the precedence relation indicated by part c) of this figure: cj1 precedes cj2 which needs only be executed if cj1 evaluates to FALSE, and cj3 comes after cj1 in case cj1 evaluates to TRUE. This graph is the "cond_tree" associated with node N1. This precedence relation of the conditional branches of a program-graph node is just a logical precedence, not a temporal one - all operations inside a node are executed in parallel in the same clock cycle.

The non-branch operations are actually related to the cond_tree; if an operation op is moved from node N4 to N1 then it needs only be executed if c1 evaluates to FALSE; this fact will become important if cj1 is moved higher up in the program graph - in this case op needs not be copied in the path from cj1 to cj3. However, in the following we will not associate non-branch operations with the cond-tree. This will be interesting mainly in the context of speculative execution where it is necessary to perform this association.

The second core transformation, move_cj is shown in figure 23 on page 51. The algorithm below shows how it can be realized and combined with the unification of copies of cj.

Move_cj Core-Transformation:

- Does cj read a variable which is written by an operation in M?

  yes: • no move possible; exit.

  no: • Build a copy N_f of N and delete cj and its "TRUE" subtree T_t in N_f.

  • Build a copy N_t of N and delete cj and its "FALSE" subtree T_f in N_t.

  • Has N another predecessor besides M?

    yes: • Create a copy of N (if that copy has not been created before) and link all predecessors except M to that.

  • Delete the edge from M to N and delete N.

  • Does M contain a copy cj' of cj?

    no: • Insert cj in M at the bottom of M's conditional tree where the successor link to N was before.

  • Insert an edge from cj in M to N_f (the "FALSE"-edge) if N_f is not empty.

  • Insert an edge from cj in M to N_t (the "TRUE"-edge) if N_t is not empty.

  • Update all dependence and liveness information in nodes where changes occurred.

Algorithm 14: Move_cj Core-Transformation, Extended Version

There is no need for a separate unify core-transformation - it is part of move_op and move_cj now. Whenever an operation op or conditional jump cj is moved, it is unified with its copies if there are any in the destination node or in other successors of the destination node.

The algorithm for the "delete" core-transformation, shown in figure 25 on page 54, is quite simple:

Delete Core-Transformation:

We want to delete a node N in the program graph.

• Is N empty?

   yes: • Remove all links to N and update them to links to N's successor (since N contains no conditional-branch operation it can have at most one successor);

      • Delete N.

    Algorithm 15: Delete Core-Transformation

12.3.3.2 Core Transformations for Multicycle Operations

In the following, extensions to Percolation Scheduling for supporting multicycle operations (see subsection 12.2.6) are described. The main characteristics of multicycle operations and their representations, the *multicycle_reps* (see figure 34, 35, and 36 on page 95), in the program graph are:

• Each cycle of the execution phase of a multicycle operation is represented by one multicycle_rep.

• If a node N contains the multicycle_rep for the i-the cycle of a n-cycle operation op ($n > i$) then each successor node of N contains the multicycle_rep for the (i+1)st cycle of op.

• All multicycle_reps carry the same data-dependence and liveness information.

• All multicycle_reps carry the same resource usage information.

• All multicycle_reps of an operation are linked.

• There are aggregate multicycle_reps representing more than one cycle; these are used for limiting program-graph size. They will not be considered below.

For moving multicycle_reps we can make use of some useful characteristics which can be derived from figure 42.

The multicycle operation op_k in figure 42 needs 4 cycles (compare figure 36). If we want to move op_k one level higher, we will move $op_k.1$ into node N_0, $op_k.2$ into node N_1, $op_k.3$ into nodes N_2 and N_3, $op_k.4$ into nodes N_4 and N_5 (the latter for the path via node N_3). Thus, the graph in part a) is transformed to the graph in part b) of figure 42. This figure helps to derive the properties of multicycle_reps for moving an operation op_k:

• The node receiving the first multicycle_op ($op_k.1$ in node N_0 in part b) of the figure) has to be checked for dependences, liveness, and resources as in move_op.

• For moving the other multicycle_reps, in all other cases there is already a multicycle_rep in the node (e.g. N_1 hosts $op_k.1$ before the move); when the move is performed, the multicycle_rep currently in the node is replaced by the multicycle_reps for op_k in the successor nodes. However, those have the same dependence, liveness, and resource usage; thus, all these characteristics need not be checked (except for the node N_0 above which contains no multicycle_rep before the move).

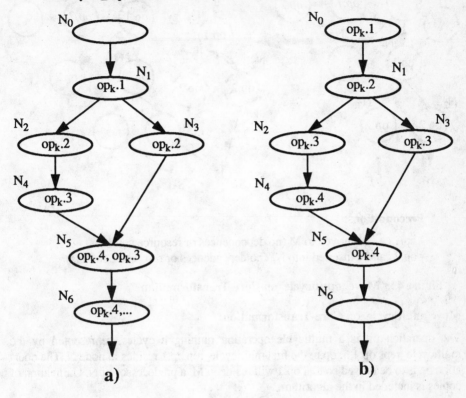

Figure 42: Moving multicycle_ops

• The last node, N5 in the example, will contain no multicycle_rep any more after the move; thus, dependence, liveness, and resource usage information will have to be updated in N_5. Node N_5 has also to be checked for deletion - it is the only one which may become empty by the move.

All these properties help moving multicycle_reps. Figure 43 and algorithm 14 describe the transformation:

In figure 43, op.1 residing in N shall be moved to node M; op.2 will thus be moved to N, and op.1 in node N_4 will be unified with op.1 in M, while op.2 is moved from N_5 to N_4.

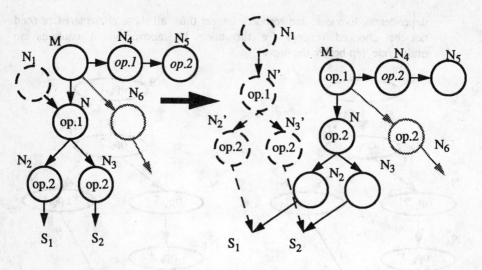

Preconditions:

- op.1 can be moved to M (no dependences or resource conflicts)
- op.2 can be inserted into N_6 (no dependences or resource conflicts)

Figure 43: Move_multicycle_op Core-Transformation

Move_multicycle_op Core-Transformation:

The operation op is a multicycle operation running n cycles, represented by the multicycle_reps op.1 ... op.n; the first multicycle_rep op.1 resides in node N. The operation op is to be moved so that op.1 will reside in M, a predecessor of N. Unification of copies is included in the algorithm.

- Is there any (including off-live) dependence between op.1 and M?

  yes: • Is there a copy op'.1 of op.1 in M?

     yes: • Remove op'.1 from M; if M is empty, delete it, relink its predecessors and successors and exit.

     no: • Are all these dependences off-live dependences and are they due to a copy $op_k.1$ of op.1 in all these successors N4 of M ($N4 \neq N$)?

        no: • No move possible; exit.

- Make a list L of all these successors N4 of M containing a copy of op.1.

- Are there sufficient resources for op.i in M and all successors of M (except N) and their successors in distance 1, ..., n-2?

  no: • No move possible; exit.

- Insert op.1 in M and add all corresponding attributes.

- Has N any other predecessor besides M (like N1 in figure 43)?

    yes: • Try to move op.1 to all these predecessors in the same way as it is moved to M. If this is not possible, make a copy N' of node N and all its successors containing the other multicycle_reps of op, including all attributes and edges, unless such a copy has been made before.

    • Relink all edges from node(s) N2 where op.1 cannot be inserted to N' instead of N.

- Add N to the list L (all nodes in L are successors of M containing copies of op.1).

- For each node K in L and their successor nodes in distance i for i = 1, ..., n-2:

    • These nodes contain op.(i+1); change op.(i+1) to op.(i+2), the (i+2)nd multicycle-representative.

- For each node K in L:

    • Delete op.n in all successor nodes in distance (n-1). Delete empty nodes.

- Recompute data-dependence and liveness information for all nodes where changes occurred.

   Algorithm 16: Move_multicycle_op Core-Transformation

In some architectures, conditional branches (just the branches without comparisons) may require more than one clock cycle to execute. In these cases we need a core transformation to move such multicycle operations: move_multicycle_cj. Figure 44 describes the transformation.

We want to move a conditional branch operation cj which needs more than one cycle to execute; in figure 44 we assume two cycles. We have a node N where the first cycle of cj resides; this multicycle_op is to be moved to N's predecessor M. The last multicycle_op of cj resides in node P. It is the one where control flow is affected, where the actual branch to two possible successors occurs, one connected via the FALSE-edge and the other via the TRUE-edge. The algorithm is quite similar to move_cj:

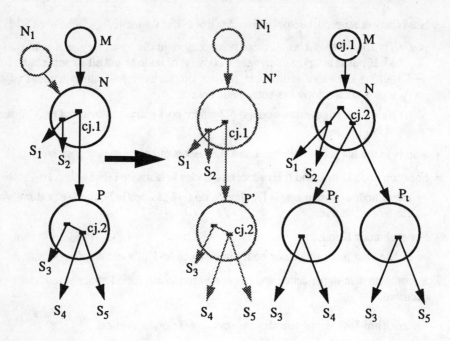

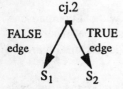

This is a cj-tree whose nodes (■) are conditional jumps and the edges point to program-graph nodes with operations being executed if the branch condition evaluates to FALSE resp. to TRUE.

Figure 44: Move_multicycle_cj

Move_multicycle_cj Core Transformation:

- Does cj read a variable which is written by an operation in M?

  yes: • no move possible; exit.

- Are there sufficient resources for op.i in M and all successors of M (except N) and their successors in distance 1, ..., n-2?

  no: • No move possible; exit.

- Is there a copy cj'.i (the i-th cycle) of cj.1 in M?

  yes: • Has N other predecessors besides M?

  yes: • Try to move cj.1 to these predecessors without further considering M, in the same way as here described for the move to M; exit.

  no: • Delete all cj.i (for i = 2,...,n) connected as multicycle_reps to cj.1 and

> delete cj.1.
>> • Delete empty nodes. Exit.
• Has N other predecessors beside M?

> yes: • Try to move cj.1 to these predecessors in the same way as described for M.
>> • Are there any of these predecessors where cj.1 cannot be moved?

>> yes: • Make a copy of all nodes containing cj.i for i=1,...,n, i.e. N and the subtree headed by N.
>>> • Relink all these predecessors to the copy of N (N1 in figure 44) instead of N.

• Insert cj.1 into M at the bottom of M's conditional tree where the successor link to N was before.

• For each successor K of M which contains cj.1 or a copy of it and all successors of these nodes K in distance i for i = 1, ..., n-2:

> • Change cj.(i+1) to cj.(i+2).

• Build a copy P_f of P (P is N's successor in distance n-1 containing cj.n) and delete cj and its "TRUE" subtree T_t in P_f.

• Build a copy P_t of P and delete cj and its "FALSE" subtree T_f in P_t.

• Q is P's predecessor on the path from N to P. Link all predecessors of P except Q to both, P_f and P_t.

• Delete the edge from Q to P and delete P.

• Insert an edge from cj.n in Q to P_f (the "FALSE"-edge) if P_f is not empty.

• Insert an edge from cj.n in Q to P_t (the "TRUE"-edge) if P_t is not empty.

• Update all dependence and liveness information in nodes where changes occurred.

Algorithm 17: Move_multicycle_cj Core-Transformation

12.3.4 Extended Percolation Scheduling - Structure

In the original definition of Percolation Scheduling in [Nicolau 85], a structure of six layers is proposed. However, only layer 0 with the core transformations, is described there in detail. These transformations are methods to move an operation from one node to a preceding node, maintaining program semantics. However, this is just the base for the transformations we want to perform. The sequence of operations considered for moving has an influence on the performance achieved by these movements as the example: in figure 45 shows.

Assume that we can move both, the operation from node N3 to node N2 in figure 45, as well as the operation from node N4 to node N2. If we move the operation from node N3 then no operation from the right subtree of N writing to r5 can be moved in or above node N2. If we move the operation from N4 to N2 then we cannot move operations from its left successor path writing to r7 in or above node N2. This may have a significant influence on performance - one subtree of N2 may e.g. be very small and the other one very high, with many candidates to move, using e.g. register r7 as first in a chain of operations.

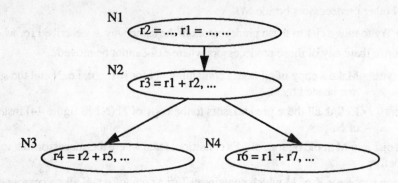

Figure 45: The sequence of Operations to Move

In [Ebcioglu/Nicolau 89] this problem is tackled in a general way. For each node N in the program graph, the set unifiable_ops(N) is determined, containing all operations which can be moved from any other node to N. A cost function representing the performance increase by the move is applied to determine which operations will be moved into N. This yields an optimum, however it is quite costly to determine and update the set unifiable_ops(N) and not practicable for realistic programs.

Thus, for optimizing program run time with Percolation Scheduling, we have to determine in which sequence the transformations are applied. The main items to specify for an actual application of Percolation Scheduling are:

- Determine in each program graph the sequence of *nodes* for the application of the core transformations.

- Determine in each program graph the sequence of *operations* to be considered for application of the core transformations.

- These sequences may be determined statically or may be determined dynamically during the transformation process.

The upper levels of Percolation Scheduling are redefined here to get suitable strategies for determining the above sequences. The following definition presents a new version of Percolation Scheduling:

Def. 16: Percolation Scheduling

Percolation Scheduling is a set of methods for program transformation, structured in levels:

- Level 0: This level of PS comprises a set of core transformations for moving operations between adjacent nodes, for deleting nodes, and for merging operations; the core transformations are described in subsections 8.4.1, 12.3.3.1, and 12.3.3.2.

- Level 1: Comprises control tactics specifying how the core transformations are applied to a set of operations or nodes inside a window around a node N specified by a control strategy (level 2).

- Level 2: Comprises control strategies determining the sequence of nodes or operations to which the core transformations are applied using particular control tactics from level 1.

- Level 3: The higher levels of Percolation Scheduling, level 3 upwards, comprise methods for higher-level constructs, e.g. methods for loop transformations described in subsection 8.5.

These levels are applied in a top-down sequence, i.e. first the high-level transformations like software pipelining are applied. Then, for each program graph, control strategies of level 2 determine the sequence of nodes and operations to which the core transformations are applied. After this, the control tactics determine how the core transformations are applied, which are then finally executed. The following subsections describe the upper layers (> 0) of Percolation Scheduling.

12.3.5 Extended Percolation Scheduling - Control Tactics

The control-tactics level (level 1) of Percolation Scheduling determines

- how far an operation is moved
- from which node to which node the operations are moved.

The application of the core transformations is performed inside a window for reasons of complexity. There are two ways to apply control tactics, either *node oriented* or *operation oriented*.

12.3.5.1 Node-Oriented Tactics

Two kinds of node-oriented tactics were developed: *pull_n* and *push_n*. These tactics take a node N and try either to fill N with operations from below N or they try to move all operations out of N to predecessors.

The node-oriented tactics consider nodes as sources or destinations of moves. The node N where control tactics will be applied has been determined in the strategy level. Now, the tactics level has to determine which operations will be moved into N or out of N. Both tactics, pull_n and push_n, actually comprise sets of tactics.

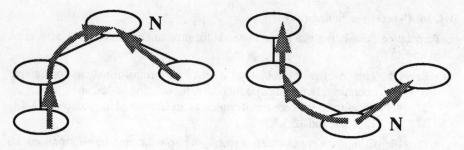

Figure 46: Pull_n with Window Size 2   Push_n with Window Size 2

Pull_n:

First, *pull_n* determines the set of all nodes in a distance up to n in the program graph's subtree rooted by N (see figure 46). Only operations from this subtree will be moved into N. This distance "n" is the "window" for applying the tactics. The window size may be determined statically or it may be changed dynamically. Several ways may be used to determine the operations to be moved into N:

1. Optimum Moves

    • Determine the set of all operations inside the window which may be moved to N.

    • Determine for each of these operations the value of a cost function.

    • The cost function may e.g. be the average execution time, assuming the corresponding operation is moved into N.

    • Choose those operations with optimum cost-function values and move them into N; their number is restricted by N's resources.

2. Top-down Moves

    • Loop until all resources in N are exhausted:

        • Loop for level = 1, ..., n (i.e. start with N's successors):

            • Loop for all nodes N' in window at distance "level" from N:

                • Loop for all operations op in N':

                    • Apply *move_op* "level" times to move op from N' to its predecessor, and so on, up to N.

3. Bottom-up Moves

    The same as top-down moves, but starting at the bottom of the window; i.e. the second loop of the algorithm is now:

        • Loop for level = n, ..., 1, (-1):

    The rest is the same as in 2.

4. Minimum Copy Code

    • Like 2. or 3., but choose the source so that the number of copy nodes is minimum.

5. Combined Moves
   - Check for each operation op in the window if a node can be deleted by moving op into N. If there is such an op, perform the move and delete the node.
   - Repeat the above until no more node can be deleted.
   - Perform one of the other methods for the other moves.

Algorithm 18: Pull_n Control Tactics

Many other tactics are possible and can be developed accordingly.

Push_n:

First, *push_n* determines the set of all nodes in a distance up to n in the program graph's subgraph with N as leaf, i.e. it takes N, then N's predecessors (on distance 1), then their predecessors (distance 2), and so on, up to distance n (see figure 46). Then, it tries to move all operations from N into one of the other nodes of the subgraph. Several ways may be used to determine the targets for moving operations from N:

1. Optimum Moves
   - Determine for each operation op in N the target nodes N' where it may be moved.
   - Determine for each such move the value of a cost function.
   - The cost function may e.g. be the average execution time, assuming the corresponding operation is moved into N'.
   - Determine for each operation op in N which can be moved its destination node so that the cost function is optimum.

2. Moving Far
   - Choose the next operation op in N randomly.
   - Move op as highly up in the window as possible by applying move_op repeatedly.

3. Moving Near
   - Choose the next operation op in N randomly.
   - Move op to upwards to the first node where it can be inserted.

4. Minimum Copy Code
   - Like 2. or 3., but choose the destination so that the number of copy nodes is minimum.

5. Combined Moves
   - The above methods may be combined.

Algorithm 19: Push_n Control Tactics

While data dependences have to be checked between op and each node on its way up, resource constraints have to be checked only between op and its destination node. In this manner, operations can be passed even through nodes with insufficient resources.

Pull_n is a suitable tactics to consider resource constraints while filling nodes with operations. *Push_n* aims at emptying nodes. Thus, it reduces compiler runtime by early deletion of nodes.

12.3.5.2 Operation-Oriented Tactics

Operation-oriented tactics take an operation and try to move it. We start with an operation op in a node N. The following figure shows the three tactics *move_to_all_preds*, *migrate_within_trace*, and *migrate*:

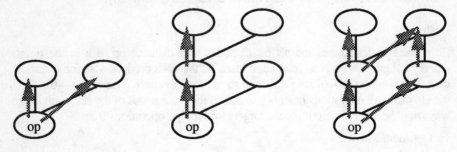

Figure 47: move_to_all_preds   migrate_within_trace   migrate

Move_to_all_preds:

• Determine the window as above as the set of all nodes preceding N in a distance up to n.

• Loop for i = 1, ..., level:

  • Can op be moved to *all* nodes on this level?

    yes: • Move op to *all* nodes on this level; exit loop.

  • End loop "for i = 1, ..., level".

Algorithm 20: Move_to_all_preds Control Tactics

The application of this tactics prevents the creation of copy code; however, moves are only performed if an operation can be moved to all predecessors.

Migrate_within_trace:

• Determine the window as above, as the set of all nodes preceding N in a distance up to n.

• Determine a trace from the node N to the top of the window, e.g. as:

  • longest path from N to the top of the window

  • most probable path from N to the top of the window

  • path of nodes containing the longest chain of data-dependent operations.

- Move op upmost in the window along the chosen trace.

Algorithm 21: Migrate_within_trace Control Tactics

Migrate:

Similar to move_to_all_preds, this strategy tries to move an operation upmost in the window on each path. Thus, in the algorithm for move_to_all_preds just the upper and lower bounds of the loop and the loop exit have to be changed.

12.3.5.3 Which Tactics for what Application?

The control-tactics level gives the opportunity to taylor scheduling methods to program characteristics. There are some general examples:

- For scientific or similar code with "regular" behaviour the node-oriented tactics can be applied, pull_n if resources are scarce in the machine architecture, push_n otherwise.
- In small regions with loops optimum_move should be applied.
- Otherwise, combined_moves might be best, however, only if there are no scarce resources.
- In case of long chains of data-dependent operations top_down resp. move_near are the best methods; they allow to move the whole chains by starting with the topmost of these chained instructions inside the window, allowing to move the other operations in the chain one by one.
- For applications which are not very regular, we may get a lot of copy code when core transformations are applied; thus, the operation-oriented tactics where the creation of copy code can be prevented or limited are preferable.
- In applications where many alternative traces through the program exist, migrate_within_trace can be applied if probabilities for the alternatives can be determined.

12.3.5.4 Control Tactics for Specific Code Patterns

There are particular patterns in the code of application programs which occur quite frequently and for which specific tactics can be developed. Such patterns may e.g. cause unnecessary copy code when the standard methods are used or prevent transformations unnecessarily by resource constraints.

Figure 48 shows a "diamond" structure in a program graph. Such a structure is very common in programs - it represents an if-then-else construct in a high level language where the "if-statement" resides in node N1. The statements in the "else" path are e.g. in the left successor node, N2, and the statements in the "then" path are in the right successor nodes, N3 and N4. The next statement after the if-then-else construct, where the two paths rejoin, resides in node N5. Now let's apply a core transformation to an operation op in N5. When we move op to N2 then we get a copy node N5' of N5 as successor of N4; moving op to N4 instead will lead to a copy node N5', too, as successor of N2. Similarly, we will get copy nodes N2' when moving op out of N2 (because N2 has more than 1 predecessor), N4' when moving op to N3 (because N4 has more than 1 predecessor), and finally a N3'. We can rejoin op from both successor paths of N1 when we move it to N1, but the copy nodes remain. These copy nodes increase code size and thus miss-rates in caches which leads finally to lower performance. There are some more problems occurring with this frequent code structure: when moving op upwards in both paths (via N2 and N4), it might get stuck somewhere. This might occur e.g. if there are not sufficient resources in N3 to move op there; in this case we get one copy of op in N2 and one in N4. Both consume resources, e.g. a PE, register, busses, etc. These resources are wasted in cases where we can move op to N1 - where the two copies in the both paths from N5 up to N1 could be rejoined.

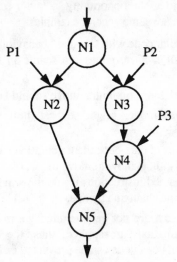

Figure 48:   Code Patterns: A Diamond Structure

An "intelligent", dedicated transformation for diamond structures would move op directly from N5 to N1, checking dependences on both paths upwards, but without checking any resources. Using this transformation would thus save at least the resources for the copy of op and the copy node N5'.

This transformation can be implemented by using a special parameter which allows to use core transformations with and without application of resource management. Control tactics may be applied which detect diamond patterns and apply the core transformations so that operations are always moved from the bottom of a diamond structure to the top without checking resources in between. The number of copy nodes has to be controlled accordingly.

Another structure which deserves some attention is shown in figure 49.

This program-graph structure looks like a stair; such a pattern is created by a sequence of if-then-statements. Of course there are also more general kinds of these stairs, e.g.

with several nodes in certain steps. The stair is just like the diamonds above a code structure occurring frequently.

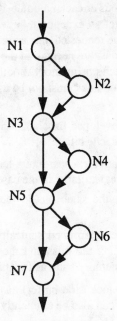

Figure 49: Code Patterns: Stair Structure

When moving an operation upwards from the bottom of the stair we get copy nodes at each node with more than one predecessor, i.e. N3, N5, N7. Similarly, unification of operations may be blocked by scarce resources.

This means that resources are wasted for copies of the operation. The creation of copy nodes and wasting of resources due to copies of operations which cannot be rejoined can be prevented if we move the operation from the bottom of the stairs to its top in one step. Control tactics for this purpose have to identify stair structures in the program graph and apply the core transformations without creating copy nodes and without allocating resources in the nodes between the source node where the operation resides and the target node.

There are frequent structures like stairs and diamonds for which dedicated control tactics may gain performance. Such structures can be identified by analyzing a variety of program graphs of application programs.

12.3.5.5 Control Tactics Considering Resources

So far, consideration of resources has not been described. Resources are all those parts of the system architecture which are used for processing an application, e.g. processing elements, registers, memory locations, busses, pages, page table entries, etc. For resources like busses and caches, scheduling can decrease waiting time.

Consider a load operation which in case of a cache hit may take two cycles in which the busses are utilized. During these two cycles no other load or store operation can be processed which uses the same bus or cache module. A cache miss may have a latency of 30 clock cycles. Either we get an exception, anyway, so that the processor has to wait after the cache miss until the requested data arrive from memory, or the processor can proceed until the requested data are needed. In the latter case no other load or store operation must use the same cache or memory module during these 30 cycles; similarly, the busses between these modules must not be used concurrently to the transmission of these data.

Several control tactics can be developed for considering caches and busses to caches, assuming "t" clock cycles for a cache hit:

- In the case of set-associative caches: move loads/stores using the same cache set as far apart as possible; similarly, in the case of direct-mapped caches.
- Move loads/stores using the same bus to their cache module(s) at least "t" nodes apart.
- In cases where it can be determined statically that a cache miss will occur, move the operation causing the miss and the next load/store using the same cache module or bus or memory bank as far apart as possible.

Misses in the TLB (translation lookaside buffer) can be considered similarly. Other resources like physical registers can also be efficiently considered by control tactics.

12.3.6 Extended Percolation Scheduling - Control Strategies

Control strategies determine the sequence of nodes considered for application of control tactics. Such strategies are e.g.:

Top-down strategy:

The nodes in a region are ordered by a depth-first search and processed top-down.

Bottom-up strategy:

Nodes are processed bottom-up. The bottom nodes are determined as nodes whose successors are not in the same region or are already visited in the current phase or nodes which are reachable only via back edges. Such bottom nodes can be determined by a depth-first search.

Path-oriented strategy:

The region is separated into sequences of critical paths. Such a critical path may be determined as:

- The longest path in the region.
- The path of nodes with (presumably) high execution frequencies.
- The path comprising the longest chain of data-dependent operations in the region.

12.3.7 Moving Operations out of Regions and Functions

Scheduling is so far restricted to regions, i.e. operations may only be moved inside these regions and not beyond their boundaries. However, it may be useful to consider moves across these boundaries, too. The main reasons for region boundaries are:

- loops
- loop-like structures caused by "goto" statements
- irreducible subgraphs
- the strictness of the algorithm for determining the regions (see section 12.3.2)
- function boundaries.

Loops should only be processed with loop-specific methods as presented in section 8.5. Analyzing loops once more at this place and trying to find some more possibilities for moves is a very high effort offering little reward. The second reason for these boundaries, loop-like structures caused by goto statements, will better be analyzed in the scheduler's front-end and treated like loops. Various kinds of code patterns can be created by making use of many goto statements, and these are hard to be categorized for finding general scheduling methods. The patterns which can be recognized as forming loops are those which can be treated best using the loop-scheduling methods.

Irreducible flow-graphs need thorough analysis to be treated accordingly; in many cases semantic analysis may be necessary. This is left for further research.

The strict algorithm from section 12.3.2, however, can be enhanced so that we get less regions as shown in figure 50.

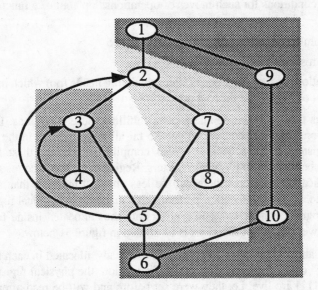

Figure 50: Program-Graph Regions

Our algorithm separates the program graph into the regions: {1, 9, 10}, {2, 7, 8}, {3, 4}, {5}, {6}. The nodes 3 and 4 have to be in a of their own because they form a separate loop; similarly, the nodes 2, 5, 7, and 8 must not be part of the set {1, 9, 10} because they are part of the loop with header 2. The nodes 5 and 6 form regions of a single node each - this is not necessary and prevents unnecessarily moving operations from node 6 to 10 and 5. The above figure shows that tail nodes of outer loops (node 5 above) will not be part of the loops' regions, neither inner nor outer ones when nodes from the inner and outer loop (i.e. from different regions) are predecessors. We can add these tail nodes to the outer loop's region and enhance our chances for moving operations. The method to achieve this is not too hard:

We have to determine that such a node (e.g. node 5 above) is not part of an irreducible subgraph and that it belongs to an outer loop. Both conditions can be checked using algorithms from [Aho/Sethi/Ullman 88]. Similarly, node 6 in figure 50 can be added to the region {1, 9, 10}. This can be accomplished in the same way as before by considering the region with the program graph's root node as outer loop. Thus, we get the regions:

{1, 9, 10, 6}, {2, 7, 8, 5}, {3, 4}.

Moving operations out of functions can be useful in several cases. For relatively small functions which are called from not too many other functions, inlining will be the best way to increase chances of scheduling (see section 12.2.8); thus, all information about this function will be intraprocedurally and can be gained more efficiently. For other functions, moving an operation from the called function into the calling function is only feasible in cases where we have sufficient resources available in the nodes of the caller. Thus, the conditions for such moves of operations "op" out of a function "foo" to the callers are:

- a small number of places from where foo is called
- sufficient resources for op in these places
- few operations in foo's root node (after scheduling inside foo) which may all be moved out of foo so that the root node can be deleted.

In most programs there will not be many cases fulfilling these conditions. However, there is an additional case not considered yet. So far all registers used in the program are symbolic registers. In the scheduler's (resp. compiler's) back-end these symbolic registers have to be mapped to physical registers. Registers are a scarce resource and for realistic application programs there will be less physical registers than symbolic registers available. Register allocation performs this mapping to physical registers; it works on the program graphs, too, and registers are thus allocated inside functions. The situation between different functions is illustrated in figure 51 below.

We assume a situation where physical registers are already allocated in each function. The function "fy" calls "foo" and after the call operation, the physical registers r[5], r[8], r[10], and r[12] are live, i.e. they were set before and will be read after the call (the return register of "foo" is not used here). Similarly, function "fum" calls "foo" and after the call, registers r[6], r[9], r[10], and r[12] are live. The function "foo" uses several physical registers, too: r[5], r[9], r[11], and r[12]. Thus, functions "fy" and "fum" will not find the expected values in their registers r[5], r[9], and r[12] after the return from "foo", but the values set by "foo".

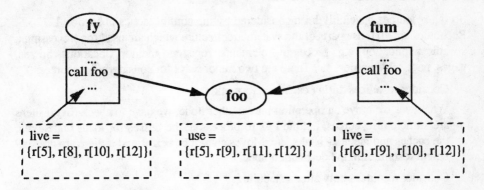

Figure 51: Saving Registers at Function Calls

Therefore, we have to restore after the return from "foo" the values which were in the registers before the call. There are two strategies for saving and restoring these registers:

- caller save:

  the calling functions ("fy" and "fum") save the registers before the call to "foo" and restore them after the return; the registers to be saved are those which are live after the call.

- callee save:

  the called function, "foo", saves the registers it uses right at its beginning and restores them at the end, before the return operations in "foo".

In case of the caller-save strategy, too many registers are saved and restored - these are the registers which are live after the call operation (in "fy" or "fum") but not used in the called function, in the above figure these are r[8], r[10] in "fy" and r[6], r[10] in "fum". These operations could be removed by an optimizer in the register allocator. In the case of a callee-save strategy there are also redundant loads and stores; these are those for registers used in "foo" but not live in any of the functions calling "foo" after the call operation. In the figure above this is r[11].

By moving the store operations of callee-saves to the calling functions ("fy" and "fum") we can eliminate also stores which are only partially redundant, e.g. the "store r[9]" moved to "fy" can be removed while it cannot be removed in "fum". Thus, we can try to move all callee-saves to the calling functions, eliminating as many as possible, and delete the node with these callee-saves in "foo". By moving the stores to the calling functions we get the chance to move them higher up in those functions, considering busy busses, cache hits, etc. there.

A function performing such moves of operations out of functions has to be applied after register allocation, i.e. in the back-end.

12.3.8 Resource Management

So far, resources have only been considered by the control tactics in section 12.3.5.5. Resources are all those parts of the system architecture which are used for processing a specific application, e.g. processing elements, registers, memory locations, busses, pages, page table entries, etc. There are two major ways for considering resources:

1. Consider resources during each transformation.

   Whenever we move an operation into another node, we have to check first if there are sufficient resources, i.e. the PEs to process it, the busses for loads and stores, the caches and memory banks, etc. Moves cannot be performed if there are not suf-ficient resources in the destination node.

2. Consider resources only after scheduling.

   All scheduling is performed as if there were infinite resources; thus, we get a high parallelization. However, after scheduling we have to check each program-graph node for resource shortage. For nodes with insufficient resources we have to per-form a rescheduling.

Case 1. is very time consuming; in many cases the time consumption can be intolera-bly high. It also may prevent scheduling an operation from a node to a preceding node at a distance greater one if in any intermediate node the lack of resources prevents fur-ther moves.

Case 2. creates highly parallelized schedules, however resources may be overutilized in particular nodes. In these nodes we have to perform a rescheduling. However, if we perform rescheduling according to i) or ii) we will get the same problems as before and may find ourselves in a vicious circle. The solution chosen was to perform reschedul-ing inside a window around the particular node. If there are not sufficient resources in this window then new nodes will have to be inserted (e.g. for moving a register's con-tent to memory so that the register can be used for another purpose and moving the earlier content in again afterwards) - causing additional execution time and perfor-mance degradation!

Systematic resource management is presented in section 13. A thorough description, theoretical foundation, and practical application can be found in [KarlR 93].

12.4 The Scheduler's Back-End

The scheduler's back-end performs essentially the same tasks as a compiler back-end. However, some of these tasks are different from those of a standard compiler, and there are some additional tasks to perform. The back-end gets program graphs for each function as input; it performs all actions to derive the load program's object-code representation and provides the object file as load file for the simulator. Figure 52 shows the back-end's main tasks:

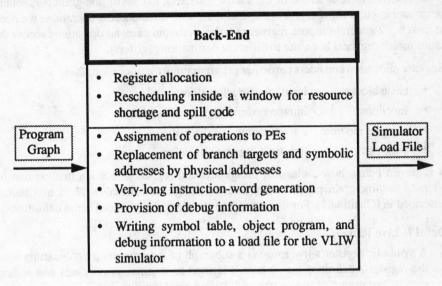

Figure 52: The Scheduler's Back-End

The diagram shows:

Program Graph → **Back-End**

- Register allocation
- Rescheduling inside a window for resource shortage and spill code
- Assignment of operations to PEs
- Replacement of branch targets and symbolic addresses by physical addresses
- Very-long instruction-word generation
- Provision of debug information
- Writing symbol table, object program, and debug information to a load file for the VLIW simulator

→ Simulator Load File

12.4.1 Register Allocation

Register allocation is a special kind of resource management; it is treated here separate from general resource allocation because various algorithms for register allocation exist which can well be adapted to architectures with fine-grain parallelism. In RISC processors only load and store operations access memory while the other operations' operands are located in registers. In CISC architectures many operations may get their operands from memory. Accesses to registers are in most architectures faster than accesses to cache memory, at least faster than accesses to secondary cache or memory (in cases of cache misses). Therefore, system performance is increased when the number of memory accesses in a program is minimized by using registers efficiently. This is the task of register allocation. It is usually more effective on RISC processors because they have considerably more registers than CISC processors.

Register allocation maps symbolic to physical registers; this is a well-known technique for compilers. Most of the current methods used for register allocation were developed in the context of RISC processors. The performance features of these architectures can be utilized best by application programs if a good register allocation limits the number of memory accesses by keeping as many variables as possible inside registers. The main global (i.e. beyond basic block boundaries) register-allocation algorithms are described in [Briggs et al 89], [Chaitin 82], [Chow 88], [Chow/Hennessy 84], [Chow/Hennessy 90], [Gupta/Soffa/Steele 89], [Proebsting/Fischer 92], [Rau 92], [Santhanam/Odnert 90], [Sweany/Beaty 90], and [Wall 86].

For three-address architectures we need at least three general-purpose registers, two for the source operands and one for the destination operand (if the destination register is not always the same as one of the source registers). In case of fine-grain parallelism on an architecture using n processing elements with three-address operations we need at least n + 2 general-purpose registers (in the minimum case, all operations access the same source registers but write to different destination registers).

Register allocation considers particular program units for allocation; these are:

- basic blocks: local register allocation
- functions: intraprocedural register allocation
- compile modules: interprocedural register allocation
- program: link-time register allocation.

It is shown below how a classical intraprocedural register-allocation method can be adopted for fine-grain parallel architectures, the graph coloring method of Chaitin, described in [Chaitin 82]. For understanding the algorithm we need some definitions:

Def. 17: Live Range

A symbolic register's live range is a subgraph of the program graph, starting with the register's definition (i.e. where it is used as destination operand) and ending with its last usage (as source operand) before a redefinition.

Def. 18: Interference Graph

The nodes of an interference graph represent symbolic registers; there is an edge between two nodes if the registers' live ranges overlap, i.e. if the corresponding subgraphs are not disjoint.

Def. 19: Node Degree

A node of a graph has the degree d if it is linked to d "neighbour nodes".

In Chaitin's algorithm we may consider each live range as separate symbolic register, in accordance with register renaming (see section 12.2.3). In cases where we have not sufficient physical registers available we have to use a single physical register for several symbolic registers inside their live ranges. Consider a physical register p assigned to symbolic register r[i] at a particular place in the program; r[i] has been defined (written) before and will be used (read) later. Let's assume, the succeeding operation's symbolic destination register r[j] needs a physical register - and there is none available. In such a case we write the contents of p to memory, use p for the symbolic register r[j], and reload p's earlier contents before the symbolic register r[i] is used as source register again. The code for storing and reloading these register contents is called *spill code*. Below, Chaitin's register-allocation algorithm is described:

Register Allocation:

1. Repeat until the whole graph of the function f can be colored:

    1.1 Build the interference graph.

    1.2 Reduce the interference graph.

    1.3 Is the interference graph reduced, i.e. empty?

    > no: • Insert spillcode.
    >
    > • Update the live ranges of f.

2. Color the graph, i.e. assign physical registers.

Ad 1.1: Building the interference graph of a function f means:

- Determine the live ranges in f (e.g. using def-use-chains, see [Aho/Sethi/Ullman 88]) and create a node for each live range.
- For each node N:
    - Create nodes N' representing live ranges overlapping with N.
    - Create an edge between N and N'.

Ad 1.2: Reducing the interference graph means:

- Remove each node N from the interference graph with less neighbors than physical registers available (i.e. its degree is less than the number of physical registers).
- Push N onto the stack S.
- Repeat this until no more node can be removed.

Ad 1.3: Inserting spillcode means:

- Use cost functions to determine the register to be spilled; a series of such cost functions have been proposed in the literature, see e.g. [Bernstein et al 89].
- Insert store operations at the appropriate places, i.e. in the range between the last usage or definition of the old variable and before the new definition for the new symbolic variable.
- Insert load operations at the appropriate places, i.e. in the range between the last usage of the new symbolic variable and the next usage of the old symbolic variable.

Ad 1.3: Updating live ranges means:

- Determine the def-use chains according to [Aho/Sethi/Ullman 88] for all live ranges changed.

Algorithm 22: Register Allocation via Graph Coloring

There are particular differences between constraints on registers for sequential processors and for architectures with fine-grain parallelism. The minimum number of physical registers is higher and we must allow concurrent access while keeping program semantics, i.e. considering dependences.

Another problem area concerns spill code. Let's assume a physical register p is allocated to a symbolic register r[i] and shall be reused in a certain range for symbolic register r[j]. Conventionally, this means that we insert a "store r[i]" operation after the last definition of r[i] before this range and a "load r[i]" operation before the first reuse after the range. In case of fine-grain parallelism we have now more than one operation per node. Two cases can happen here which are not possible for sequential architectures:

- the operation with the (last) definition of r[i] and reuse of r[i] are in subsequent nodes
- the reuse of r[i] and the definition of r[j] reside in the same nodes.

Figure 53 below shows such a case where spilling does not solve the problem:

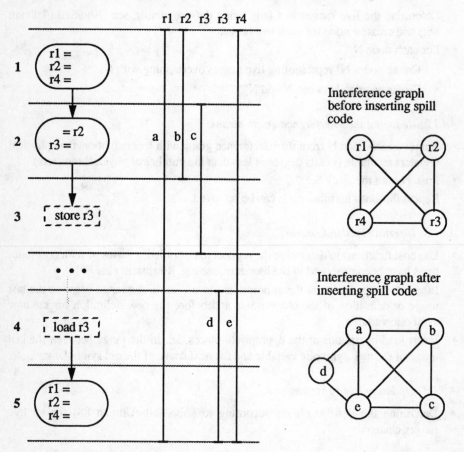

Figure 53: Problems with Spill-Code Insertion

In figure 53 we assume that we have three physical registers available for the symbolic registers (live ranges) r1, r2, r3, and r4; Chaitin's algorithm determines the places to insert the spill code - however, we still have four live ranges active at the same time in node 2. This problem will be just the same in cases with n (> 3) physical registers available and n+1 statements in the pattern shown above - in all these cases we cannot assign physical registers to symbolic registers because we can't find places where to insert the spill code. The reason is that several statements are executed in parallel which need the registers at the same time. There is no way to assign the registers conventionally.

We can solve this kind of problems by splitting the corresponding program-graph nodes. Figure shows the problem in the example from figure 53 solved by splitting node 2 into the new nodes 2 and 3; thus, the interference graph can be reduced and we don't even need spill code. However, this method may cost performance - splitting a node into two means needing an additional cycle execution time. In this example we even don't decrease performance because the node splitting saves the insertion of spill code.

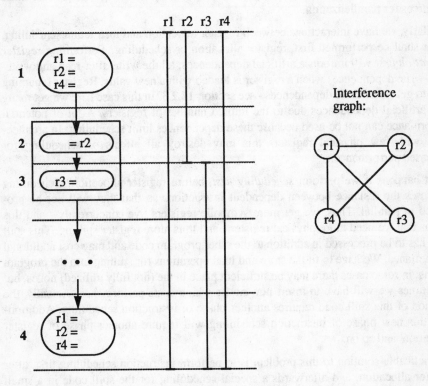

Figure 54: Solution of the Spill-Code Problem

Considering a node's operations, splitting this node can be guided by the rule that operations starting more live ranges than ending them should be moved into the upper node (node 2 in figure) and operations causing not more live ranges to end than to begin should be moved into the lower node, node 3 in the example. Thus, the goal of node splitting here is live-range reduction.

The adoption of Chaitin's register-allocation algorithm to fine-grain parallel architectures is described in [Baumann 93].

12.4.2 Interactions Between Register Allocation and Instruction Scheduling

One of the principal problems in compiler optimizations and other program transformations is to determine the sequence of optimizations because most of them interact. The combined application of two optimizations can increase or decrease program performance, depending on the sequence of their application. For some optimizations, the optimum sequence can be determined because they interact in a unique way. An example for this are dead-code elimination and parallelization. Having dead code in the program occupies resources; eliminating this code before scheduling will provide more resources for parallelization.

Similarly, we have interactions between register allocation and instruction scheduling. What shall be performed first, register allocation or scheduling? Performing *register allocation first* will introduce artificial dependences, all the write-after-read and write-after-write dependences when a register is loaded with a new value. Register renaming tries to get rid of these dependences - see section 12.2.3. In this case here we get many new artificial dependences due to the limited number of registers. A lot of potential performance can not be used because these dependences limit scheduling. In architectures with few physical registers this may destroy all effects of scheduling for increased performance.

What happens if we perform *scheduling first*, before register allocation? Scheduling increases the distance between dependent instructions so that they will not be processed in parallel. Thus, we get more symbolic registers live concurrently - and this means that we need more physical registers, and thus more register spilling. This spill code has to be processed in addition to the other program code and may cost additional performance. We have to fit the store and load operations for spilling into the program graphs; in some cases there may be sufficient place in the (not fully utilized) nodes, but sometimes we will have to insert new nodes which costs performance. Actually, the creation of this spill code requires another phase of instruction scheduling. Additionally, this new phase of instruction scheduling will require another phase of register allocation, and so on.

A practicable solution to this problem is to perform instruction scheduling first, after register allocation, and afterwards a special scheduling for the spill code in a small environment inside the specific area of the program graph where the spill code has to be placed. Such a "limited scheduling" will first try to find sufficient resources in the node where the spill code has to be placed or in neighbors of these nodes. Only if no such resources in existing program-graph nodes can be found, a new node will be created for the spill code.

However, there is a third possibility; we can try to *integrate scheduling and register allocation*. For local scheduling and local register-allocation such a method was proposed in [Bradlee et al 91]. Schedule costs, i.e. the execution time for a scheduling unit (basic block or, in our case, a program graph) have to be estimated as well as spill costs. These costs are balanced iteratively in order to find a register limit, a number of symbolic registers live concurrently, so that the schedule costs are low. However, this method is quite costly w.r.t. execution time. The comparisons in [Bradlee et al 91] show that the performance gain is small compared to a method performing register allocation after scheduling.

Another way is to consider the needs of register allocation during scheduling in the control tactics and strategy layers (see 12.3.5 and 12.3.6). To consider diamond structures and stairs (see section 12.3.5.4) reduces the amount of copy nodes and thus the number of register live ranges active concurrently. Thus, the number of physical registers needed is reduced. When operations are selected for scheduling we can choose them so that the number of concurrent live ranges is reduced. In node-oriented tactics we can choose nodes with many active live ranges first. This will reduce spill code further. Thus, the most effective method will be:

- Perform instruction scheduling first.
- Consider register allocation during scheduling in the control tactics and strategy layers.
- Perform register allocation after scheduling.
- Perform a limited scheduling for spill code afterwards.

12.4.3 Rescheduling

The interactions between several kinds of code transformations may lead to significant performance degradation of the compiling/scheduling process or even to infinite sequences of actions. The same problems as with interactions between register allocation and scheduling presented in the previous section may occur for other program transformations, too. Such transformations are e.g. those for resource management as described in section 13.

The previous section showed that from the perspective of register allocation the sequence

> instruction scheduling ⇢ register allocation ⇢ limited rescheduling

will offer the best relation between achieved performance and scheduling cost. But how can this rescheduling be performed? Let's have a look at an example in figure 55.

In this figure, symbolic register r3 is used several times, first it is written in node N1, then read several times, including nodes N2 and N5. Between N2 and N3 register r3 is not used. In node N3, symbolic register r4 is written and read afterwards, between N3 and N4. Between N4 and N5, neither of the two symbolic registers is used. We assume that our register allocator maps both symbolic registers to the same physical register r.

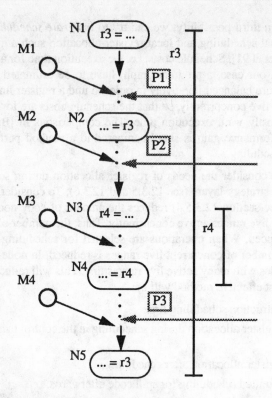

Figure 55: Spill Code and Rescheduling

Now, where to put the spill code? The register allocation algorithms have relatively simple methods for determining this place. But we will take a closer look at the constraints for its determination.

The store for register r3 has to occur somewhere between N1 and N3, i.e. between the beginning of the both live ranges, excluding the ends N1 and N3. The reload of r3 has to occur somewhere between N4 and N5, i.e. between the ends of the live ranges, excluding the end nodes N4 and N5.

This rule is quite simple. However, we have to consider paths entering the linear node sequence {N1, N2, N3, N4, N5} from the outside, like the one from node M1. Obviously, r3 must be written in M1 or one of its predecessors because it is read in N2. This value of r3 must be retained, too, thus the store operation has to be inserted after the entry point from M1 (unless N1 is a predecessor of M1 and r3 is not written between N1 and M1). There is a certain point P1 in our linear node sequence, not after N2, where the last entry point of such a M1 may occur. Between P1 and N3 is the place where to insert the store operation for r3.

The next case to check is an entry like the one from node M2, occurring between N2 and N3. Register r3 is live in M2, like in M1. Here, we either have to move the point

P1 below this entry point, to P2, or we have to insert spill code in that path, too, using the same method as here. A register allocator will place the store for r3 immediately before N3 in a node N3' and redirect all predecessors of N3 to N3'.

Now we consider the case of an entry between N3 and N4, like from node M3 above. Like in the other cases, r3 has to be live on this path. We don't have to care about this path if N1 is the only predecessor of M3 where r3 is written (the same holds for the previous cases). Otherwise, we have to insert a store operation for r3 in the path from M3, using the same method as before.

Finally, we have to consider the case of an entry between N4 and N5, like from M4 in figure 55. Like in all these cases, r3 has to be live on this path. We can determine a point P3 where the first entry to the sequence occurs where r3 is live but not written. Between N4 and P3 is the place where to put the reload operation. A register allocator will usually put the reload immediately after N4.

Now we are ready to determine an algorithm for rescheduling and spill code placement; we use the same naming as in the example above, i.e. registers r3 and r4 are to be mapped to the same physical register r and our task is to find the place where to insert spill code. Generally, we can determine the places as:

- The store operation is inserted in a node between P1 and N3 with sufficient resources. If there is a node like M2, we will try to insert a store operation in the path from M2; if that is not possible, P1 is set to P2 for the insertion of the store operation. If there are not sufficient resources left, we have to create a new node N' as immediate predecessor of N3 containing the store operation. We may apply Percolation Scheduling then to the nodes between N' and N5, trying to move as many operations as possible to N' in order to delete a node between N' and N5.

- The load operation is inserted uppermost between N4 and P3 if there are sufficient resources. In case there are not, a new node N' is inserted as successor of N4, containing the load operation. We may apply Percolation Scheduling then to the nodes between N' and N5, trying to move as many operations as possible to N' in order to delete a node between N' and N5.

Algorithm 23: Spill-Code Placement

12.4.4 Assignment of Operations to PEs

Each operation has to be processed by a particular processing element. This constraint can easily be kept in case of single-cycle independent operations. However, for multicycle operations one specific PE has to be reserved for all cycles of such an operation. Figure 56 shows some of the problems connected with the assignment of PEs.

In this example we have to assign several multicycle operations op_1, op_2, op_3 to processing elements so that an operation stays on the same functional unit during all its execution cycles. For two processing elements a valid assignment is op_1 on PE_1, op_2 on PE_2, and op_3 on PE_1. Generally, we have to consider a particular environment of a

node N for PE assignment (the closure of the set of nodes containing multicycle operations with representations in N). Local assignment of operations in N_5, for instance,
may map op_2 to PE_1, yielding a conflict in N_4 where op_1 has been assigned to PE_1, too.

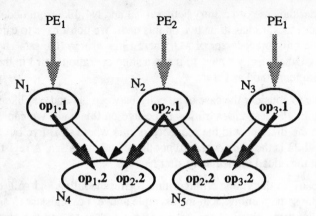

Figure 56: PE Assignment

The problem of assigning multicycle operations to functional units is similar to the
register assignment problem, and can thus be solved by graph coloring. For our problem the nodes of the interference graph are the multicycle operations and the colors are
the PEs. Similarly, a multicycle operation with all its representatives corresponds to a
variable's live range. If no coloring is possible, new program-graph nodes have to be
inserted containing multicycle representations which caused conflicts.

Similar problems occur for dependent operations. In the MIPS instruction set, multiplication operations write the result into specific registers and with another machine
operation these results are moved to a general-purpose register. These specific registers
(HI and LO) exist once in each PE. Thus, we have to execute the multiplication and the
move operation on the same PE and have to take care that dependences are considered,
i.e. that such a register is not overwritten by another multiplication before the previous
result is moved to a general-purpose register. The problem is solved in the same way as
the mapping of multicycle operations to PEs.

This kind of PE assignment is straight-forward and heuristic. A more systematic
approach to PE assignment is presented in section 13.4.

12.4.5 Instruction-Word Generation

For VLIW architectures we have to map the machine operations to very long instruction words. Each program-graph node is mapped to one instruction word. An operation
assigned to the first PE is mapped to the first field in the instruction word, an operation
assigned to the second PE is mapped to the second field, etc. Fields of the instruction
word remaining empty are filled with "noops", operations performing no action.

For other kinds of architectures, mainly superscalar ones, the operations are written in sequences, keeping the operations from the program-graph nodes together.

So far, no jumps occur in the code - they are represented by edges in the program graph and the operations have to be inserted in the back end. Doing this earlier means updating jumps during scheduling - and that would be a lot more costly than inserting them here. The problem where to insert jumps is shown in the following figure:

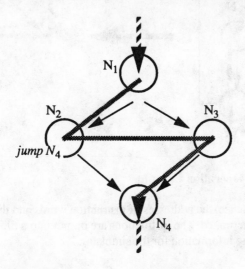

Figure 57: Jump Operations

In figure 57, a sequence of VLIWs may be N_1, N_2, N_3, N_4 where N_1 contains a branch operation (with fall-through node N_2 if the branch condition evaluates to FALSE or a branch to N_3 if the evaluation delivers TRUE). So, the instruction word generated from N_2 must contain a *"jump N_4"*. Another sequentialization may be N_1, N_3, N_2, N_4 with an operation *"jump N_4"* inserted into N_3 and *"branch N_2 if condition = FALSE"* into N_1. The sequence mentioned first contains one jump less than the second one. Therefore, algorithms were developed that determine a sequentialization of the program-graph nodes so that the number of jumps is near minimum. Figure 58 demonstrates an optimization integrated in the routine computing this sequentialization. On the left side of figure 58 the sequence is N1, N2, N3, ..., N4 where "jump N2" is to be inserted in the VLIW containing N4. This jump can be avoided if the sequence N1, N3, ..., N4, N2 is chosen. There, the instructions represented by N3 up to N4 are placed in front of those from N2.

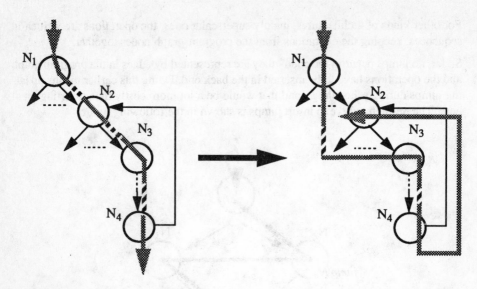

Figure 58: Jump Operation Creation

According to this sequence, the addresses of instruction words and the targets for multiway branches are determined. The instructions are output into a file together with the symbol table and debug information for the simulator.

12.4.6 Debug Information

This section lists some features needed for debugging parallelized code. There are two kinds of users for such a debugger:

- The developer of new scheduling algorithms wants to test the algorithms and find out if these scheduling algorithms cause erroneous code.
- Users want to find bugs in application programs.

For basic tests users are advised to work with non-parallelized programs; they run slower but it will be easier to identify bugs. However, it will be necessary to test application programs in the parallelized version, too, because some bugs in the application may only occur there while they may be hidden in the sequential code.

Breakpoints:

Breakpoints are basic elements of most debugging activities. A user will set a breakpoint e.g. at a source code line. The compiler maps this source code line first to a sequence of machine-code lines. It is easy to map the breakpoint to this sequence - it is just the place before the first machine operation in the sequence. But how can this mapping be performed when the machine operations created from the source-code statement are scattered across the whole procedure by scheduling? Some may be merged with machine operations from other source-code statements or even be deleted or duplicated during scheduling.

To support setting breakpoints in scheduled code the following actions are performed:

- A mapping of each source-code statement to all the machine operations created from it; it is created before scheduling and updated after scheduling.
- When a breakpoint to a source-code statement is set, it will be mapped to internal breakpoints to all machine operations this source-code statement is mapped to (resp. instruction words containing these machine operations).
- There are three strategies for executing the breakpoint:
  - Stop before the first of these operations is executed, which ever will be the first one dynamically.
  - Stop before the execution of each of these machine operations.
  - Stop after the last machine operation belonging to the source-code statement.

The first strategy is best used as default while the other ones may be interesting for developers.

A breakpoint to a function has to be mapped not only to the first statement of the function itself but also to each place where this function was inlined. However, in cases where statements are moved out of functions by scheduling, no correct stopping at the function is possible at places where the function was inlined.

More debugging features can be offered if the parallelized code is running on a simulator; in [Böckle/Trosch 90] several methods are described. The simulator can check for each operation if the expected operands are used. Each variable in the program and each memory address accessed is assigned a unique number. Each register a variable is written to is attributed by the corresponding number. For each machine operation the numbers of the source operands and those in the registers containing the source operands are compared during execution. Thus, we can find out if the correct source operands are used.

13 Resource Management

One of the problem areas of parallel architectures is resource management. This has not been considered before for sequential architectures because it was not necessary. Theoretical research typically doesn't consider resource management - in the cases considered there, the machine model has typically infinite resources. However, in real-world applications resources are limited and have to be managed efficiently.

The main resources to be considered here are:

- Processing elements.
- Shared pipeline stages e.g. in multipliers.
- In floating point units certain actions can be overlapped while others are sequential - these stages in the floating-point pipeline have to be considered as resources.
- The interconnect system, mostly busses.
- Register banks and register-bank ports.
- Memory banks and memory-bank ports.
- Caches, cache ports, and sometimes cache-controller functions

These resources can be managed dynamically by corresponding hardware control. However this control often decreases performance; several agents accessing the same bus need some cycles for arbitration each time they access the bus - even when there is no other agent active. Planning the sequence of resource usage statically at compile time will reduce the number of collisions for using the same resource, even in presence of hardware control (which may be needed in some cases for security reasons). In the Multiflow TRACE machines (see section 4.1 or [Colwell et al 88] or [Fisher 87]) the busses are controlled statically by software. This saves the cycles for bus arbitration and provides fast access to memory.

The delay slots in RISC pipelines constitute another kind of these resources, see section 8.

Resource management is actually a planning method - the usage of resources by actions has to be planned in advance so that efficient usage can be made of these resources and so that the actions can be performed efficiently.

There are many interactions between scheduling and resource management; each time we move an operation from one program-graph node to another, this is a user of resources being moved. A program graph node contains operations which are processed in parallel and thus, also the resource usage at the corresponding clock cycle. Some examples for resource restrictions on the types and number of operations in a node are:

- The architecture offers two multipliers; this means that not more than two multiplication operations can be placed in a program-graph node. If a multiplication takes t cycles then no third multiplication must occur in the next t successor nodes, i.e. not more than two multicycle_reps of multiplications must occur in the same node.

- The architecture offers m memory banks; this means that not more than m loads and stores can be placed into a program-graph node.

- The architecture offers one single bus to a particular memory bank; this means that not more than one access to this memory bank must occur in a program-graph node. For guaranteeing this, memory-reference disambiguation is necessary (see 12.2.4).

Moving an operation from one node to another means that the resources used are released and that resources in the destination node have to be assigned. This assignment may cause conflicts with other operations in that node. For a proper assignment in cause of a conflict we have to determine a new assignment for all operations in the destination node and for all other nodes containing multicycle_reps of multicycle operations present in this node. This is extremely costly and prevents moving an operation from one node to a predecessor via an intermediate node with insufficient resources. Such an intermediate node prevents moving the operation further ahead - although the resources won't be needed after the next move.

The interactions between scheduling and resource management make it hard to determine their sequence so that the objectives of both are fulfilled. We get similar problems as above in section 12.4.3 for the combination of scheduling and register allocation (which is a special kind of resource management, anyway).

Performing resource management before scheduling:

- Restricts the Percolation Scheduling control-strategies significantly (e.g. to Trace Scheduling).

- Restricts the application of the core transformations by additional dependences (e.g. for register allocation as described in section 12.4.3) and blocking of their further applications.

- Doesn't capture operations which are created during or after scheduling like those in copy nodes (created e.g. by move_op) or the jump operations inserted during code generation (see section 12.4.5).

Performing resource management after scheduling:

- Will encounter nodes with insufficient resources.
- Has to split such nodes or perform a rescheduling (compare section 12.4.3).
- Will degrade performance.

Combining resource management and scheduling:

- May increase complexity and cost significantly.
- May be solved partially by specific scheduling-control strategies like the resource-controlled IBM-method (see [Ebcioglu/Nicolau 89]) or Compact_global (see [Aiken 88] and [Werner 91]).

In [KarlR 93] a new method for resource management is presented which tries to combine scheduling and resource management by splitting the tasks of resource management. First, *resource allocation* is performed by attributing each operation with the set of symbolic resources used. Such a symbolic resource represents a specific *class* of physical resources; one class is e.g. the set of all PEs which can perform multiplications. A multiply operation will be attributed with the symbolic resource representing this class; this allocation is not a commitment to one specific member of this class, any of them can process the operation.

The actual *resource assignment* is performed after scheduling. This assignment maps each symbolic resource to a physical resource of the corresponding class. However, it is not guaranteed that a properly performed resource allocation guarantees a proper assignment.

We can distinguish between active resources like PEs or busses and passive resources like registers or memory. For passive resources there are already specific methods for resource management as e.g. the one described in section 12.4.1. In the sequel the management of active resources is described.

13.1 Machine Description

Resource management depends heavily on the machine architecture and the way this architecture is described. For a proper resource management we need a concise and comprehensive machine model.

For each operation we can define a resource allocation by a matrix; figure 59 below shows such a resource-allocation matrix for a 4-cycle operation.

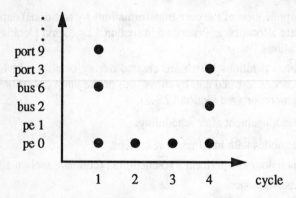

Figure 59: Resource Allocation Matrix for an Operation

This operation uses for this specific allocation PE 0 during all 4 cycles while in cycle 1 bus 6 and port 9 are used, and during the fourth cycle bus 2 and port 3 are used. Of course this is only one specific allocation of many possible allocations of the architecture. The set of all possible resource allocations of an operation comprises all these resource-allocation matrices which are valid for this operation (alternative-resource allocation matrix, ARA).

Alternatively, *resource-allocation expressions* can be used to specify a machine operation's resource allocation, i.e. its requirements on the machine architecture. Such a resource allocation expression (RAE) comprises the name of a resource and the cycles this resource is used. This time qualification is specified by the sign '. Two RAEs may be combined as alternative characterized by the character I and as conjunction characterized by the character &. For specifying that n resources out of a set of equal resources are occupied by an operation, we restrict the set by specifying a suffix @n; this will e.g. be used for an operation needing two read ports. Generally, the RAEs can be described as:

RAE = RESOURCE_NAME['TIME_QUALIFICATION];

RAE = RAE I RAE;

RAE = RAE & RAE;

RAE = (RAE);

RAE = (RESOURCE_NAME I ... I RESOURCE_NAME) @ n, n $\in$ N (natural numbers);

RAE = (RESOURCE_NAME I ... I RESOURCE_NAME)'TIME_QUALIFICATION;

RESOURCE_NAME $\in$ {pe0, ..., bus0, ..., port0, ...};

TIME_QUALIFICATION = n $\in$ N;

TIME_QUALIFICATION = TIME_QUALIFICATION, TIME_QUALIFICATION;

TIME_QUALIFICATION = n-m; n,m $\in$ N;

The example from figure 59 can be expressed as RAE:

pe0'1-4 & (bus6 & port9)'1 & (bus2 & port3)'4

These RAEs are just a convenient form to express an operation's resource allocation. Thus, we have ways to describe a machine so that we can perform resource management and other operations based on this description.

The preconditions for resource management have to be satisfied in the front end by creating the machine description for the machine architecture M:

M = (resources, {(o, resource_usage(o)) I for all operations o})

The vector *resources* contains the number of physical resources available for each resource class. There are two kinds of resource classes, base classes and combined classes. Base classes are the resources we know already: PEs, busses, caches, etc. Combined classes are built for specific operations, e.g. the class of all PEs which can perform integer additions or the class of all PEs which can perform both, integer additions and integer multiplications. For each machine operation we have a resource-allocation matrix determining the resources used in each clock cycle. These matrices can be compressed to vectors if the operations' resource usage of is not distinguished for different clock cycles.

13.2 Operators and Functions for Resource Management

Proceeding from the resource allocation matrices RA we can define operations on such RAs. We take two RAs, $A = A_{(i,j)}$ and $B = B_{(i,j)}$ as resource allocation matrices of the same dimensions and combine them to create new resource allocation matrices:

$$R = A \oplus B \Leftrightarrow \quad R(i,j) = \begin{cases} 1 & \text{if } A_{(i,j)} = 1 \text{ } or \text{ } B_{(i,j)} = 1 \\ 0 & \text{else} \end{cases} \quad \forall \text{ } i,j$$

$$R = A \ominus B \Leftrightarrow \quad R(i,j) = \begin{cases} 1 & \text{if } A_{(i,j)} = 1 \text{ } and \text{ } B_{(i,j)} = 0 \\ 0 & \text{else} \end{cases} \quad \forall \text{ } i,j$$

$$R = A \otimes B \Leftrightarrow \quad R(i,j) = \begin{cases} 1 & \text{if } A_{(i,j)} = 1 \text{ } and \text{ } B_{(i,j)} = 1 \\ 0 & \text{else} \end{cases} \quad \forall \text{ } i,j$$

$$R = A \Delta V \Leftrightarrow \quad R(i,j) = \begin{cases} 1 & \text{if } A_{(i,j)} = 1 \text{ } and \text{ } V_{(i)} = 1 \\ 0 & \text{else} \end{cases} \quad \forall \text{ } i,j$$

The operator $\oplus$ adds two resource allocation matrices to a common one while the operator $\ominus$ subtracts them. The operator $\otimes$ can be used to determine if two operations require common resources. The operator Δ applies a mask vector V to a resource allocation A to select specific resources. In all cases we may use sets of alternative-resource allocations instead of single resource allocation matrices by applying the operator to each element of the set.

In [KarlR 93] it is shown how these operators can be used to perform the functions needed for resource allocation.

For compressing a matrix to a vector over the time axis we need the auxiliary function *compress*; starting from a set A of resource allocations of dimension x × y the function produces a set of resource allocation vectors of dimension x by compressing the time dimension y to 1 by adding the columns $a_{(,t)}$ of a resource matrix a for each t.

compress (A):
- $R := \emptyset$;
- Repeat for all $a \in A$:
  - $r := (0)_{(x)}$;
  - for t from 1 to y do: $r := r \oplus a_{(,t)}$;
  - $R = R \cup r$;

The following function, likely_pe (op) determines for an operation op the set of PEs which can be used for its execution (with *maxres* as maximum number of resources available and ARA the set of alternative-resource allocations of op).

likely_pe (op):

- pe_mask := $(0)_{(maxres)}$;
- Repeat for all h ∈ (compress (ARA(op) Δ resource_type ("PE"))):
    - pe_mask = pe_mask ⊕ h;

For resource assignment we need the function *likely_resources* which determines a mask vector r_mask specifying the set of resources of a specific type which can be utilized during a specific clock cycle; this function is applied to a set A of alternative-resource allocation matrices (ARA). (In this notation, $h_{(,cycle)}$ is the column number "cycle" in matrix h.)

likely_resources (A, type, cycle):

- r_mask := $(0)_{(maxres)}$;
- Repeat for all h ∈ A:
    - r_mask := r_mask ⊕ $(h_{(,cycle)}$ Δ resource_type(type));

The function *remaining_resources* determines for a set A of alternative-resource allocations the resulting set R after allocating a resource z in cycle cyc to a specific operation.

remaining_resources (A, z, cyc):

$$R = \bigcup_{h_{(z,cyc)} = 1} h \qquad \forall\, h \in A$$

13.3 Resource Allocation

Resource allocation is performed during scheduling. Initially, during program-graph construction (see section 12.2) each program-graph node N is assigned the set of all resources available. The node N gets an attribute resource_scoreboard (N) which is initialized with the vector *resources*.

During instruction scheduling two functions are applied to this resource_scoreboard:

When an operation op is moved from a node N to a node M then we determine:

resource_scoreboard(N) := resource_scoreboard(N) ⊖ resource_usage (op);

resource_scoreboard(M) := resource_scoreboard(M) ⊕ resource_usage (op);

The operations ⊖ and ⊕ represent element-wise subtraction and element-wise addition, respectively. For single-cycle operations, resource_usage (op) is just a vector; for a multicycle_op op representing the i-th cycle we take the vector

resource_usage$_{(,i)}$(op). For moving multicycle operations the allocation and deallocation have to be performed for all multicycle_reps. In case of operations where all
multicycle_reps have the same resource usage, i.e. where all resources are reserved
during the whole processing, an allocation has to be performed for the target node M
only where op$_1$ (the multicycle_rep for the first cycle) is moved to, and a deallocation
for the last node, containing the multicycle_rep for the last cycle as in algorithms 16
and 17.

A program-graph transformation moving an operation op from a node N to a preceding
node M under consideration of resources is only allowed if the predicate *overflow (op,
N)* evaluates to FALSE. This predicate is determined as:

$$\text{overflow (op, N)} = \begin{cases} \text{TRUE} & \text{if } \exists \text{ k: resource\_scoreboard (N)}_{(k)} - \\ & \quad \text{resource\_usage (op)}_{(k)} < 0 \\ \text{FALSE} & \text{else} \end{cases}$$

For scheduling-control strategies and tactics it might be useful to consider resource
management e.g. by moving operations into nodes with low resource utilization. For
this purpose we define the utilization of a node N with respect to a resource k as:

$$\text{utilization (N, k)} = 1 - \frac{\text{resource\_scoreboard (N)}_{(k)}}{\text{resources}_{(k)}}$$

13.4 Resource Assignment

Resource assignment is performed on the scheduled program graph, i.e. in the back
end, replacing the more heuristic approach of assigning operations to PEs as described
in section 12.4.4.

As described above, we can assign to each operation the resources needed using the
function *likely_resources. (op)*. In the following, methods for assigning PEs to operations are presented first.

13.4.1 Assignment of Processing Elements

Assigning resources is not difficult if all resources of a class are identical, i.e. if all PEs
can perform all machine operations. Otherwise, we can formulate the problem more
generally as described in [KarlR 93]. First, we consider single-cycle operations only;
this case can be solved with common graph algorithms.

We have to assign the operations op of a set O to resources (PEs) from a set R. For
each operation op $\in$ O we have a subset *likely_resources(op)* determining which elements of R may be assigned to op.

The problem can be generalized as:

We have a graph G = (V,E); the set V of vertices consists of two disjoint subsets O and
R: V = O $\cup$ R, O $\cap$ R = $\varnothing$. For the set E of edges with E $\subseteq$ O $\times$ R and (op $\in$ O, r $\in$ R)
we have:

$(op \leftrightarrow r) \in E \Leftrightarrow likely\_resources(op)_{(r)} = 1.$

This graph is bipartite, i.e. the edges always connect a node of set O with a node of set R. Our task is to find a set of edges complying with the constraints of the functions likely_resources(op) for all operations op so that the number of these edges is maximized (a maximum assignment). The following example shows such a bipartite assignment-problem for a program-graph node N:

resource_type ("PE") =	(1, 1, 1, 1, 0, 0, ..., 0)	... this part of the machine
likely_resources (op1) =	(0, 1, 0, 0, 0, 0, ..., 0)	description specifies four
likely_resources (op2) =	(1, 1, 1, 0, 0, 0, ..., 0)	PEs and four operations
likely_resources (op3) =	(0, 1, 1, 0, 0, 0, ..., 0)	(op1, ..., op4) and the PEs
likely_resources (op4) =	(0, 0, 1, 1, 0, 0, ..., 0)	which can execute the operations.

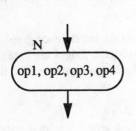 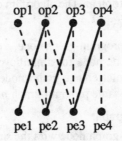 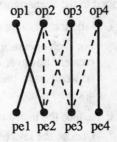

non-maximum assignment   maximum assignment

Figure 60: Bipartite Assignment Problem

In figure 60 a machine description specifies four PEs and four operations op1, ..., op4. A program-graph node N contains the four operations op1, ..., op4. The bipartite assignment problem in node N is shown next to the node, the relations specified by the function *likely_resources (op)* represented as edges. The solid edges specify actual assignments and the dashed edges possible assignments. The left-hand graph offers no actual assignment for op1 while the one on the right-hand side assigns each operation one PE, a maximum assignment.

The maximum assignment problem can be solved in polynomial time. There are several algorithms for such an optimization which are described in books about graph theory and in [KarlR 93].

The formulation of resource assignment as bipartite assignment-problem is adequate for single-cycle but not for multicycle operations. A multicycle operation starting on a specific PE will continue during the subsequent cycles on the same PE. For superpipelined superscalar processors we may also have to model the single pipeline stages, i.e. we have to assign a sequence of these pipeline stages to an operation for the sequence of execution cycles. However, for all integer PEs and most floating-point PEs it will be sufficient to use the model described here. Thus, we assume that a n-cycle operation occupies one particular PE for all these n cycles. This model encompasses most standard pipelines, e.g. those where after stage i a stage k = i + 1 is occupied. The model can be extended for more general pipelines, too.

The problem of assigning operations to PEs can be modeled by graph coloring like register assignment (see section 12.4.1). We model each operation as node in an interference graph and get an edge between two nodes if the execution of the two operations overlaps and if they can be executed on the same PE. An assignment of operations to PEs is then equivalent to coloring the interference graph with colors representing the PEs. coloring means that each node in the interference graph gets a color so that adjacent nodes (i.e. those connected via an edge) have different colors. In cases where no coloring can be performed, nodes have to be split to allow for a coloring.

For understanding the algorithm, we assume first that each operation can be executed on each PE. In [KarlR 93] the graph-coloring algorithm from [Briggs et al 89] is applied to the PE assignment problem. The algorithm consists of the following steps:

i. Build the interference graph:

   For each operation in a program-graph node, a node of the interference graph is created, however only one node for a multicycle operation. Edges are created between each pair of interference-graph nodes where representations of the operations appear in the same program-graph nodes.

ii. Reduce the interference graph:

   Choose the interference-graph node with the smallest degree, i.e. with the least number of neighbors. Remove it from the interference graph and put it onto a stack. The degree of all neighbour nodes is thus decremented. This is continued until all nodes are linearized on the stack.

iii. Color the interference graph:

   The nodes on the stack are assigned colors, starting with the critical ones, i.e. those with most neighbors (nodes with less neighbors than colors available can be colored anyway). The assignment of colors may be performed according to a strategy like round-robin. The algorithm stops when all nodes are colored so that two adjacent nodes always have different colors. If there are any nodes left on the stack which cannot be colored then they have to be split. Strategies for splitting are similar to those in 12.4.1. After splitting the algorithm continues with step i.

Algorithm 24: Graph-Coloring Algorithm for PE Assignment

This algorithm can easily be extended for more general architectures where not all PEs can perform each operation. We enlarge the interference graph by adding one (pseudo)node for each PE, colored with the color corresponding to this PE. Each node representing an operation which cannot be performed on a particular PE gets an edge to the new node representing this PE. Thus, we assure that this operation is not assigned to that PE, i.e. gets not that color. The pseudo-nodes representing PEs are of course not reduced during step ii.

This algorithm is quite fast, linear in the number of edges, $O(|E|)$. In [KarlR 93] another algorithm is presented which is adopted from [Gupta 87] resp. [Gupta/Soffa 91]. This algorithm can color the interference graph with less node splittings, however requiring higher complexity; in extreme cases it is up to quadratic in the graph size.

The algorithm adopted from Gupta is then performed as:

i. Build the interference graph:

Each edge is attributed with its number of conflicts, i.e. the number of program-graph nodes in which the operations (corresponding to the nodes) interfere. The pseudo-nodes representing the PEs are added as described above.

ii. Determine all urgencies:

This is a measure on the nodes (see below).

iii. Color the most urgent node; continue with step ii. until all nodes are considered.

iv. The algorithm stops when all nodes are colored; otherwise, split the most urgent node of the uncolored ones and continue with step i.

Determining the next node to be colored for an optimum coloring is a task needing exponential execution time. Thus, a heuristic is used based on the "urgency" the node needs a coloring. Such an urgency of a node N is proportional to the number of conflicts between N and other nodes which are already colored. If the most urgent node were not colored next, it might become uncolorable at the next step, thus causing node splittings. The urgency of a node is inverse proportional to the number of remaining colors, available for the actual coloring. Thus, we get the formula:

$$ urgency\,(N) \;=\; \frac{\sum conflicts\,(M \rightarrow N)}{remaining\_colors\,(N)}\,, \qquad \forall\, M \in S_a \text{ with } (M \rightarrow N) \in E $$

with S_a as set of all colored nodes. In cases of disjoint subgraphs and for the first node of the graph we need an initial node for coloring because the urgency measure is only greater than zero for nodes with at least one colored neighbour. This initial node N_{init} is defined by the edge with the highest number of conflicts:

$$ \max_{N_i \;\; \forall\,(N_i \rightarrow N_j)} \quad \sum conflicts\,(N_i \rightarrow N_j) $$

This algorithms allows to place long multicycle operations early to avoid splitting nodes containing such long multicycle operations.

One characteristic of graph coloring for PE assignment is worthwhile noticing: In a program graph like the one in figure 61, we can assign op_2 and op_3 to the same PE although they share the same node (N_4). These two operations start on two alternative paths through the program graph and can never been executed at the same time - the branching in node N_1 can either go left or right, not to both directions at once! Thus, two colors are sufficient for coloring the interference graph in figure 61. This will however not be applicable to VLIW architectures and architectures with conditional execution.

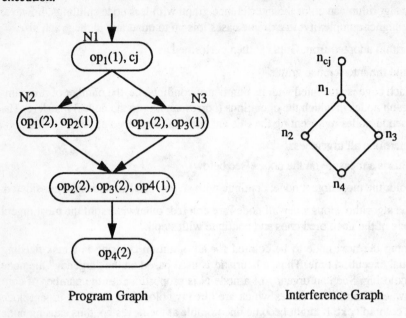

Program Graph   Interference Graph

Figure 61: PE Assignment in Alternative Program-Graph Paths

So far, we have only considered the assignment of PEs which are certainly the most important resources for processing. However, paths to memory (resp. cache), register-bank and memory-bank ports are important resources, too, albeit for special instructions like loads and stores.

13.4.2 Assignment of General Resources

For general resource assignment we have to consider that resources are not independent. A specific PE may e.g. have busses to certain memory banks only; assigning this PE to a load operation means that we have a certain subset of all busses which can be used for accessing memory and this assignment is only allowed if this PE is connected to the memory module accessed. For loads and stores where we don't know the memory address at compile time only such PEs may be assigned which have paths to each memory bank which may perhaps be accessed. These dependences between resources have to be considered during assignment.

Assignment of general resources can be performed using generalized interference graphs as for the special case of PEs as only resources. Figure 62 shows an example of such a general resource assignment. We want to perform resource assignment in a node with three operations op_1, op_2, op_3. The alternative-resource allocations are shown as vectors $RA(o_i)$ for each operation o_i. We have four possible resource allocations $ra_{1,1}$, ..., $ra_{1,4}$ in $RA(o_1)$, three resource allocations $ra_{2,1}$, ..., $ra_{2,3}$ in $RA(o_2)$, and three resource allocations $ra_{3,1}$, ..., $ra_{3,3}$ in $RA(o_3)$. Each resource allocation is entered as a node $ra_{i,j} \in N$ in a conflict graph $G = (N,E)$. We have two kinds of edges in E:

- Between all nodes $n_{i,j}$ representing alternative-resource allocations of the same operation o_i:

  $(n_{i,k} \leftrightarrow n_{i,j}) \in E \; \forall \; k,j$ with $k \neq j$ and $n_{i,j}, n_{i,k} \in RA(o_i)$

- between all nodes where the corresponding operations interfere, i.e. are processed (at least partially) in parallel:

  $(n_{i,k} \leftrightarrow n_{j,l}) \in E \Leftrightarrow o_i$ and o_j interfere and $ra_k(o_i) \otimes ra_l(o_i) \neq (0)$.

$$RA(o_1) = \left\{ \begin{array}{l} ra_{1,1} = (0,1,0,0,0,0,1,0,0) \\ ra_{1,2} = (0,1,0,1,0,0,0,0,0) \\ ra_{1,3} = (0,1,0,0,0,0,0,1,0) \\ ra_{1,4} = (0,0,1,0,1,0,0,0,0) \end{array} \right. \qquad RA(o_2) = \left\{ \begin{array}{l} ra_{2,1} = (0,0,1,1,0,0,0,0,0) \\ ra_{2,2} = (0,0,1,0,0,0,0,0,1) \\ ra_{2,3} = (1,0,0,0,0,1,0,0,0) \end{array} \right.$$

$$RA(o_3) = \left\{ \begin{array}{l} ra_{3,1} = (0,0,1,1,0,0,0,0,0) \\ ra_{3,2} = (0,0,1,0,1,0,0,0,0) \\ ra_{3,3} = (1,0,0,0,0,1,0,0,0) \end{array} \right.$$

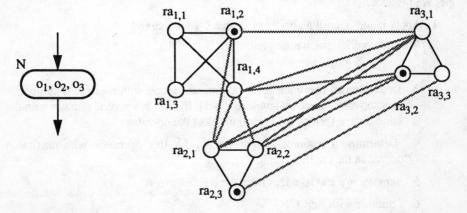

Program Graph Node　　　　　Marked Conflict Graph for Program Graph Node N

Figure 62: Conflict Graph for General Resource Assignment

In figure 62 we see the square representing the four alternative-resource allocations of operation op_1 and the two triangles representing the alternative-resource allocations of operations op_2 and op_3. The shaded lines represent the interactions. An actual assignment is then a marking of the nodes in the conflict graph; the goal of resource assignment is a marking with one marked node per operation for each conflict graph. The conflict-graph nodes belonging to the same operation can be combined to one new node, yielding an interference graph as we had above.

For marking nodes we consider mainly two cases:

i. A conflict-graph node $n_{i,k}$ with degree 0, i.e. no neighbors. This represents the only possible resource assignment of an operation o_i. Such a node has no conflicts with other nodes and can be marked.

ii. A conflict-graph node $n_{i,k}$ with degree 1. This only edge ($n_{i,k} \leftrightarrow n_{j,l}$) may either be of the first kind, i.e. representing one of two alternative-resource assignments of an operation o_i ($i = j$). Since there are no conflicts (i.e. edges) with other operations (i.e. to other nodes), the node $n_{i,k}$ is marked and the other node $n_{j,l}$ deleted. In the other case this edge ($n_{i,k} \leftrightarrow n_{j,l}$) is of the second kind, representing a resource conflict. The node $n_{i,k}$ which has only one resource assignment in this case ($i \neq j$) is marked and the neighbour node $n_{j,l}$ is deleted.

Strategies for marking a conflict graph will stepwise delete nodes from the graph until the remaining nodes can be marked. The nodes to be deleted are those with a high probability of not being markable. These are the nodes with a high degree because marking a node makes all neighbors unmarkable. Deleting a node means omitting the represented resource assignment for the corresponding operation, which is not critical if sufficient alternative-resource assignments are available. In [KarlR 93] two strategies are presented:

1. Apply i. and ii. until all nodes of degree ≤ 1 are marked.

2. Are any conflict-graph nodes left?

yes:

3. Determine an operation o_i in the program graph with maximum number of alternative-resource assignments (> 1). If there are several choices with the same degree then step 4 is used to select the operation.

4. Determine a resource assignment $n_{i,k}$ for this operation with maximum degree in the conflict graph.

5. Remove $n_{i,k}$ and its edges from the conflict graph.

6. Continue with step 1.

no: exit.

Algorithm 25:   Resource Assignment by Marking Conflict Graphs, Strategy 1

This algorithm ends because in each loop through 1. - 6. the number of nodes is reduced. It will try to leave at least one possible resource allocation for each operation in the graph (step 3.). For operations which get no assignment we have to split program-graph nodes as described above. One split may offer sufficient resources for more than one non-assigned operation if it is performed accordingly.

Another strategy marks in each step one node among nodes with low degrees which make neighboring nodes with high degree unmarkable; nodes with a small number of alternative-resource assignments are chosen first. This is performed with the following strategy:

1. Apply i. and ii. until all nodes of degree ≤ 1 are marked.
2. Are any conflict-graph nodes left?

   yes:

   3. Determine the set of all conflict-graph nodes with minimum degree.

   4. Choose a node from this set for which the sum of the degrees of its neighbour nodes is maximum.

   5. Mark this node and delete all its neighbors.

   6. Continue with step 1.

   no: exit.

Algorithm 26: Resource Assignment by Marking Conflict Graphs, Strategy 2

These strategies for marking graphs can be applied for general resource assignments and similar problems. However, where problems can be reduced, like e.g. assignment of single resource types, like PEs or application of single-cycle operations only, the corresponding simpler algorithms should be applied because conflict graphs tend to get quite complex.

14 Exceptions

When machine operations are reordered globally, new problems arise with respect to exceptions. Exceptions are events other than branches (including calls etc.) which change the control flow of program execution. In [Hennessy/Patterson 90] the most important exceptions are listed and explained. Among those, page faults and I/O-device requests are not altered by instruction scheduling. However, faults, i.e. exceptions like arithmetic overflow or memory-protection violation can be affected by global instruction scheduling. The following example will show the main problem.

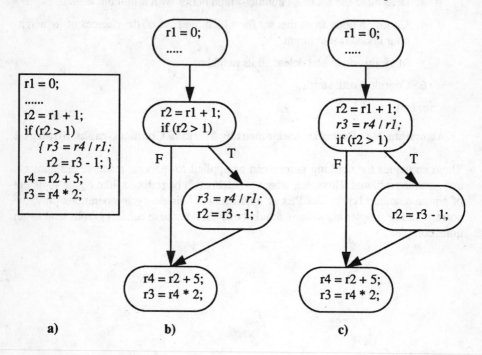

Figure 63: Exceptions in Reorganized Code

In figure 63 a small part of a program is shown in a); in b) we see the corresponding part of the program graph. The scheduler may move the operation "r3 = r4 / r1" to the preceding node because there is no dependence on that node and r3 is not live in the other successor path of that node (r3 is overwritten in the other successor node: r3 = r4 * 2). The content of r3 is not used in the FALSE-path of the branch. This works fine, but what happens if r1 is 0? In the original program, the division "r3 = r4 / r1" will not be executed in this case but in the reordered case c) the division will be executed and will cause an exception due to dividing by 0. This exception will cause the program erroneously to stop.

In the Multiflow TRACE machines this problem is solved by delaying exceptions. Each register is attributed a valid-bit which is usually set. An exception like the one in our example will set the valid-bit of the destination register r3 to 0. When this register is used again by an interruptible operation, the exception will be executed; i.e. whenever a register with valid bit 0 is used as source register an exception will occur.

This is perhaps the most elegant solution to this problem. Another one would be to analyze all exception-causing operations statically and find out if their movement above a particular branch may cause an exception like in our example. Such a movement would then be prevented as well as movements of instructions for which the analysis would fail. Another possibility is to use checkpointing hardware as described in [Hwu/Patt 87] or in [Vassiliadis et al 92].

15 Vertical Instruction-Scheduling

Originally, for RISC architectures (vertical) instruction scheduling means filling branch delay slots and load delay slots; a series of local instruction-scheduling methods have been developed so far which offer pretty good results (see section 8). However, for architectures with deep pipelines some new vertical instruction-scheduling methods may turn out useful.

Considering the development of architectures so far, we see that for some time a trend towards long pipelines occurred, exemplified by the development of the MIPS R4000. At that time there was some controversy about the best way to exploit most parallelism: vertically or horizontally. Most microprocessors chose horizontal parallelism in the form of superscalar processors. However, it seems that a combination of both methods were appropriate; it is useful for many superscalar architectures to split the decode stage so that we can predecode instructions as early as possible.

This section gives an overview how the methods of percolation scheduling can be applied to "Very Deep Pipeline Architectures". The methods presented below apply to machine instructions which are dependent and must not be started successively. In current architectures machine instructions which have to be separated by a certain distance are:

- Branches and the subsequent instructions.
- Load instructions and instructions using the loaded data.
- Integer multiply/division and instructions using the results.
- Floating-point instructions and instructions using the results.
- Other, mostly rare, multicycle instructions and instructions using the results.

In future architectures with very deep pipelines, there may be more kinds of instructions which have to be separated.

We assume an operation O needs $n(O)$ pipeline stages to complete. In its r-th pipeline stage $r(O)$, it reads its source operands, and in its w-th pipeline stage it writes its destination operand. Thus, after w cycles the destination operand is ready for succeeding operations to be used as their source operand. For architectures with bypassing, that will be one cycle earlier, assuming one cycle delay for writing the destination operand in its register. For capturing both, architectures with and without bypassing, we set $w(O)$ as the cycle when the destination operand can be used by succeeding operations as source operand. Whenever $w(O) - r(O) > 1$, instruction scheduling will enhance the system's performance. For floating-point operations and for potential future long pipelines this may be significant. In architectures where load (or store) operations must not be issued subsequently, we have the same situation. In the following, we set
$D = \max (w(O) - r(O)), \forall O$.

For considering dependences between operations, condition codes are treated the same way as other operands: a compare operation writes a condition code and a conditional-branch operation reads it.

Instruction-scheduling methods will be presented which reorder the instructions so that no instruction has to wait for its source operands to become ready. For this purpose we use a variant of the program graph defined in def. 8 where a node contains only one operation and no conditional tree. On this program graph, transformations are performed which we will derive from the Percolation Scheduling core-transformations. A few additional definitions will be necessary.

Def. 20: Successors and Predecessors in the Program Graph

A program graph contains a set of nodes and a set E of edges. An edge is a pair of nodes (M,N). A node N contains one operation O and the sets read(N) and write(N) of variables read and written by the operation O.

A node M is a predecessor of a node N in the program graph if there is a edge $(M,N) \in E$ in the program graph's set E of edges.

The set of predecessors of a node N in the program graph is called *pred(N,1)*. The i-th predecessor set of node N is the set $pred(N,i) = pred(pred(N,i-1),1)$ *for i > 1.*

First, the program graph is constructed for each function. Then, for each node N we insert (w(N) - r(N) - 1) nodes after N in the program graph. These nodes contain noops and the same sets read(N) and write(N) as the node N. The last inserted node will have the previous successors of N now as its own successors.

During this transformation of the program graph, each node gets an additional attribute, the architecture module it is using, respectively the pipeline stage, e.g. pre_decode, ALU or multiplier. We call it the "resource attribute". In this context, we define a new kind of dependence, resource dependence.

Def. 21: Resource Dependence

Two operations are called resource dependent if their nodes have the same resource attribute.

15.1 Vertical Core Transformations

The Vertical Percolation Scheduling transformations are applied in the same sequence as in subsection 12.3.4. Starting with the uppermost level, loop handling transformations are applied and the others described in section 8.5. Next, the core transformations described below are applied, first move_cj_vertical and then move_op_vertical. Finally, the delete_vertical core transformation is applied to the program graph.

Delete_Vertical Core Transformation:

We consider a node N containing an operation O.

- If O is not a noop, exit.
- If N has no successors and its resource attribute is 0, delete N.
- If there is no dependence (considering all kinds of dependences, including resource dependences) between O and N's successor nodes, delete N and link its predecessors to its successors.

Algorithm 27: Delete_Vertical Core Transformation

Figure 64 shows the move_op_vertical core transformation. This program-graph transformation tries to move an operation op from a node N to a preceding node M where it replaces a noop or a copy of op.

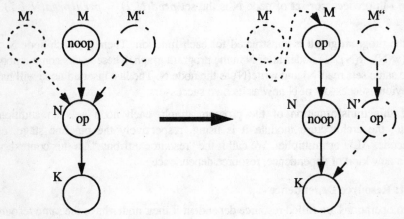

Let the operation in M' be independent of the noop in M and the operation in M" dependent on the noop in M.

Figure 64: Move_op_Vertical Core-Transformation

Move_op_Vertical Core Transformation:

We consider a node N and a predecessor node M of N; N contains an operation op (which is not a noop) and M either a copy of op or a noop. The construction and the transformations of the program graph guarantee that op is independent from all operations in preceding nodes N' ∈ pred(N,i) for i = 1, ..., d(N') with
d(N') = w(N') - r(N') - 1.

- If op is dependent on any operation in the nodes pred(M,d(N)) exit.

- Has N other predecessors M' besides M?

   yes: • Is the operation in M independent from operations in all other predecessors M' of N and in all X ∈ pred(M',i) for i=1, ..., d(pred(M')) and i ≤ D?

       yes: • Relink the nodes M' to point to M as successor instead of N.

            • Set the corresponding attributes of all nodes succeeding N in distance d(N) containing a noop to 0.

       no: • Make a copy N' of N (with all attributes).

           • Relink all M' not fulfilling the above condition to N' instead of N.

           • Relink all M' fulfilling the above condition to M instead of N.

- Replace the noop in M by op (if there is a noop) and set the corresponding attributes.

- Replace op in N by a noop and set the corresponding attributes.

Algorithm 28: Move_op_Vertical Core-Transformation

The following figure 65 displays the move_cj_vertical core-transformation. It tries to move a conditional jump cj from a node N to a preceding node M. Additionally, a predecessor M' of N is shown with an operation independent from the noop in M, and a predecessor M" of N with an operation dependent on the noop in M.

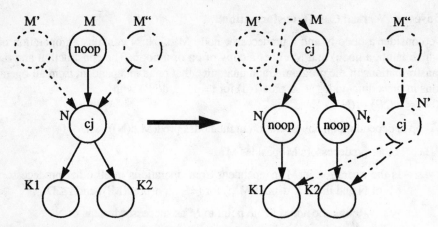

Let the operation in M' be independent of the noop in M and the operation in M" dependent on the noop in M.

Figure 65: Move_cj_Vertical Core-Transformation

Move_cj_Vertical Core-Transformation:

We consider a node N and a predecessor node N of M; N contains a conditional branch cj and M either a copy of cj or a noop. The construction and the transformations of the program graph guarantee that cj is independent from all operations in preceding nodes $N' \in pred(N,i)$ for $i = 1, ..., d(N')$ with $d(N') = w(N') - r(N') - 1$.

- If cj is dependent on any operation in the nodes pred(M,d(N)) exit.

- Has N other predecessors M' besides M?

  yes: • Is the operation in M independent from operations in all other predecessors M' of N and in all $X \in pred(M',i)$ for $i=1, ..., d(pred(M'))$ and $i \leq D$:

    yes: • Relink the nodes M' to point to M as successor instead of N.

      • Set the corresponding attributes of all nodes succeeding N in distance d(N) containing a noop to 0.

    no: • Make a copy N' of N.

      • Relink all predecessors of N not fulfilling the above condition to N' instead of N.

      • Relink all M' fulfilling the above condition to M instead of N.

- Replace the noop in M by cj and set the corresponding attributes.

- Replace the cj in N by a noop and set the corresponding attributes.

- Make a copy N_t of N.

- Delete the TRUE-successors from N.

- Mark N as FALSE-successor of M.
- Delete the FALSE-successors from N_t.
- Link N_t as TRUE-successor of M.

Algorithm 29: Move_cj_Vertical Core-Transformation

All these transformation algorithms can also be specified so that an operation op or a conditional jump cj may be moved as far as possible instead of just one level up in the program graph. Similarly, the delete transformation can be extended to delete several succeeding nodes.

16 Conclusion

In this book, methods were presented which increase the performance of computer systems by making use of the parallelism which can be found in application programs. These methods provide a way to employ the fast increasing potential of new hardware for current and new demanding applications.

The techniques described shall provide computer architectures and compiler writers, as well as students insight into the manifold aspects to be considered. In particular, a systematic for instruction scheduling is presented together with new instruction-scheduling methods. The characteristics of specific processors can be confined to specific places, namely to the machine description and a single scheduling-level. The other scheduling levels can thus be reused for other architectures.

Altogether, the book tried to provide:

- An overview of the methods for (fine-grain) parallelization by architecture and compiler.
- Insight into the multitude of areas which have to be considered for scheduling.
- A structure which decomposes the functionality of scheduling so that major parts are independent of machine and application and can thus be reused.
- A thorough description of current and new scheduling techniques.
- A systematic approach to resource management.

The areas of further research in this area are mainly:

- Creating machine-specific parts of the scheduler for various specific processors.
- Refined exception handling.
- Combination of coarse-grain and fine-grain parallelization to provide the combined performance potential for application programs.

17 References

[Aho/Sethi/Ullman 88]   A.V. Aho, R. Sethi, J.D. Ullman:
Compilers: Principles, Techniques, and Tools
Addison-Wesley 1988.

[Aiken 88]   Alexander Aiken:
Compaction-Based Parallalization
PhD Thesis, Cornell Univ., TR 88-922, June 1988

[Aiken/Nicolau 88]   Alexander Aiken, Alexandru Nicolau:
Optimal Loop Parallelization
Technical Report No. 88-905, Cornell University, March 1988

[Aiken/Nicolau 88a]   Alexander Aiken, Alexandru Nicolau:
A Development Environment for Horizontal Microcode
IEEE Trans. on Software Engineering, Vol. 14, No. 5, May 1988

[Aiken/Nicolau 88b]   Alexander Aiken, Alexandru Nicolau:
Perfect Pipelining: A New Loop Parallelization Technique
Proc. European Symp. on Prog. , Springer 1988

[Aiken/Nicolau]   Alexander Aiken, Alexandru Nicolau:
Fine-Grain Parallelization and the Wavefront Method
Univ. of Irvine, Tech. Report

[Banger et al 89]   Michael Banger et. al.:
TROPIC - Transformation and Optimization Into Parallel Instruction Code
Abschlußbericht der Projektgruppe "Übersetzerbau für Parallelrechner", 1988/1989, Universität-GH Paderborn

[Baumann 93]   Uli Baumann:
Registerallokation kombiniert mit globalem Scheduling für Rechner mit feinkörniger Parallelverarbeitung
Diplomarbeit, Techn. Univ. Chemnitz-Zwickau, März 1993

[Beck et al 93]   Gary R. Beck, David W.L. Yen, Thomas L. Anderson:
The Cydra 5 Minisupercomputer: Architecture and Implementation
Special Issue on Instruction-Level Parallelism of The Journal of Supercomputing, Vol. 7, No. 1/2, 1993, pp. 143 - 180

[Bernstein 88]   D. Bernstein:
                          An Improved Approximation Algorithm for
                          Scheduling Pipelined Machines
                          Proc. Intern. Conf. on Parallel Proc. St. Charles, Aug.
                          1988

[Bernstein et al 89]   D. Bernstein et al.:
                          Spill Code Minimization Techniques for Optimizing
                          Compilers
                          Proc. SIGPLAN '89 Conference of Programming
                          Language Design and Implementation, ACM Press
                          1989, pp. 258 - 263

[Bernstein/Rodeh 91]   D. Bernstein, M. Rodeh:
                          Global Instruction Scheduling for Superscalar
                          Machines
                          ACM SIGPLAN 91, Toronto, Canada, 1991

[Bode/Händler 83]   A. Bode, W. Händler:
                          Rechnerarchitektur II, Strukturen
                          Springer Verlag, Berlin, 1983

[Bodin/Charot 90]   François Bodin, François Charot:
                          Loop Optimization for Horizontal Microcoded
                          Machines
                          Proc. Int. Conf. on Supercomputing, 1990

[Böckle 88]   Günter Böckle:
                          VLIW-Architekturen und -Compiler: Ein Beispiel für
                          Entwicklung aus Systemarchitektur-Perspektive
                          Siemens Corporate Research Techn. Report No.
                          SYS5-04/88/Bc, Feb. 1988

[Böckle 92]   Günter Böckle:
                          A Development Environment for Fine-Grained
                          Parallelism Exploitation
                          Proc. 3rd Workshop on Compilers for Parallel
                          Computers, Vienna, July 1992

[Böckle et al 91]   Günter Böckle, Christof Störmann, Isolde Wildgruber:
                          Horizontal Instruction Scheduler Description
                          Siemens Corporate Research Technical Report No.
                          BeG041/92, Nov. 1991

[Böckle et al 93]   Günter Böckle, Christof Störmann, Isolde Wildgruber:
                          Instruction Scheduling for Fine-Grain Parallelism
                          Siemens Corporate Research Technical Report No.
                          053/93, 1993

[Böckle et al 93a]   Günter Böckle, Christof Störmann, Isolde Wildgruber:
                             Methods for Exploitation of Fine-Grain Parallelism
                             in A. Bode, M. dal Cin (ed.): Parallel Computer
                             Architectures,
                             Lecture Notes in Computer Science 732, Springer
                             Verlag, 1993, pp. 118-131

[Böckle/Trosch 89]   Günter Böckle, Siegfried Trosch:
                             Ein   Simulator   für   VLIW-Architekturen:
                             Leistungsbeschreibung und Modulspezifikation
                             Siemens Corporate Research Technical Report No.
                             SYS5-BeJ014/89/Bc/T, 1989

[Böckle/Trosch 90]   Günter Böckle, Siegfried Trosch:
                             A Simulator for VLIW Architectures
                             Tech. Univ. Munich Tech. Report, SFB-Bericht Nr.
                             342/16/90 A, Sept. 1990

[Borkar et al 88]   Shekhar Borkar, Robert Cohn, George Cox, Sha
                             Gleason, Thomas Gross, H.T. Kung, Monica Lam,
                             Brian Moore, Craig Peterson, John Pieper, Linda
                             Rankin, P.S. Tseng, Jim Sutton, John Urbanski, Jon
                             Webb:
                             iWarp: An Integrated Solution to High-Speed Parallel
                             Computing
                             Proc. Supercomputing Conf. 1988, Orlando, Florida

[Bradlee et al 91]   David G. Bradlee, Susan J. Eggers, Robert R. Henry:
                             Integrating Register Allocation and Instruction
                             Scheduling for RISCS
                             Proc. 4th Int. Conf. on Archit. Support for Prog. Lang.
                             and Oper. Systems (ASPLOS), April 1991

[Breternitz 91]   Mauricio Breternitz:
                             Architecture   Synthesis   of   High-Performance
                             Application-Specific Processors
                             PhD Dissertation, Carnegie Mellon Univ., Research
                             Report No. CMUCDS-91-5, April 1991

[Breternitz/Nicolau 89]   Mauricio Breternitz, Alexandru Nicolau:
                             Trade-offs   between   Pipelining   and   Multiple
                             Functional   Units   in   Fine-grain   Parallelism
                             Exploitation
                             Proc. 3rd Conf. on Arch. Support for Prog. Lang. and
                             Oper. Systems (ASPLOS III), Boston, MA, April 1989

168   17 References

[Briggs et al 89]   Preston Briggs, Keith D. Cooper, Ken Kennedy, Linda
                                  Torczon:
                                  Coloring Heuristics for Register Allocation
                                  Proc. SIGPLAN 89 Conf. on Prog. Lang. Design and
                                  Impl., ACM Press, July 1989

[Butler et al 91]   Michael Butler, Tse-Yu Yeh, Yale Patt, Mitch Alsup,
                                  Hunter Scales, Michael Shebanow:
                                  Single Instruction Stream Parallelism Is Greater than
                                  Two
                                  Proc. 18th Comp. Arch. Symp, ACM SIGARCH,
                                  Comp. Arch. News, Vol. 19, No. 3, May 1991

[Callahan 88]   D. Callahan:
                                  The Program Summary Graph and Flow-Sensitive
                                  Interprocedural Data-Flow Analysis
                                  Proc. of the SIGPLAN '88 Conference on
                                  Programming Language Design and Implementation,
                                  Atlanta 1988

[Chaitin 82]   G.J.Chaitin:
                                  Register Allocation Via Graph Coloring
                                  Proc. SIGPLAN '82 Symp. on Compiler Constr.,
                                  SIGPLAN Notices, Vol. 17, No. 6, June 1982

[Chang et al 91]   Pohua P. Chang, Scott A. Mahlke, William Y. Chen,
                                  Nancy J. Warter, Wen-mei W. Hwu:
                                  IMPACT: An Architectural Framework for Multiple-
                                  Issue Processors
                                  Proc. 18th Comp. Arch. Symp., ACM SIGARCH,
                                  Comp. Arch. News, Vol. 19, No. 3, May 1991

[Chang/Lavery/Hwu 91]   Pohua P. Chang, Daniel M. Lavery, Wen-mei W. Hwu:
                                  The Importance of Prepass Code Scheduling for
                                  Superscalar and Superpipelined Processors
                                  Center   for   Supercomputing   Research   and
                                  Development, Univ. of Illinois at Urbana-Champaign
                                  CSRD Report No. 1144

[Chow 88]   Fred C. Chow:
                                  Minimizing Register Usage Penalty at Procedure Calls
                                  Proc. SIGPLAN '88 Conf. on Prog. Lang. Design and
                                  Implem. Atlanta, GO, 1988

[Chow/Hennessy 84]   Fred C. Chow, John Hennessy:
                                  Register Allocation by Priority-based Coloring
                                  Proc. SIGPLAN '84 Symposium on Compiler Constr.,
                                  SIGPLAN Notices Vol. 19, No. 6, June 1984

[Chow/Hennessy 90]	Fred C. Chow, John Hennessy: The Priority-Based Coloring Approach to Register Allocation ACM Transactions on Prog. Lang. and Systems, Vol. 12, No. 4, Oct. 1990
[Clancy et al 87]	Patrick Clancy, Benjamin F. Cutler, J. Christopher Dodd, Douglas W. Gilmore, Robert P. Nix, John J. O'Donnell, Christopher P. Ryland: Unix^{TM} on a VLIW Proc. Summer Usenix Conf. 1987
[Clancy 88]	Patrick Clancy: Virtual Memory Extensions in Trace/Unix Proc. USENIX 1988 Supercomputer Workshop
[Colwell et al 88]	Robert P. Colwell, Robert P. Nix, John O'Donnell, David B. Papworth, Paul K. Rodman: A VLIW Architecture for a Trace Scheduling Compiler IEEE Transactions on Computers, C-37(8), pp. 967-979, August 1988
[Cooper et al 86]]	Keith D. Cooper, Ken Kennedy, Linda Torczon: Interprocedural Optimization: Eliminating Unnecessary Recompilation Proc. SIGPLAN '86 Symp. on Compiler Constr., ACM, Palo Alto, CA, January 1986
[Danelutto/Vanneschi 90]	Marco Danelutto, Marco Vanneschi: VLIW-in-the-large: A Model for Fine-Grain Parallelism Exploitation on Distributed Memory Multiprocessors Proc. 23rd Ann. Worksh. on Microprog. and Microarch., micro 23, Nov. 1990
[Dehnert 88]	Jim Dehnert: Overlapped Loop Optimization for a VLIW Architecture Cydrome Inc., Milpitas, CA, 1988
[Dehnert/Towle 93]	James C. Dehnert, Ross A. Towle: Compiling for the Cydra 5 Special Issue on Instruction-Level Parallelism of The Journal of Supercomputing, Vol. 7, No. 1/2, 1993, pp. 181 - 227

[Ebcioglu 87]   Kemal Ebcioglu:
                                 A Compilation Technique for Software Pipelining of
                                 Loops with Conditional Jumps
                                 IEEE Micro, No. 20, 1987, pp. 69-79

[Ebcioglu 88]   Kemal Ebcioglu:
                                 A Wide Instruction Word Architecture for Fine-Grain
                                 Parallelism
                                 Proc. Conf. on Algor. and Hardw. for Parallel Proc.,
                                 COMPAR 88, Manchester, UK, 1988

[Ebcioglu 88a]   Kemal Ebcioglu:
                                 Some Design Ideas for a VLIW Architecture for
                                 Sequential-Natured Software
                                 Proc. IFIP Working Conf. on Par. Proc., Pisa, April
                                 1988

[Ebcioglu 90]   Kemal Ebcioglu:
                                 Some Global Compiler Optimizations and
                                 Architectural Features for Improving Performance of
                                 Superscalars
                                 IBM T.J.Watson Research Center Technical Report
                                 RC 16145 (#71759), 1990

[Ebcioglu/Nakatani 89]   Kemal Ebcioglu, Toshio Nakatani:
                                 A New Compilation Technique for Parallelizing
                                 Loops with Unpredictable Branches on a VLIW
                                 Architectures
                                 Proc. 2nd Workshop on Parallel Computation, Urbana,
                                 IL, 1989

[Ebcioglu/Nicolau 89]   Kemal Ebcioglu, Alexandru Nicolau:
                                 A global resource-constrained parallelization
                                 technique
                                 Proc. ACM SIGARCH Intern. Conf. on
                                 Supercomputing, Crete, June 1989

[Ellis85]   J.R.Ellis:
                                 Bulldog: A Compiler for VLIW Architectures
                                 MIT Press, 1985

[Fernandes et al 92]   Edil S.T. Fernandes, Claudson F. Bornstein, Claudia
                                 M.D. Pereira:
                                 Parallel Code Generation for Superscalar
                                 Architectures
                                 Microprocessing and Microprogramming 34, 1992

[Ferrante et al 87]   Jeanne Ferrante, Karl J. Ottenstein, Joe D. Warren:
                            The Program Dependence Graph and its Use in
                            Optimization
                            ACM Transact. on Prog. Lang. and Sys., Vol. 9, No. 3,
                            July 1987

[Fisher 80]   Joseph A. Fisher:
                            2^N-Way Jump Microinstruction Hardware and an
                            Effective Instruction Binding Method
                            IEEE 1980

[Fisher 81]   Joseph A. Fisher:
                            Trace Scheduling: A Technique for Global Microcode
                            Compaction
                            IEEE Transactions on Computers, Vol. C-30, No. 7,
                            July 1981

[Fisher 83]   Joseph A. Fisher:
                            Very Long Instruction Word Architectures and the
                            ELI-512
                            Proc. 10th Annual Intern. Conf. on Computer
                            Architecture, Stockholm, June 1983

[Fisher 84]   Joseph A. Fisher:
                            The VLIW Machine: A Multiprocessor for Compiling
                            Scientific Code
                            IEEE Computer, July 1984, pp. 45-53

[Fisher 87]   Joseph A. Fisher:
                            A New Architecture For Supercomputing
                            Proc. 32nd IEEE Computer Society Intern. Conf.
                            (COMPCON), Feb. 1987

[Fisher/O'Donnell 84]   Joseph A. Fisher, John J. O'Donnell:
                            VLIW Machines: Multiprocessors We Can Actually
                            Program
                            Proc. 28th IEEE Computer Society Intern. Conf.
                            (COMPCON), San Francisco, 1984

[Fisher et al 84]   Joseph A. Fisher, John R. Ellis, John C. Ruttenberg,
                            Alexandru Nicolau:
                            Parallel Processing: A Smart Compiler and a Dumb
                            Machine
                            Proc. SIGPLAN '84 Symp. on Compiler Constr.,
                            SIGPLAN Notices, Vol. 19, No. 6, June 1984

[Franklin/Sohi]   Manoj Franklin, Gurindar S. Sohi:
                           The Expandable Split Window Paradigm For
                           Exploiting Fine-Grain Parallelism
                           Proc. 19th Ann. Symp. Comp. Arch., SIGARCH
                           Comp. Arch. News, Vol. 20, No. 2, May 1992

[Gasperoni 91]   Franco Gasperoni:
                           Scheduling for Horizontal Systems: The VLIW
                           Paradigm in Perspective
                           PhD Diss, Courant Institute of Math. Sciences, New
                           York Univ., May 1991

[Gibbons/Muchnick 86]   Philip B. Gibbons, Steven S. Muchnick:
                           Efficient Instruction Scheduling for a Pipelined
                           Architecture
                           Proc. SIGPLAN '86 Symp. on Compiler Constr., June
                           1986, SIGPLAN Notices , Vol. 21, No. 7

[Glass 90]   David N. Glass:
                           Compile-time Instruction Scheduling for Superscalar
                           Processors
                           Proc. 35th Comp. Soc. Nat. Conf, COMPCON 90,
                           1990

[Grishman/Bogong 83]   Ralph Grishman, Su Bogong:
                           A Preliminary Evaluation of Trace Scheduling for
                           Global Microcode Compaction
                           IEEE Transactions on Computers, Vol. C-32, No. 12,
                           Dec. 1983

[Gupta 87]   Rajiv Gupta:
                           A Reconfigurable LIW Architecture and its Compiler
                           PhD Dissertation, Univ. of Pittsburgh, 1987

[Gupta 90]   Rajiv Gupta:
                           A Fine-Grained MIMD Architecture based upon
                           Register Channels
                           Proc. 23rd Workshop on Microprog., micro 23, Nov.
                           27-29, 1990

[Gupta/Soffa/Steele 89]   Rajiv Gupta, Mary Lou Soffa, Tim Steele:
                           Register Allocation Via Clique Separators
                           SIGPLAN Notices, Vol. 24, No. 7, 1989

[Gupta/Soffa 91]   Rajiv Gupta, Mary Lou Soffa:
                           Compile-Time Techniques for Improving Scalar
                           Access Performence in Parallel Memories
                           IEEETrans. on Parallel and Distributed Systems, Vol.
                           2, No. 2, April 1991

[Hahne et al 89]   Klaus Hahne, Burkhard Scherf, Karl-Josef Thürlings:
Anwendung des VLIW-Prinzips auf PROLOG, LISP, SQL und C
Siemens Corporate Research Technical Report No. SYS5-BeJ012/89/Hh/S/Th, 1989

[Hendren/Nicolau 89]   Laurie J. Hendren, Alexandru Nicolau:
Parallelizing Programs With Recursive Data Structures
Proc. Int. Conf. on Parallel Processing ICPP, 1989

[Hennessy/Gross 83]   John L. Hennessy, Thomas Gross:
Postpass Code Optimization of Pipeline Constraints
ACM Transact. on Prog. Lang. and Sys., Vol. 5, No. 3, 1983

[Hennessy/Patterson 90]   John.L. Hennessy, David A. Patterson:
Computer Architecture - A Quantitative Approach
Morgan Kaufmann Publishers Inc., 1990

[Horwitz et al 89]   Susan Horwitz, Phil Pfeiffer, Thomas Reps:
Dependence Analysis for Pointer Variables
Proc. SIGPLAN '89 Conf. on Compiler Constr., 1989

[Hsu/Davidson 86]   Peter Y.T. Hsu, Edward S. Davidson:
Highly Concurrent Scalar Processing
Proc. 13th Intern. Symp. on Computer Architecture, Tokyo, 1986

[Hsu/Bratt 88]   Peter Y.T. Hsu, Joseph P. Bratt:
Architectural Support for Overlapped Loops on the Cydra 5
Cydrome Inc., Milpitas, CA, 1988

[Hwu/Patt 87]   W.W.Hwu, Y.N.Patt:
Checkpoint Repair for High-Performance Out-of-Order Execution Machines
IEEE Trans. Computers, Vol. 36, pp. 1496 - 1514, Dec. 1987

[Hwu et al 93]   Wen-Mei W. Hwu, Scott A. Mahlke, William Y. Chen, Pohua P. Chang, Nancy J. Warter, Roger A. Bringmann, Roland G. Ouellette, Richard E. Hank, Tokuzo Kiyohara, Grant E. Haab, John G. Holm, Daniel M. Lavery:
The Superblock: An Effective Technique for VLIW and Superscalar Compilation
Special Issue on Instruction-Level Parallelism of The Journal of Supercomputing, Vol. 7, No. 1/2, 1993, pp. 229 - 248

[Johnson 91]
Mike Johnson:
Superscalar Microprocessor Design
Prentice-Hall Inc., 1991

[Jouppi 89]
Norman P. Jouppi:
The Nonuniform Distribution of Instruction-Level and
Machine Parallelism and its Effect on Performance
IEEE Transactions on Computers, Vol. 38, No. 12,
Dec. 1989

[Jouppi/Wall 89]
Norman P. Jouppi, David W. Wall:
Available instruction-Level Parallelism for Super-
scalar and Superpipelined Machines
Proc. 3rd Int. Conf. Arch. Supp. Prog. Lang. Oper.
Syst. (ASPLOS III), April 1989
Long Version: DEC Western Research Lab WRL
Research Report 89/7

[KarlR 93]
Ralf Karl:
Ressourcenverwaltung für Rechner mit feinkörniger
Parallelverarbeitung
Diplomarbeit der Technischen Universität Chemnitz-
Zwickau, Mai 1993

[KarlW 93]
Wolfgang Karl:
Parallele Prozessorarchitekturen - Codegenerierung
für superskalare, superpipelined und VLIW-
Prozessoren
BI Verlag, Reihe Informatik, Band 93, 1993

[Karplus/Nicolau 85]
Kevin Karplus, Alexandru Nicolau:
Efficient Hardware for Multi-Way Jumps and Pre-
Fetches
IEEE 1985

[Keckler/Dally 92]
Stephen W. Keckler, William J. Dally:
Processor Coupling: Integrating Compile Time and
Runtime Scheduling for Parallelism
Proc. 19th Ann. Symp. Comp. Arch., SIGARCH
Comp. Arch. News, Vol. 20, No. 2, May 1992

[Krishnamurthy 90]
Sanjay M. Krishnamurthy:
A Brief Survey of Papers on Scheduling for Pipelined
Processors
SIGPLAN Notices Vol. 25, No. 7, July 1990

[Labrousse/Slavenburg 88]
Junien Labrousse, Gerrit A. Slavenburg:
CREATE-LIFE: A Design System for High
Performance VLSI Circuits
Proc. Int. Conf. Comp. Design, ICCD 1988

[Lah/Atkins 83]	Jehkwan Lah, Daniel E. Atkins: Tree Compaction of Microprograms Proc. 16th Annual Microprogramming Workshop (MICRO 16), Downington, PA, Oct. 1983
[Laird 92]	Michael Laird: A Comparison of Three Current Superscalar Designs ACM SIGARCH Comp. Arch. News, Vol. 20, No. 3, June 1992
[Lai/Lee/Lee 90]	Feipei Lai, Hung-Chang Lee, Chun-Luh Lee: Optimization on Instruction Reorganization Proc. 23rd Symp. on Microprog., micro 23, Nov. 27-29, 1990
[Lam 87]	Monika S.Lam: A Systolic Array Optimizing Compiler PhD Thesis, Carnegie Mellon Univ., Techn. Report No. CMU-CS-87-187, May 1987
[Lam 88]	Monika S. Lam: Software Pipelining: An Effective Scheduling Technique for VLIW Machines Proc. SIGPLAN '88 Conf. on Prog. Lang. Design and Impl., Atlanta, GO, June 1988
[Lam 90]	Monika S. Lam: Instruction Scheduling for Superscalar Architectures Ann. Rev. Comp. Sci. Vol. 4, 1990
[Lam/Wilson 92]	Monika S. Lam, Robert P. Wilson: Limits of Control Flow on Parallelism Proc. 19th Ann. Symp. Comp. Arch., SIGARCH Comp. Arch. News, Vol. 20, No. 2, May 1992
[Landi/Ryder 92]	William Landi, Barbara G. Ryder: A Safe Approximate Algorithm for Interprocedural Pointer Aliasing ACM SIGPLAN '92 Conf. on Prog. Lang. Design and Impl., San Francisco, CA, 1992
[Liebl 92]	Martin Liebl: Implementierung von Algorithmen zur Optimierung von Schleifen für den VLIW-Scheduler mit bedingtem Ausführungsmodell Diplomarbeit, Techn. Univ. München, May 1992
[Lilja 91]	David J. Lilja: Architectural Alternatives for Exploiting Parallelism IEEE Computer Society Press, 1991

[Linn 83]   Joseph L. Linn:
                             SRDAG Compaction - A Generalization of Trace
                             Scheduling to Increase the Use of Global Context
                             Information
                             Proc. 16th Annual Microprogramming Workshop
                             (MICRO 16), Downington, PA, Oct. 1983

[Love/Jordan]   Carl E. Love, Harry F. Jordan:
                             An Investigation of Static Versus Dynamic Scheduling
                             Proc. 17th Int. Symp. on Comp. Arch., May 1990

[Lowney et al 93]   P. Geoffrey Lowney, Stefan M. Freudenberger,
                             Thomas J. Karzes, W.D. Lichtenstein, Robert P. Nix,
                             John S. O'Donnell, John C. Ruttenberg:
                             The Multiflow Trace Scheduling Compiler
                             Special Issue on Instruction-Level Parallelism of The
                             Journal of Supercomputing, Vol. 7, No. 1/2, 1993, pp.
                             51 - 142

[Melvin/Patt 91]   Stephen Melvin, Yale Patt:
                             Exploiting Fine-Grained Parallelism Through a
                             Combination of Hardware and Software Techniques
                             Proc. 18th Comp. Arch. Symposium, ACM
                             SIGARCH Comp. Archit. News, Vol. 19, No. 3, May
                             1991

[Müller 91]   Reiner Müller:
                             Implementierung von Algorithmen zur Optimierung
                             von Schleifen mit Hilfe von Software-Pipelining
                             Techniken
                             Diplomarbeit, Techn. Univ. München, TUM-I9117,
                             SFB-Bericht Nr. 342/12/91 A, June 1991

[Nakatani/Ebcioglu 90]   Toshio Nakatani, Kemal Ebcioglu:
                             Using a Lookahead Window in a Compaction-Based
                             Parallelizing Compiler
                             Proc. 23rd Annual Microprogramming Workshop
                             (MICRO 23), Orlando FL, 1990

[Nakatani/Ebcioglu 90a]   Toshio Nakatani, Kemal Ebcioglu:
                             "Combining" as a Compilation Technique for VLIW
                             Architectures
                             Microprogramming Workshop, Dublin 1990

[Nicolau 84]   Alexandru Nicolau:
                             Parallelism, Memory Anti-Aliasing And Correctness
                             For Trace Scheduling Compilers
                             PhD Dissertation, Yale University, 1984

[Nicolau 85]   Alexandru Nicolau:
                    Percolation Scheduling: A Parallel Compilation
                    Technique
                    Cornell Univ. Techn. Report TR 85-678, May 1985

[Nicolau 87]   Alexandru Nicolau:
                    Loop Quantization or Unwinding Done Right
                    Proc. 1st Int. Conf. on Supercomputing, June 1987

[Nicolau 88]   Alexandru Nicolau:
                    Loop Quantization: A Generalized Loop Unwinding
                    Technique
                    Journal of Parallel and Distributed Computing No. 5,
                    1988, pp. 568-586

[Nicolau 89]   Alexandru Nicolau:
                    Run-Time Disambiguation: Coping with Statically
                    Unpredictable Dependencies
                    IEEE Trans. on Computers, Vol. 38, No. 5, May 1989

[Nicolau/Fisher 81] Alexandru Nicolau, Joseph A. Fisher:
                    Using an Oracle to Measure Potential Parallelism in
                    Single Instruction Stream Programs
                    Proc. 14th Annual Microprogramming Workshop
                    (MICRO 14), Oct. 1981

[Nicolau/Fisher 84] Alexandru Nicolau, Joseph A. Fisher:
                    Measuring the Parallelism Available for Very Long
                    Instruction Word Architectures
                    IEEE Transactions on Computers, Vol. C-33, No. 11,
                    Nov. 1984

[Nicolau/Potasman 90] Alexandru Nicolau, Roni Potasman:
                    Realistic Scheduling: Compaction for Pipelined
                    Architectures
                    Proc. 23rd Workshop on Microprogramming, micro
                    23, Nov. 1990

[Nicolau/Pingali/Aiken 88] Alexandru Nicolau, Keshav Pingali, Alexander Aiken:
                    Fine-grain compilation for Pipelined Machines
                    Journal of Supercomputing, November 1988

[Nowka/Flynn 89]   Kevin J. Nowka, Michael J. Flynn:
                    The Pipelined Processor as an Alternative to VLIW
                    Proc. 3rd Conf. on Arch. Support for Prog. Lang. and
                    Oper. Systems (ASPLOS III), Boston, MA, April 1989

[Oyang 90]   Yen-Jen Oyang:
                    Exploiting Multiway Branching to Boost Superscalar
                    Processor Performance
                    ACM SIGPLAN Notices, Vol. 26, No. 3, March 1991

[Proebsting/Fischer 92]   Todd A. Proebsting, Charles N. Fischer:
                           Probabilistic Register Allocation
                           ACM SIGPLAN '92 Conf. on Prog. Lang. Design and
                           Impl. San Francisco, 1992

[Paulin/Knight 89]   Pierre G. Paulin, John P. Knight:
                           Force-Directed Scheduling for the Behavioral
                           Synthesis of ASICS
                           IEEE Transactions on CAD, Vol. 8, No. 6, June 1989

[Rau 88]   B. Ramakrishna Rau:
                           Cydra^{TM} 5 Directed Dataflow Architecture
                           Cydrome Inc., Milpitas, CA, 1988

[Rau 92]   B. Ramakrishna Rau, M. Lee, P.P. Tirumalai, M.S.
                           Schlansker:
                           Register Allocation for Software Pipelined Loops
                           ACM SIGPLAN '92 Conf. on Prog. Lang. Design and
                           Impl., San Francisco, 1992

[Rau/Fisher 93]   B. Ramakrishna Rau, Joseph A. Fisher:
                           Instruction-Level Parallel Processing: History,
                           Overview, and Perspective
                           Special Issue on Instruction-Level Parallelism of
                           The Journal of Supercomputing, Vol. 7, No. 1/2, 1993,
                           pp. 9-50

[Rau/Yen/Towle 89]   B. Ramakrishna Rau, David W.L. Yen, Wei Yen, Ross
                           A. Towle:
                           The Cydra 5 Departmental Supercomputer: Design
                           Philosophies, Decisions and Trade-offs
                           Cydrome Inc., Milpitas, CA, 1989

[Santhanam/Odnert 90]   Vatsa Santhanam, Daryl Odnert:
                           Register Allocation Across Procedure and Module
                           Boundaries
                           Proc. ACM SIGPLAN '90 Conf. on Prog. Lang.
                           Design and Impl., June 199

[Scherf 90]   Burkhard Scherf:
                           Percolation Scheduler Specification
                           Siemens Corporate Research Tech. Report SYS5-
                           BeJ003/90/S, Feb. 1990

[Schepers 92]   Jörg Schepers:
                           Lokale Schedulingverfahren für superskalare und
                           superpipelined Mikroprozessoren
                           Siemens Corporate Research Tech. Report BeG 048/
                           92, Jan. 1992

[Schepers 92a]   Jörg Schepers:
                         Local Instruction Scheduling for Modern RISC
                         Architectures
                         Siemens Corporate Research Tech. Report BeG 051/
                         93, Oct. 1992

[Schlansker/McNamara 88] Michael Schlansker, Michael McNamara:
                         The Cydra^{TM} 5 Computer System Architecture
                         Proc. Conf. on Computer Design, ICCD, 1988

[Schubert 90]   Axel Schubert:
                         Vergleich von Verfahren zur automatischen Erzeugung
                         paralleler Programme für VLIW-Architekturen
                         Diplomarbeit Techn. Univ. München, Mai 1990

[Schuette/Shen 93]   Michael A. Schuette, John P. Shen:
                         Instruction-Level Experimental Evaluation of the
                         Multiflow TRACE 14/300 VLIW Computer
                         Special Issue on Instruction-Level Parallelism of The
                         Journal of Supercomputing, Vol. 7, No. 1/2, 1993, pp.
                         249 - 271

[Schuette/Shen 94]   Michael A. Schuette, John P. Shen:
                         Exploiting Instruction-Level Parallelism for Integrated
                         Control-Flow Monitoring
                         IEEE Transactions on Computers, Vol. 43, No. 2, pp.
                         129-140, Febr. 1994

[Schwiegelshohn 89]   Uwe Schwiegelshohn:
                         On Optimal Loop Parallelization
                         IBM T.J. Watson Research Center Technical Report
                         RC 14595(#65335), 5/3/89

[Schwiegelshohn et al 90] U. Schwiegelshohn, F. Gasperoni, K. Ebcioglu:
                         On Optimal Loop Parallelization
                         Proc. Microprogramming Workshop, Dublin, 1990

[Schwiegelshohn et al 91] U. Schwiegelshohn, F. Gasperoni, K. Ebcioglu:
                         On Optimal Parallelization of Arbitrary Loops
                         Journal of Parallel and Distr. Comp. 11, 1991

[Slavenburg/Labrousse 90] Gerrit A. Slavenburg, Junien Labrousse:
                         LIFE-1: A Single Chip Integer VLIW Processor Core
                         Hot Chips Symposium, 1990

[Smith 92]   Michael David Smith:
                         Support for Speculative Execution in High-
                         Performance Processors
                         Stanford University Tech. Report CSL-TR-93-556,
                         Nov. 1992

[Smith/Lam/Horowitz 90]	Michael D. Smith, Monica S. Lam, Mark A. Horowitz Boosting Beyond Static Scheduling in a Superscalar Processor Proc. 17th Symp. on Comp. Arch., Seattle, May 28-31, 1990
[Steven/Gray/Adams89]	G.B. Steven, S.M. Gray, R.G. Adams: HARP: A parallel pipelined RISC processor Microprocessors and Microsystems, Vol. 13, No. 9, Nov. 1989
[Su/Ding/Jin 84]	Bogong Su, Shiyuan Ding, Lan Jin: An Improvement of Trace Scheduling for Global Microcode Compaction Proc. 17th Annual Microprogramming Workshop (MICRO 17), Dec. 1984
[Su/Ding 85]	Bogong Su, Shiyuan Ding: Some Experiments in Global Microcode Compaction Proc. 18th Annual Microprogramming Workshop (MICRO 18), Pacific Grove, CA, Dec. 1985
[Sweany/Beaty 90]	Philip Sweany, Steven Beaty: Post-Compaction Register Assignment in a Retargetable Compiler Proc. 23rd Workshop on Microprogramming, micro 23, Nov. 27-29, 1990
[SYS 52 90]	ZFE IS SYS 52: Diskussionsergebnisse und Präsentationsergebnisse der VLIW-Klausur Internal Report, Siemens AG, Dep. ZFE IS SYS 52, 1990
[Thornton 70]	J.E. Thornton: Design of a Computer: The Control Data 6600 Foresman and Company, 1970
[Tomasulo 67]	R.M. Tomasulo: An Efficient Algorithm for Exploring Multiple Arithmetic Units IBM Journal of Research and Development, 11(1), Jan. 1967
[Trosch 91]	Siegfried Trosch: Pipeline Simulator User's Manual Siemens Corporate Research Technical Report No. BeG040/92, 1992

[Vassiliadis et al 92]   Stamatis Vassiliadis, Bert Blaner, Richard E.
                           Eickemeyer:
                           On the Attributes of the SCISM Organization
                           Computer Architecture News, Vol. 20, No. 4, Sept. 92

[Wall 86]   David W. Wall:
                           Global Register Allocation at Link Time
                           Proc SIGPLAN '86 Symp. on Compiler Constr., Palo
                           Alto, CA, June 1986

[Wall 86]   David W. Wall:
                           Post-Compiler Code Transformation
                           ACM SIGPLAN '02 Conf. on Prog. Lang. Design and
                           Impl., June 1992, Tutorial

[Wall 91]   David W. Wall:
                           Limits of Instruction-Level Parallelism
                           Proc. ACM ASPLOS IV, Santa Clara, CA, 1991

[Warren 90]   H.S. Warren, Jr.:
                           Instruction Scheduling for the IBM RISC System /
                           6000 Processor
                           IBM Journal. Res. Develop., Vol. 34, No. 1, 1990

[Werner 91]   Michael Werner:
                           Implementierung von Algorithmen zur Kompakti-
                           fizierung von Programmen für VLIW-Architekturen
                           Diplomarbeit, Techn. Univ. München, TUM-I9116,
                           SFB-Bericht Nr. 342/11/91 A, June 1991

[Windheiser/Jalby 91]   D. Windheiser, W. Jalby:
                           Behavioral Characterization of Decoupled Access/
                           Execute Architectures
                           Proc. Int. Conf. on Supercomputing 1991

[Wolfe/Shen 91]   Andrew Wolfe, John P. Shen:
                           A Variable Instruction Stream Extension to the VLIW
                           Architecture
                           Proc. ACM ASPLOS IV, Santa Clara, CA, 1991

[Yen/Rau 88]   David W. Yen, B. Ramakrishna Rau:
                           A Detailed Look of a Parallel-Pipelined Minisuper-
                           computer - Part II: The Numeric Processor and the
                           High-Bandwidth Memory System
                           Cydrome, Inc. Milpitas, CA, 1988

[Zima/Chapman 91]   Hans Zima, Barbara Chapman:
                           Supercompilers for Parallel and Vector Computers
                           ACM Press, 1991

Figures

1 Introduction

2 Kinds of Parallelism

    Figure 1: Parallelism by Replication 3

3 Architectures for Fine-Grain Parallelism

    Figure 2: Base Architecture Pipeline 8

    Figure 3: VLIW Architecture 10

    Figure 4: Superscalar Processor Architecture 11

    Figure 5: Pipeline of an Architecture with Vertical Parallelism (MIPS R4000)   13

    Figure 6: Superscalar Processor Pipeline Structure (with four PEs) 14

    Figure 7: VLIW Processor Pipeline Structure 14

    Figure 8: iWarp Component Architecture ([Borkar et al 88]) 16

4 VLIW Machines

    Figure 9: TRACE 7/200 Architecture ([Colwell et al 88]) 18

    Figure 10: IBM's VLIW Architecture ([Ebcioglu 88]) 20

    Figure 11: Cydra 5 System Architecture ([Rau/Yen/Towle 89]) 22

    Figure 12: Cydra 5 Numeric Processor Architecture ([Rau/Yen/Towle 89]) 23

    Figure 13: LIFE Processor Architecture ([Slavenburg/Labrousse 90]) 25

    Figure 14: LIFE Multiport Memory ([Slavenburg/Labrousse 90]) 25

    Figure 15: XIMD Architecture ([Wolfe/Shen 91]) 26

5 Constraints on VLIW Architectures

6 Architectural Support for Exploitation of Fine-Grain Parallelism

    Figure 16: Superscalar Processor Architecture, Detailed 33

7 Constraints for Instruction Scheduling

    Figure 17: Off-live Dependence and Incorrect Reordering 39

8 Instruction-Scheduling Methods

    Figure 18: Branch Delay Slot 40

    Figure 19: Bulldog Compiler Structure 44

    Figure 20: Bookkeeping 46

    Figure 21: Program-Graph Node and Conditional Tree 48

    Figure 22: Move_op Core Transformation 50

    Figure 23: Move_cj Core Transformation 51

    Figure 24: Unify Core Transformation 53

    Figure 25: Delete Core-Transformation 54

    Figure 26: Loop Unrolling 56

    Figure 27: Loop Unrolling with Register Renaming 57

    Figure 28: Software Pipelining 58

    Figure 29: Perfect Pipelining 60

9 Developing Instruction-Scheduling Methods

10 Tools for Instruction Scheduling

    Figure 30: Tools for Fine-Grain Parallelism Exploitation 63

11 The Machine Model

12 The Horizontal Instruction-Scheduler

Figure 31: Horizontal Instruction-Scheduler Structure 67
Figure 32: The Scheduler's Front-end.. 69
Figure 33: Example Program for Memory-Access Analysis 86
Figure 34: Insertion of Multicycle-reps.. 93
Figure 35: Inserting Multicycle-reps in Loops.. 94
Figure 36: Inserting Multicycle-reps into a diamond structure...................... 95
Figure 37: Interference of Scheduling with Standard Optimizations................ 101
Figure 38: The Scheduler's Central Part 103
Figure 39: a) Program Graph with Loop, b) Irreducible Program-Graph 105
Figure 40: Move_op, Extended Version 107
Figure 41: Conditional Trees.. 108
Figure 42: Moving multicycle_ops 111
Figure 43: Move_multicycle_op Core-Transformation 112
Figure 44: Move_multicycle_cj 114
Figure 45: The sequence of Operations to Move 116
Figure 46: Pull_n with Window Size 2, Push_n with Window Size 2.............. 118
Figure 47: move_to_all_preds, migrate_within_trace, migrate 120
Figure 48: Code Patterns: A Diamond Structure... 122
Figure 49: Code Patterns: Stair Structure.. 123
Figure 50: Program-Graph Regions 125
Figure 51: Saving Registers at Function Calls 127
Figure 52: The Scheduler's Back-End 129
Figure 53: Problems with Spill-Code Insertion... 132
Figure 54: Solution of the Spill-Code Problem... 133
Figure 55: Spill Code and Rescheduling.. 136
Figure 56: PE Assignment... 138
Figure 57: Jump Operations 139
Figure 58: Jump Operation Creation 140

13 Resource Management

Figure 59: Resource Allocation Matrix for an Operation 144
Figure 60: Bipartite Assignment Problem.. 149
Figure 61: PE Assignment in Alternative Program-Graph Paths...................... 152
Figure 62: Conflict Graph for General Resource Assignment 153

14 Exceptions

Figure 63: Exceptions in Reorganized Code... 156

15 Vertical Instruction-Scheduling

Figure 64: Move_op_Vertical Core-Transformation 160
Figure 65: Move_cj_Vertical Core-Transformation 162

16 Conclusion

17 References

Subject Index

A

alternative resource-allocation matrix 145
anti-dependence 38
Astronautics ZS-1 15
automatic parallelization 6

B

back-end 129
basic block 39
binary instructions 71
bookkeeping 46
bottom trees 46
bottom-up strategy 124
branch prediction 35
branch_on_coprocessor instructions 72
branch-delay slot 40
breakpoints 140
BULLDOG 43
bypassing 30

C

case instructions 73
central instruction-window 32
central part 103
coarse-grain parallelism 5
code patterns 121
compact_global 54
compare_and_branch instructions 72
compare_and_set instructions 72
conditional execution 16, 21
conditional tree 47, 108
constraints for instruction scheduling 38
constraints on VLIW architectures 28
control strategies 124
convert instructions 72
core transformation 50–54, 106–115, 159–163
Cydra architecture 22

D

data dependences 38
data-dependence analysis 90–92
data-flow analysis 96–100
debugging 140
decoupled access / execute architectures 15
delete 53, 110

delete_vertical 160
dependence mechanisms 34
diamond structure 121
directed-dataflow architecture 22
disambiguation 44
distributed-memory architecture 7
dominator 78
dynamic-instruction scheduling 32

E

exception handling 33
exceptions 156
extended percolation-scheduling 115

F

fine-grain parallelism 6
float_compare instructions 72
flow dependence 38
front-end 68
funnel file 24

G

general-resource assignment 153
global instruction-scheduling 42
graph coloring 131, 150
guarded operations 26

H

horizontal parallelism 8
horizontal-instruction scheduler 63

I

IBM's VLIW architecture 20
improved trace-scheduling 46
instruction completion 36
instruction decode 35
instruction fetch 34
instruction issue 35
instruction retirement 36
instruction tree 21
instruction window 32
instruction-scheduling methods 40
instruction-word generation 138
interactions scheduling / register allocation 134
interference 101
interference graph 130
irreducible program-graph 105
iWarp 15

J

jump instructions 73
jump_and_link instructions 72

L

leaves 49
LIFE architecture 24
list scheduling 42
load instructions 72
load_immediate instructions 72
local instruction-scheduling 42
loop parallelization 55, 104
loop unrolling 56

M

machine description 144
machine model 65
memory access 36
memory-access analysis 81–90
migrate 54, 121
migrate_within_trace 120
MIMD 6
MISD 6
move_cj 51, 109
move_cj_vertical 162
move_from_coprocessor instructions 72
move_multicycle_cj 114
move_multicycle_op 112
move_op 50, 107
move_op_vertical 160
move_to_all_preds 120
move_to_coprocessor instructions 72
moving multicycle_ops 111
multicycle operations 92
Multiflow TRACE 18
Multiflow TRACE architecture 18
multiway branch 30

N

node-oriented tactics 117

O

off-live dependence 38, 39
operation-oriented tactics 120
output-dependence 38

P

path-oriented strategy 124
PE assignment 137, 150

percolation scheduling 49, 117
perfect pipelining 59, 60
pipeline scheduler 64
pipeline simulator 64
PRISM 6
program graph 47
program-graph regions 104, 125
pull_n 118
push_n 119

R

read-after-write dependence 38
region 104, 125
register allocation 129–134
register renaming 34, 75
rescheduling 135
reservation station 32
resource allocation 147
resource assignment 148
resource management 128, 142–155
resource-allocation expression 145
resource-allocation matrix 144

S

scheduler structure 67
scheduling tools 63
scoreboarding 34
shared-memory architecture 7
SIMD 6
SISD 6
software pipelining 58
speculative execution 16
spill code 132, 137
splitting a program graph 106
SRDAG 47
stair structure 122
start node 49
structured memory-access machine 15
superpipelined 12
superscalar 11–12
superscalar-processor architecture 33
superscalar-processor pipeline 14

T

top node 49
top trees 46
top-down strategy 124
trace scheduling 43–46

true dependence 38

U

unifiable_ops 55
unify 52

V

vertical core transformation 159
vertical parallelism 8
vertical-instruction scheduling 158
VLIW architecture 9–10
VLIW machines 18–27
VLIW simulator 64
VLIW-processor pipeline 14

W

write-after-read dependence 38
write-after-write dependence 38

X

XIMD architecture 26

Lecture Notes in Computer Science

For information about Vols. 1–865
please contact your bookseller or Springer-Verlag

Vol. 866: Y. Davidor, H.-P. Schwefel, R. Männer (Eds.), Parallel Problem Solving from Nature - PPSN III. Proceedings, 1994. XV, 642 pages. 1994.

Vol 867: L. Steels, G. Schreiber, W. Van de Velde (Eds.), A Future for Knowledge Acquisition. Proceedings, 1994. XII, 414 pages. 1994. (Subseries LNAI).

Vol. 868: R. Steinmetz (Ed.), Multimedia: Advanced Teleservices and High-Speed Communication Architectures. Proceedings, 1994. IX, 451 pages. 1994.

Vol. 869: Z. W. Raś, Zemankova (Eds.), Methodologies for Intelligent Systems. Proceedings, 1994. X, 613 pages. 1994. (Subseries LNAI).

Vol. 870: J. S. Greenfield, Distributed Programming Paradigms with Cryptography Applications. XI, 182 pages. 1994.

Vol. 871: J. P. Lee, G. G. Grinstein (Eds.), Database Issues for Data Visualization. Proceedings, 1993. XIV, 229 pages. 1994.

Vol. 872: S Arikawa, K. P. Jantke (Eds.), Algorithmic Learning Theory. Proceedings, 1994. XIV, 575 pages. 1994.

Vol. 873: M. Naftalin, T. Denvir, M. Bertran (Eds.), FME '94: Industrial Benefit of Formal Methods. Proceedings, 1994. XI, 723 pages. 1994.

Vol. 874: A. Borning (Ed.), Principles and Practice of Constraint Programming. Proceedings, 1994. IX, 361 pages. 1994.

Vol. 875: D. Gollmann (Ed.), Computer Security – ESORICS 94. Proceedings, 1994. XI, 469 pages. 1994.

Vol. 876: B. Blumenthal, J. Gornostaev, C. Unger (Eds.), Human-Computer Interaction. Proceedings, 1994. IX, 239 pages. 1994.

Vol. 877: L. M. Adleman, M.-D. Huang (Eds.), Algorithmic Number Theory. Proceedings, 1994. IX, 323 pages. 1994.

Vol. 878: T. Ishida; Parallel, Distributed and Multiagent Production Systems. XVII, 166 pages. 1994. (Subseries LNAI).

Vol. 879: J. Dongarra, J. Waśniewski (Eds.), Parallel Scientific Computing. Proceedings, 1994. XI, 566 pages. 1994.

Vol. 880: P. S. Thiagarajan (Ed.), Foundations of Software Technology and Theoretical Computer Science. Proceedings, 1994. XI, 451 pages. 1994.

Vol. 881: P. Loucopoulos (Ed.), Entity-Relationship Approach – ER'94. Proceedings, 1994. XIII, 579 pages. 1994.

Vol. 882: D. Hutchison, A. Danthine, H. Leopold, G. Coulson (Eds.), Multimedia Transport and Teleservices. Proceedings, 1994. XI, 380 pages. 1994.

Vol. 883: L. Fribourg, F. Turini (Eds.), Logic Program Synthesis and Transformation – Meta-Programming in Logic. Proceedings, 1994. IX, 451 pages. 1994.

Vol. 884: J. Nievergelt, T. Roos, H.-J. Schek, P. Widmayer (Eds.), IGIS '94: Geographic Information Systems. Proceedings, 1994. VIII, 292 pages. 19944.

Vol. 885: R. C. Veltkamp, Closed Objects Boundaries from Scattered Points. VIII, 144 pages. 1994.

Vol. 886: M. M. Veloso, Planning and Learning by Analogical Reasoning. XIII, 181 pages. 1994. (Subseries LNAI).

Vol. 887: M. Toussaint (Ed.), Ada in Europe. Proceedings, 1994. XII, 521 pages. 1994.

Vol. 888: S. A. Andersson (Ed.), Analysis of Dynamical and Cognitive Systems. Proceedings, 1993. VII, 260 pages. 1995.

Vol. 889: H. P. Lubich, Towards a CSCW Framework for Scientific Cooperation in Europe. X, 268 pages. 1995.

Vol. 890: M. J. Wooldridge, N. R. Jennings (Eds.), Intelligent Agents. Proceedings, 1994. VIII, 407 pages. 1995. (Subseries LNAI).

Vol. 891: C. Lewerentz, T. Lindner (Eds.), Formal Development of Reactive Systems. XI, 394 pages. 1995.

Vol. 892: K. Pingali, U. Banerjee, D. Gelernter, A. Nicolau, D. Padua (Eds.), Languages and Compilers for Parallel Computing. Proceedings, 1994. XI, 496 pages. 1995.

Vol. 893: G. Gottlob, M. Y. Vardi (Eds.), Database Theory – ICDT '95. Proceedings, 1995. XI, 454 pages. 1995.

Vol. 894: R. Tamassia, I. G. Tollis (Eds.), Graph Drawing. Proceedings, 1994. X, 471 pages. 1995.

Vol. 895: R. L. Ibrahim (Ed.), Software Engineering Education. Proceedings, 1995. XII, 449 pages. 1995.

Vol. 896: R. N. Taylor, J. Coutaz (Eds.), Software Engineering and Human-Computer Interaction. Proceedings, 1994. X, 281 pages. 1995.

Vol. 897: M. Fisher, R. Owens (Eds.), Executable Modal and Temporal Logics. Proceedings, 1993. VII, 180 pages. 1995. (Subseries LNAI).

Vol. 898: P. Steffens (Ed.), Machine Translation and the Lexicon. Proceedings, 1993. X, 251 pages. 1995. (Subseries LNAI).

Vol. 899: W. Banzhaf, F. H. Eeckman (Eds.), Evolution and Biocomputation. VII, 277 pages. 1995.

Vol. 900: E. W. Mayr, C. Puech (Eds.), STACS 95. Proceedings, 1995. XIII, 654 pages. 1995.

Vol. 901: R. Kumar, T. Kropf (Eds.), Theorem Provers in Circuit Design. Proceedings, 1994. VIII, 303 pages. 1995.

Vol. 902: M. Dezani-Ciancaglini, G. Plotkin (eds.), Typed Lambda Calculi and Applications. Proceedings, 1995. VIII, 443 pages. 1995

Vol. 903: E. W. Mayr, G. Schmidt, G. Tinhofer (Eds.), Graph-Theoretic Concepts in Computer Science. Proceedings, 1994. IX, 414 pages. 1995.

Vol. 904: P. Vitányi (Ed.), Computational Learning Theory. EuroCOLT'95. Proceedings, 1995. XVII, 415 pages. 1995. (Subseries LNAI).

Vol. 905: N. Ayache (Ed.), Computer Vision, Virtual Reality and Robotics in Medicine. Proceedings, 1995. XIV, 567 pages. 1995.

Vol. 906: E. Astesiano, G. Reggio, A. Tarlecki (Eds.), Recent Trends in Data Type Specification. Proceedings, 1995. VIII, 523 pages. 1995.

Vol. 907: T. Ito, A. Yonezawa (Eds.), Theory and Practice of Parallel Programming. Proceedings, 1995. VIII, 485 pages. 1995.

Vol. 908: J. R. Rao Extensions of the UNITY Methodology: Compositionality, Fairness and Probability in Parallelism. XI, 178 pages. 1995.

Vol. 909: H. Comon, J.-P. Jouannaud (Eds.), Term Rewriting. Proceedings, 1993. VIII, 221 pages. 1995.

Vol. 910: A. Podelski (Ed.), Constraint Programming: Basics and Trends. Proceedings, 1995. XI, 315 pages. 1995.

Vol. 911: R. Baeza-Yates, E. Goles, P. V. Poblete (Eds.), LATIN '95: Theoretical Informatics. Proceedings, 1995. IX, 525 pages. 1995.

Vol. 912: N. Lavrac, S. Wrobel (Eds.), Machine Learning: ECML – 95. Proceedings, 1995. XI, 370 pages. 1995. (Subseries LNAI).

Vol. 913: W. Schäfer (Ed.), Software Process Technology. Proceedings, 1995. IX, 261 pages. 1995.

Vol. 914: J. Hsiang (Ed.), Rewriting Techniques and Applications. Proceedings, 1995. XII, 473 pages. 1995.

Vol. 915: P. D. Mosses, M. Nielsen, M. I. Schwartzbach (Eds.), TAPSOFT '95: Theory and Practice of Software Development. Proceedings, 1995. XV, 810 pages. 1995.

Vol. 916: N. R. Adam, B. K. Bhargava, Y. Yesha (Eds.), Digital Libraries. Proceedings, 1994. XIII, 321 pages. 1995.

Vol. 917: J. Pieprzyk, R. Safavi-Naini (Eds.), Advances in Cryptology - ASIACRYPT '94. Proceedings, 1994. XII, 431 pages. 1995.

Vol. 918: P. Baumgartner, R. Hähnle, J. Posegga (Eds.), Theorem Proving with Analytic Tableaux and Related Methods. Proceedings, 1995. X, 352 pages. 1995. (Subseries LNAI).

Vol. 919: B. Hertzberger, G. Serazzi (Eds.), High-Performance Computing and Networking. Proceedings, 1995. XXIV, 957 pages. 1995.

Vol. 920: E. Balas, J. Clausen (Eds.), Integer Programming and Combinatorial Optimization. Proceedings, 1995. IX, 436 pages. 1995.

Vol. 921: L. C. Guillou, J.-J. Quisquater (Eds.), Advances in Cryptology – EUROCRYPT '95. Proceedings, 1995. XIV, 417 pages. 1995.

Vol. 922: H. Dörr, Efficient Graph Rewriting and Its Implementation. IX, 266 pages. 1995.

Vol. 923: M. Meyer (Ed.), Constraint Processing. IV, 289 pages. 1995.

Vol. 924: P. Ciancarini, O. Nierstrasz, A. Yonezawa (Eds.), Object-Based Models and Languages for Concurrent Systems. Proceedings, 1994. VII, 193 pages. 1995.

Vol. 925: J. Jeuring, E. Meijer (Eds.), Advanced Functional Programming. Proceedings, 1995. VII, 331 pages. 1995.

Vol. 926: P. Nesi (Ed.), Objective Software Quality. Proceedings, 1995. VIII, 249 pages. 1995.

Vol. 927: J. Dix, L. Moniz Pereira, T. C. Przymusinski (Eds.), Non-Monotonic Extensions of Logic Programming. Proceedings, 1994. IX, 229 pages. 1995. (Subseries LNAI).

Vol. 928: V.W. Marek, A. Nerode, M. Truszczynski (Eds.), Logic Programming and Nonmonotonic Reasoning. Proceedings, 1995. VIII, 417 pages. 1995. (Subseries LNAI).

Vol. 929: F. Morán, A. Moreno, J.J. Merelo, P. Chacón (Eds.), Advances in Artificial Life. Proceedings, 1995. XIII, 960 pages. 1995 (Subseries LNAI).

Vol. 930: J. Mira, F. Sandoval (Eds.), From Natural to Artificial Neural Computation. Proceedings, 1995. XVIII, 1150 pages. 1995.

Vol. 931: P.J. Braspenning, F. Thuijsman, A.J.M.M. Weijters (Eds.), Artificial Neural Networks. IX, 295 pages. 1995.

Vol. 932: J. Iivari, K. Lyytinen, M. Rossi (Eds.), Advanced Information Systems Engineering. Proceedings, 1995. XI, 388 pages. 1995.

Vol. 933: L. Pacholski, J. Tiuryn (Eds.), Computer Science Logic. Proceedings, 1994. IX, 543 pages. 1995.

Vol. 934: P. Barahona, M. Stefanelli, J. Wyatt (Eds.), Artificial Intelligence in Medicine. Proceedings, 1995. XI, 449 pages. 1995. (Subseries LNAI).

Vol. 935: G. De Michelis, M. Diaz (Eds.), Application and Theory of Petri Nets 1995. Proceedings, 1995. VIII, 511 pages. 1995.

Vol. 936: V.S. Alagar, M. Nivat (Eds.), Algebraic Methodology and Software Technology. Proceedings, 1995. XIV, 591 pages. 1995.

Vol. 937: Z. Galil, E. Ukkonen (Eds.), Combinatorial Pattern Matching. Proceedings, 1995. VIII, 409 pages. 1995.

Vol. 938: K.P. Birman, F. Mattern, A. Schiper (Eds.), Theory and Practice in Distributed Systems. Proceedings,1994. X, 263 pages. 1995.

Vol. 939: P. Wolper (Ed.), Computer Aided Verification. Proceedings, 1995. X, 451 pages. 1995.

Vol. 941: M. Cadoli, Tractable Reasoning in Artificial Intelligence. XVII, 247 pages. 1995. (Subseries LNAI).

Vol. 942: G. Böckle, Exploitation of Fine-Grain Parallelism. IX, 188 pages. 1995.

Vol. 943: W. Klas, M. Schrefl, Metaclasses and Their Application. IX, 201 pages. 1995.